ALLEN COUNTY PUBLIC LIBRARY
D1448092

STO

A Da Capo Press Reprint Series

FRANKLIN D. ROOSEVELT AND THE ERA OF THE NEW DEAL

GENERAL EDITOR: FRANK FREIDEL
Harvard University

FARMING HAZARDS IN THE DROUGHT AREA

Division of Research
Work Projects Administration

Research Monographs

I. Six Rural Problem Areas, Relief—Resources—Rehabilitation
II. Comparative Study of Rural Relief and Non-Relief Households
III. The Transient Unemployed
IV. Urban Workers on Relief
V. Landlord and Tenant on the Cotton Plantation
VI. Chronology of the Federal Emergency Relief Administration May 12, 1933, to December 31, 1935
VII. The Migratory-Casual Worker
VIII. Farmers on Relief and Rehabilitation
IX. Part-Time Farming in the Southeast
X. Trends in Relief Expenditures, 1910-1935
XI. Rural Youth on Relief
XII. Intercity Differences in Costs of Living in March 1935, 59 Cities
XIII. Effects of the Works Program on Rural Relief
XIV. Changing Aspects of Rural Relief
XV. Rural Youth: Their Situation and Prospects
XVI. Farming Hazards in the Drought Area
XVII. Rural Families on Relief
XVIII. Migrant Families
XIX. Rural Migration in the United States
XX. State Public Welfare Legislation
XXI. Youth in Agricultural Villages
XXII. The Plantation South, 1934-1937
XXIII. Seven Stranded Coal Towns
XXIV. Federal Work, Security, and Relief Programs
XXV. Vocational Training and Employment of Youth
XXVI. Getting Started: Urban Youth in the Labor Market

Works Progress Administration
Division of Social Research
Research Monograph XVI

FARMING HAZARDS IN THE DROUGHT AREA

By R. S. Kifer and H. L. Stewart

DA CAPO PRESS • NEW YORK • 1971

A Da Capo Press Reprint Edition

This Da Capo Press edition of *Farming Hazards in the Drought Area* is an unabridged republication of the first edition published in Washington, D.C., in 1938. It is reprinted by permission from a copy of the original edition owned by the Harvard College Library.

Library of Congress Catalog Card Number 78-165600

ISBN 0-306-70348-3

Published by Da Capo Press, Inc.
A Subsidiary of Plenum Publishing Corporation
227 West 17th Street, New York, N.Y. 10011

Manufactured in the United States of America

FARMING HAZARDS IN THE DROUGHT AREA

WORKS PROGRESS ADMINISTRATION
F. C. Harrington, *Administrator*
Corrington Gill, *Assistant Administrator*

DIVISION OF SOCIAL RESEARCH
Howard B. Myers, *Director*

FARMING HAZARDS IN THE DROUGHT AREA

By
R. S. Kifer
and
H. L. Stewart
of the
Bureau of Agricultural Economics

•

RESEARCH MONOGRAPH XVI

1938

UNITED STATES GOVERNMENT PRINTING OFFICE, WASHINGTON

Letter of Transmittal

Works Progress Administration,
Washington, D. C., December 27, 1938.

Sir: I have the honor to transmit an analysis of the natural and economic factors which have determined the relief needs of farm families in 13 selected areas of the Great Plains. The counties surveyed range from fertile farm sections practically untouched by drought to counties laid waste by drought and its attendant disasters.

The report is based on an intensive analysis of the farm operations of a selected group of almost 1,000 farmers and the effect on these farmers of drought conditions. It has been possible to analyze the rural relief and rehabilitation problems of the areas surveyed in terms of specific, local conditions and to formulate suggestions for a long-time program of agricultural readjustment. This readjustment involves increasing the size of many farms in order to provide farmers with adequate incomes in good years to carry them over the frequent drought periods. Larger acreages would also permit increased pasturage in some sections and give farmers the benefit of the more stable income that comes with livestock production as opposed to crop production.

The combination of farms or redistribution of holdings necessary to effect the increase in size of farms would displace few farmers from their county of residence in most of the regions surveyed. One region studied, the Red River Valley of North Dakota, is favorably situated and could absorb many displaced farmers from the drought counties if costs of resettlement were not prohibitive.

The study was initiated by the Division of Research, Statistics, and Finance of the Federal Emergency Relief Administration in cooperation with the Division of Farm Management and Costs of the Bureau of Agricultural Economics, U. S. Department of Agriculture. It was completed by the Division of Social Research, Works Progress Administration, and the Bureau of Agricultural Economics, U. S. Department of Agriculture.

This report was prepared under the direction of Howard B. Myers, Director of the Division of Social Research, Works Progress Administration, and under the supervision of T. J. Woofter, Jr., Coordinator of Rural Research, and C. L. Holmes of the Bureau of Agricultural Economics. The data were collected and analyzed under the supervision of T. C. McCormick of the Federal Emergency Relief Administration and M. R. Cooper of the Bureau of Agricultural Economics, U. S. Department of Agriculture.

The report was written by R. S. Kifer, Senior Agricultural Economist, and H. L. Stewart, Assistant Agricultural Economist, both of the Bureau of Agricultural Economics. It was edited by Ellen Winston of the Division of Social Research, Works Progress Administration.

H. M. Pevehouse, formerly of the Works Progress Administration, assisted in collecting and analyzing the data. Credit should also be given to temporary employees of the Bureau of Agricultural Economics, U. S. Department of Agriculture, and the Federal Emergency Relief Administration who collected the data in the field.

Respectfully submitted.

CORRINGTON GILL,
Assistant Administrator.

COL. F. C. HARRINGTON,
Works Progress Administrator.

Contents

Page

Introduction - XIII

Summary - XVII

Chapter I. The Northern Great Plains - - - - - - - - - - - - - 1

Situation of farmers after the 1934 drought - - - - - - - - 2

Reduction in incomes - - - - - - - - - - - - - - - - - 2

Insolvency - 4

Farmers on relief rolls - - - - - - - - - - - - - - - - 5

Types of farming - 6

Natural factors affecting agriculture - - - - - - - - - - - 7

Topography - 7

Soils - 7

Climate - 10

Causes of crop damage - - - - - - - - - - - - - - - 16

Crop yields - 17

Organization of farms - - - - - - - - - - - - - - - - - 19

Size of operating unit - - - - - - - - - - - - - - - 20

Size of relief clients' farms - - - - - - - - - - - 21

Use of land - 23

Livestock - 26

Use of machinery and labor - - - - - - - - - - - - - 29

Farm buildings - - - - - - - - - - - - - - - - - - - 31

Indebtedness - 32

Real-estate indebtedness - - - - - - - - - - - - - - 32

Crop and feed loans - - - - - - - - - - - - - - - - 34

Tax delinquencies - - - - - - - - - - - - - - - - - 35

Relief clients' indebtedness - - - - - - - - - - - - - 36

Tenure of operators and ownership of land - - - - - - - - 37

Tenure of farm operators - - - - - - - - - - - - - - 37

Ownership of land - - - - - - - - - - - - - - - - - 39

Page

Chapter II. The Central Great Plains - - - - - - - - - - - - - - 41

Situation of farmers after the 1934 drought - - - - - - 42
Reduction in incomes - - - - - - - - - - - - - - 42
Farmers on relief and rehabilitation rolls - - - - - 44
Types of farming - - - - - - - - - - - - - - - - - - 46
Natural factors affecting agriculture - - - - - - - - - 47
Topography - - - - - - - - - - - - - - - - - - 47
Soils - 48
Climate - 50
Population movements as affected by precipitation - 53
Causes of crop damage - - - - - - - - - - - - - - 55
Crop yields - 56
Organization of farms - - - - - - - - - - - - - - - - 58
Size of operating unit - - - - - - - - - - - - - - 58
Size of relief clients' farms - - - - - - - - - - - 60
Use of land - - - - - - - - - - - - - - - - - - 60
Livestock - - - - - - - - - - - - - - - - - - - 64
Use of labor and machinery - - - - - - - - - - - - 65
Farm buildings - - - - - - - - - - - - - - - - - 66
Indebtedness - 67
Real-estate indebtedness - - - - - - - - - - - - - 67
Crop and feed loans - - - - - - - - - - - - - - - 68
Taxation and tax delinquencies - - - - - - - - - - 68
Relief clients' indebtedness - - - - - - - - - - - - 69
Ownership of land and tenure of operators - - - - - - - 69

Chapter III. The Southern Great Plains - - - - - - - - - - - - 73

Situation of farmers after the 1934 drought - - - - - - 74
Reduction in incomes - - - - - - - - - - - - - - 74
Farmers on relief and rehabilitation rolls - - - - - 76
Types of farming - - - - - - - - - - - - - - - - - - 77
Natural factors affecting agriculture - - - - - - - - - 78
Topography - - - - - - - - - - - - - - - - - - 78
Soils - 79
Climate - 79
Causes of crop damage - - - - - - - - - - - - - - 83

Page

Crop yields - 84

Organization of farms - - - - - - - - - - - - - - - - 86

Size of operating unit - - - - - - - - - - - - - - 87

Use of land - - - - - - - - - - - - - - - - - - 89

Livestock - - - - - - - - - - - - - - - - - - - 92

Use of machinery and labor - - - - - - - - - - - - 94

Farm buildings - - - - - - - - - - - - - - - - - 95

Indebtedness - 96

Real-estate indebtedness - - - - - - - - - - - - - 97

Crop and feed loans - - - - - - - - - - - - - - - 98

Taxation and tax delinquencies - - - - - - - - - - - 98

Relief clients' indebtedness - - - - - - - - - - - - 99

Ownership of land and tenure of operators - - - - - - - 99

Chapter IV. Prospects for rehabilitation of farmers - - - - - - - 103

Northwestern North Dakota and northeastern Montana - 106

Southwestern North Dakota - - - - - - - - - - - - - 107

Central North Dakota - - - - - - - - - - - - - - - 108

Central South Dakota - - - - - - - - - - - - - - - 109

Red River Valley of eastern North Dakota - - - - - - - 110

Southeastern South Dakota - - - - - - - - - - - - - 111

Loess Hills of central Nebraska - - - - - - - - - - - 112

Southwestern Wheat Area of Nebraska - - - - - - - - - 113

Southeastern Wyoming - - - - - - - - - - - - - - - 114

High Plains of eastern Colorado - - - - - - - - - - - 115

North Plains of Texas - - - - - - - - - - - - - - - 116

South Plains of the Texas Panhandle - - - - - - - - - 117

Upper South Plains of the Texas Panhandle and High Plains of eastern New Mexico - - - - - - - - - - - - 118

Appendix A. Supplementary tables - - - - - - - - - - - - 123

Appendix B. Method and scope of the study - - - - - - - - - 195

Appendix C. List of tables - - - - - - - - - - - - - - - 207

Index - 213

ILLUSTRATIONS

Figures

Figure *Page*

1. Areas represented and counties of special study xv
2. Major soil groups in the Great Plains 8
3. Extent of wind erosion in the Great Plains, 1934 9
4. Average number of days without killing frost in the Great Plains, 1895–1914 11
5. Annual and growing season precipitation, selected stations in the Northern Great Plains, 1900–1936 13
6. Normal monthly precipitation and precipitation by months, selected stations in the Northern Great Plains, 1927–1936 14
7. Average size of farm operated by relief clients and by all farmers in representative counties in the Northern Great Plains, 1935 22
8. Utilization of land on selected farms in representative counties in the Northern Great Plains, 1934 24
9. Percent of cattle purchased under the Emergency Livestock Purchase Program of the Agricultural Adjustment Administration 27
10. Average value of farm assets and amount of liabilities of selected farmers in representative counties in the Northern Great Plains, by tenure, 1935 38
11. Normal monthly precipitation and precipitation by months, selected stations in the Central Great Plains, 1927–1936 51
12. Annual and growing season precipitation, selected stations in the Central Great Plains, 1900–1936 53
13. Average size of farm operated by relief clients and by all farmers in representative counties in the Central Great Plains, 1935 60
14. Utilization of land on selected farms in representative counties in the Central Great Plains, 1934 62
15. Average value of farm assets and amount of liabilities of selected farmers in representative counties in the Central Great Plains, by tenure, 1935 71
16. Normal monthly precipitation and precipitation by months, selected stations in the Southern Great Plains, 1927–1936 81
17. Annual and growing season precipitation, selected stations in the Southern Great Plains, 1900–1936 82
18. Utilization of land on selected farms in representative counties in the Southern Great Plains, 1934 90
19. Average value of farm assets and amount of liabilities of selected farmers in representative counties in the Southern Great Plains, by tenure, 1935 102

Photographs

		Page
Looking for rain	Facing	XVI
A drought afflicted cornfield	Facing	XX
As the dust storm gathers	Facing	XXVI
No use for this harvester	Facing	18
A typical farm in the drought area	Facing	32
Twenty bushels from thirty-eight acres!	Facing	56
A typical barnyard	Facing	66
After the dust storm	Facing	84
Drying water holes force cattle sales	Facing	92
Drought refugees	Facing	106
Once an excellent farming section	Facing	114

Farming Hazards in the Drought Area

XI

INTRODUCTION

AGRICULTURAL DISTRESS had been acute in many parts of the Great Plains drought area for several years prior to 1934. Crop failures during the protracted drought of 1934, however, focused attention upon a situation that had its origins prior to the drought and even before 1928. By 1935 numbers of farmers in various parts of the Great Plains had abandoned their farms, and many of those remaining were in desperate need of financial aid.

The present survey was undertaken to analyze natural and economic factors which contributed to rural distress and agricultural maladjustment in the Great Plains with a view to determining needed changes in land use and farm organization and thus indicating the form any relief and rehabilitation program should take.

AGRICULTURE OF THE GREAT PLAINS

Development

Agricultural problems in the Great Plains drought area have arisen, in part, from the method of settlement. Settlement was the result, chiefly, of the offer of free land under the various Homestead Acts, and it increased with the penetration of the railroads. The eastern sections of the region were homesteaded about 1870, and by 1890 occupation had proceeded to the western parts of Kansas and the Dakotas. Remote and less attractive areas were not occupied until 1910 or after.

For many years following 1860 agriculture throughout most of the Western Great Plains was confined to range cattle and sheep production. A boom in the cattle industry took place between 1880 and 1895, and overstocking and overgrazing soon became a problem. A change in land use was under way by the turn of the century, and by 1919 cash-grain farming had largely replaced grazing in certain sections. The expansion of wheat production continued during the 1920's. Vast acreages of virgin soil were broken, and production of wheat became the primary enterprise for farmers in many areas of the region.

Several economic and natural factors contributed to this change in farming practices. Among them may be cited the rapid increase in population, the improvement in transportation and marketing facilities, the introduction of modern machinery, and the influence of high grain prices during the World War and post World War periods. Natural factors favoring cash-grain production were the high productivity of the loam soils of the region and the large expanses of level to rolling land which is admirably suited to large-scale grain farming.

Types of Farming

Wide differences in farming systems and farm organization are to be found in the Great Plains region although the common characteristic of moisture deficiency lends some similarity to the agriculture in all sections. Differences in temperature and in length of growing season affect crop adaptation in different latitudes. Within local areas variations in the topography and soil bring about differences in the type of production, while distance to market limits production of certain products.

In the Northern Great Plains (fig. 1) approximately one-half of the cultivated land is seeded to spring wheat. Other important crops—barley, rye, oats, and flax—are also spring-seeded.

Before the feed shortage of recent drought years forced livestock reductions, sheep, stock cattle, milk cows, and hogs were growing in importance as sources of farm income in the Northern Great Plains. In the central part of South Dakota farmers had shifted from a one-crop system of farming based on wheat to a system of farming in which wheat remained the most important crop but in which corn and feed grains replaced a large part of the former wheat acreage.

Corn is more important than wheat in those parts of South Dakota and Nebraska usually not considered in the plains region but which represent the western extension of the corn belt. Yields per acre are lower than in the eastern corn belt and crop production is less certain, but the systems of farming resemble those of the corn belt more closely than they do those of the wheat belt.

In the Central Great Plains (fig. 1) farming systems are based primarily on some combination of winter wheat, corn, barley, and oats. In central and western Kansas winter wheat dominates the agriculture. Here the topography and soil favor wheat production with large-scale equipment, and the usual system of farming approaches a one-crop system. Corn and grain sorghums are important in certain sections, particularly on the lighter soils. Spring wheat is an alternate crop to winter wheat in the northern sections of this area. Where the soils and climate are favorable for the production of corn and alfalfa hay, livestock production is important. In areas too rough for cultivation range livestock predominates.

In that portion of the Southern Great Plains considered here (fig. 1), winter wheat and grain sorghums dominate the cropping

FIG. 1 - AREAS REPRESENTED AND COUNTIES OF SPECIAL STUDY

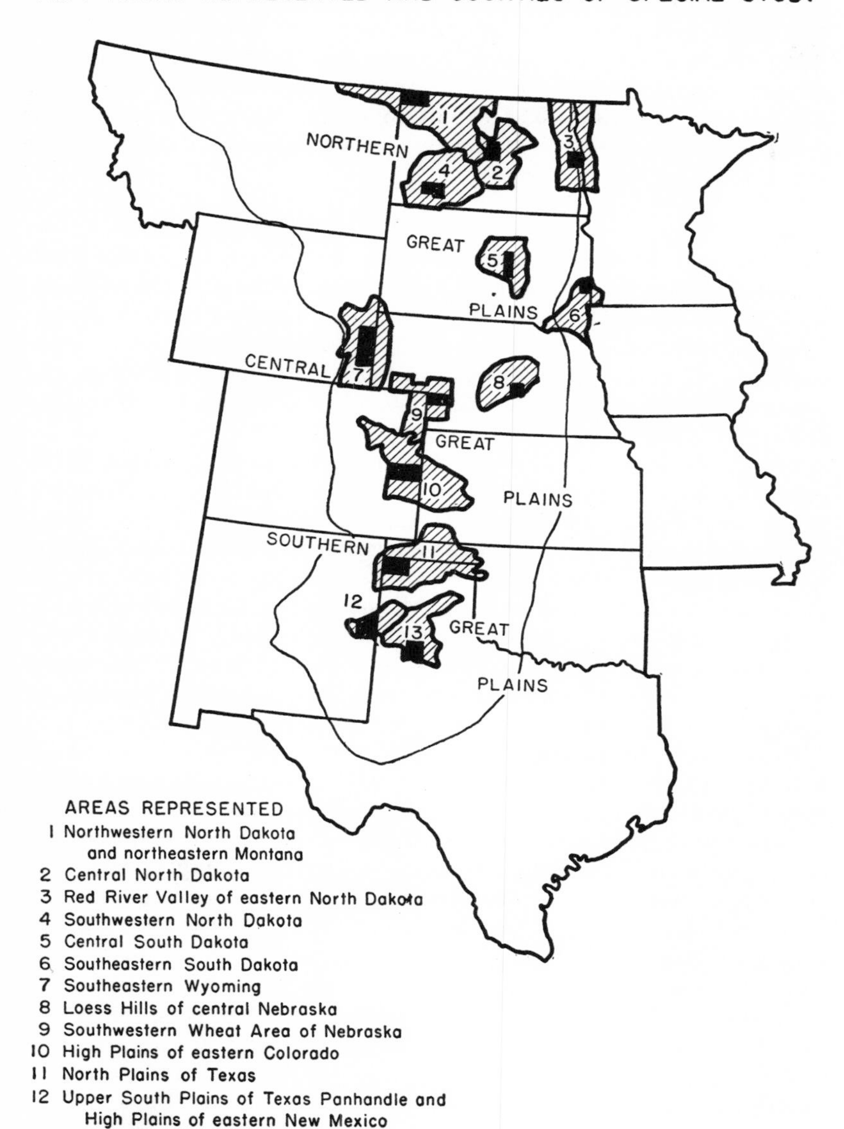

Note: Irregular line bounds the Great Plains Region as delimited by the Great Plains Committee.

AF-2709, WPA

systems with corn the alternate crop in the east and cotton the important cash crop on the light soils of the southern sections.

On rough, broken, or extremely sandy soils from the northern to the southern limits of the Great Plains region, range livestock production has been maintained. The extent to which livestock production is carried on in connection with farming is determined by the possibilities for crop production.

SELECTION OF COUNTIES FOR STUDY

The survey was made in 13 widely-separated counties in the Great Plains States (fig. 1). Each of the counties was considered broadly representative of a contiguous group of counties within the same geographic area. While the findings of this report are based on the survey of 11 counties seriously affected by drought and 2 counties affected slightly or not at all, they are believed to be generally applicable to the varied conditions in the Great Plains States.

Counties selected for the survey in the Northern Great Plains States were Divide, Hettinger, Sheridan, and Traill Counties, N. Dak., and Hyde and Moody Counties, S. Dak. In the Central Great Plains States the counties chosen for the survey were Sherman and Perkins Counties, Nebr., Goshen County, Wyo., and Cheyenne County, Colo. No representative county from the wheat areas in Kansas was studied because conditions in the distressed areas were fairly well represented by counties in adjoining States. In the Southern Great Plains States data were obtained from Dallam and Hale Counties, Tex., and Curry County, N. Mex.

In addition to general information on the agricultural situation, personal interviews with from 50 to 150 selected farmers in each county provided information relating to the farming system followed, the past record of crop yields, the financial condition of the farmers, and their financial progress since they began farming in the area. Records of almost 1,000 farmers in the Great Plains drought area were thus examined.[1]

---

[1] See Appendix B—Method and Scope of the Study.

Resettlement Administration (Rothstein).

Looking for Rain.

SUMMARY

FARMERS IN many sections of the Great Plains were in a serious financial condition in 1935 as a result of recurrent droughts and resultant low crop yields or failures. In many localities a large proportion of the farmers was receiving relief. Their 1934 incomes had been abnormally low and consisted largely of Government subventions in the form of crop and feed loans, direct relief, or payments made in connection with the livestock and crop control programs. Livestock had been drastically reduced in number throughout the Great Plains drought area.

The history of agriculture in the Great Plains indicates that the 1934 drought accentuated serious agricultural ills that had been accumulating for more than a decade. The land-use problems of the Great Plains, as well as the economic insecurity of those farming in the area, had arisen largely from the climate of the region—the light and variable rainfall, the wide fluctuations in temperature, and the recurrence of severe drought—and from the failure or inability of Great Plains farmers to adjust their farming systems to natural conditions.

THE NORTHERN GREAT PLAINS

Farmers in the central and western counties of the Northern Great Plains were dependent for the most part on Government expenditures in 1934. From two-thirds to three-fourths of the 1934 cash receipts of farmers in Divide, Hettinger, and Sheridan Counties and two-fifths of the receipts of farmers in Hyde County originated in Government expenditures, either as production control payments, emergency livestock purchases, or relief grants. In addition many farmers obtained Government crop and feed loans. An abnormally high percentage of the 1934 cash receipts in Divide, Hettinger, and Sheridan Counties came from livestock sales, most of these being made in connection with the Government's Emergency Livestock Purchase Program. Crop sales provided little or no cash receipts in 1934 to the farmers surveyed, although normally they accounted for three-fifths or more of the receipts on the farms in Divide, Hettinger, and Sheridan Counties and for more than one-third of the receipts on the farms in Hyde County.

In the eastern counties of the Dakotas, however, 1934 cash receipts were more nearly normal. In Moody County the sale of livestock and livestock products provided 64 percent of the average 1934 receipts, which was slightly less than normal. In Traill County crops provided 69 percent of the average 1934 receipts, only slightly less than normal, and the proportion of the receipts from the sale of livestock and livestock products was normal.

The relative severity of the drought in various sections of the Northern Great Plains is further indicated by the number of farmers on relief rolls. In the spring of 1935, 89 percent of the farmers in Divide County and more than 80 percent of those in Hyde County were receiving emergency relief. The proportions were 30 percent in Hettinger County and 26 percent in Sheridan County. In Moody County, in the eastern part of the region, 22 percent of the farmers received relief, and in Traill County there were no farmers on emergency relief rolls.

One farmer in five in Hyde County and one in six in Divide County reported that they were insolvent in 1935. Elsewhere insolvency was not so serious.

The much better position of the eastern counties, Traill and Moody, as compared with the central and western counties of the Dakotas in 1935, however, was not entirely because of 1934 drought effects. In the central and western counties 30 to 46 percent of the interviewed farmers reported financial losses since beginning farming in the area. On the other hand, farms in Traill and Moody Counties as small as 160 acres offered the operators something more than a bare living.

More favorable natural conditions had usually given the eastern counties an advantage over those in the central and western sections. They were able to grow a greater variety of crops, and they placed less dependence on wheat.

In three of the four central and western counties most of the farmers depended largely on wheat production. There was more livestock production in Hyde County in central South Dakota. In eastern North Dakota, represented by Traill County, farms with a variety of crops predominated. In southeastern South Dakota, represented by Moody County, livestock production predominated.

A more abundant and more stable rainfall toward the east makes possible the range of crops in Traill County and the production of corn for grain in Moody County. The central and western counties of the Dakotas, on the other hand, have to contend with a shorter growing season and less adequate but more variable moisture. Normal rainfall in these sections of the area is little more than enough for crop production, and, since it is frequently less than normal, crop failures or near failures have been frequent in the central and western portions of North and South Dakota. Droughts have occurred less frequently and have been less severe in the eastern counties. A complete crop failure caused by drought has practically never been experienced in the eastern part of these States.

In the central and western parts of the Northern Great Plains States good crop yields were reported about 1 year in 5, poor yields 1 year in 4 or 5, and failures about 1 year in 7 to 1 year in 3. In the eastern part, however, crop failures were rare and good or medium yields were reported 3 out of 4 to 4 out of 5 years.

Throughout North and South Dakota drought had been the chief cause of crop damage since the selected farmers had been operating in the area. But while it had occurred from two-fifths to more than one-half of the years in the central and western counties, it was reported in only from one-fifth to one-fourth of the years in the eastern counties. Serious or total damage was reported as frequently as 1 year in 4, or 2 years in 5, in the central and western counties, but only 1 year in 10 or 15 in the eastern counties. Other causes of crop damage, such as hail, frost, soil blowing, and insects, were not particularly serious.

In view of the natural hazards and low productivity of the central and western parts, many farms in those sections were too small for profitable operation. Although 400 acres is apparently the minimum size of farm on which farmers can operate successfully, many of the farms were only 160 or 320 acres in size. Farms of 160 or 320 acres were the most common size in the two eastern counties, but there such farms were able to show a profit.

The dry weather and unfavorable seeding conditions in 1934 had resulted in a high percentage of idle land, and there had been some tendency to replace cash crops with feed crops during the drought years. In Hyde and Divide Counties about 40 percent of the cropland was idle or fallow in 1934. Idle and fallow cropland amounted to more than 20 percent of the total in Sheridan and Hettinger Counties. On the other hand, the relative importance of the various crops in the central and western counties had not changed materially. Wheat was still the most important crop in terms of acreage, followed by barley, oats, and corn.

In contrast to the situation in the western and central counties only 18 percent of the crop acreage in Traill County, and 4 percent in Moody County, was idle or fallow in 1934. Wheat and barley occupied the largest acreages in Traill County. In Moody County corn for grain was most important, followed by oats and barley.

To return to normal operations the farmers in the central and western counties needed considerable replacements of livestock. Feed shortages had forced drastic reductions in livestock numbers in 1934 in the central and western counties. Cattle numbers were reduced to approximately one-half of normal on farms in Hyde and Divide Counties and somewhat less sharply in Hettinger and Sheridan Counties.

Hogs were reduced even more drastically. In all counties except Moody most of the farmers had no hogs. Hogs, however, had not been an important enterprise in any of the counties except Moody and Hyde, cattle usually being the most important livestock enterprise. Work stock numbers generally were maintained at near normal levels.

In most sections buildings were adequate but in need of repairs. The estimated cost of needed repairs was as high in the eastern as in the western counties, but eastern farmers were in a better position to finance their own repairs.

On many farms throughout the central and western counties minor repairs would put machinery in working condition. Some replacement of old equipment was needed.

Farmers were burdened with heavy indebtedness. From one-fourth to two-fifths of the land in the central and western counties of the Dakotas was mortgaged in 1935. Thirty-eight percent of the land in Traill County, and forty-eight percent in Moody County, was mortgaged. Federal and State lending agencies held a large proportion of the first mortgages in all areas. Unpaid feed and seed loans formed a considerable part of the farmers' obligations in the western and central areas. Indebtedness from this source was relatively slight in the eastern counties. During the years 1930–1935 tax delinquencies had increased rapidly in all of the sample drought counties except Traill and Moody, with delinquencies on more than four-fifths of the land in some counties.

Corporation holdings were not important in any of the counties. Private individuals held title to from 74 to 91 percent of the land in the Northern Great Plains. There was, however, widespread absentee ownership of land, 27 percent of the acreage in Hettinger County, 29 percent in Hyde County, 33 percent in Divide County, and 51 percent in Sheridan County being owned by nonresidents.

Tenancy had been increasing in all counties studied since 1920, and tenants were usually in a worse position financially than were owner-operators. In most areas the majority of the farmers who were insolvent were tenants, and the proportion of tenants was higher among those who reported losses than among those who had accumulated capital since beginning farming in the area. Also, a high proportion of tenants was found among the farmers on relief.

THE CENTRAL GREAT PLAINS

Farm incomes in the central part of the Great Plains were low in 1934, and from two-fifths to three-fourths of the cash receipts came directly or indirectly from Government sources. Except in the irrigated section of Goshen County, crop sales were a minor source of receipts although normally they were the source of about three-fourths of the cash receipts on farms in Perkins and Goshen Counties, one-half in Cheyenne County, and about one-third in Sherman County.

Works Progress Administration.

A Drought-Afflicted Cornfield.

The proportions of farmers on emergency relief or rehabilitation rolls in the spring of 1935 were 32 percent in Cheyenne County and about 20 percent in both Goshen and Sherman Counties. In Perkins County, however, only 7 percent of the farmers were on emergency relief rolls. Many of the farmers on relief had begun farming in the area within the preceding 5 years and, because of unfavorable conditions, had been unable to establish themselves and accumulate reserves for adverse years.

Although the Nebraska counties (Sherman and Perkins) were better situated with respect to natural factors than were the western counties (Cheyenne and Goshen), the irrigated section of Goshen County was by several indices in a much more favorable situation than most of the other sections studied in the spring of 1935. Irrigation and suitable soils make it possible for farmers to specialize in sugar-beet production with alfalfa second in importance. Although the Central Great Plains make up the major portion of the hard winter wheat area of the United States, livestock production is important in those sections of Kansas and Nebraska where corn is an important crop, and grazing predominates in sandy or rough areas not suited to cultivation.

These farming types are conditioned by natural factors except where natural limitations have been met through irrigation. As in the Northern Great Plains precipitation is more abundant and more stable in the eastern than in the western sections of the area, with the result that arid years occur less frequently in the eastern section, typified by Sherman County, than in the western section, where Perkins, Goshen, and Cheyenne Counties are located.

As a result of these factors, in the western section, typified by Goshen County, the production of small grains and early-maturing feed crops is possible, but the short growing season restricts the production of corn for grain. In Perkins and Cheyenne Counties a longer growing season gives corn and other feed crops a better chance to mature. In Sherman County, still farther east, natural conditions favor the production of grain and hay and the raising of livestock.

The period 1931–1934 was one of subnormal rainfall throughout the central part of the Great Plains, but it was by no means the first such period experienced. Precipitation records from the western portion indicate that in the 75-year period preceding 1934 there were seven drought periods of 3 or more years' duration.

In all sections drought had been the most frequent cause of crop damage. Even in the irrigated section of Goshen County scarcity of water had limited crop production. Selected farmers reported some damage from drought approximately half the years in Sherman, Perkins, and Cheyenne Counties, and from 1 year in 7 to 1 year in 3 in Goshen County. On the whole, however, the western counties experienced more years of deficient moisture with resultant low crop yields than the eastern counties.

Although crop yields in 1934 were low, if not complete failures, in all areas, yields in the immediately preceding years had been more favorable in the eastern counties and had enabled farmers better to withstand the 1934 drought. In Sherman County and the irrigated section of Goshen County farmers reported fair or good crop yields for the period 1930–1933. In Perkins County yields were low in 1931–1933 but were not complete failures, and some farmers produced crops in 1934. In the nonirrigated section of Goshen County, however, farmers reported low or scattered yields for 1931 and thereafter, and in Cheyenne County yields had been low for a 5-year period.

The size of the original homestead units still predominates in parts of the Central Great Plains. In Sherman County data secured from the Agricultural Adjustment Administration corn-hog contracts indicated that about one-half of the farms had less than 200 acres and only one-fourth to one-third had 280 acres or more. Yet, on the average, only farmers with 360 acres or more had been able to increase their capital since beginning farming in the county.

In Perkins County 22 percent of the farms with corn-hog contracts were less than 281 acres in size and 46 percent had less than 440 acres. Yet, according to farmers' estimates, a farm, to be profitable, should be not less than 400 acres in size in southwestern Nebraska.

In Cheyenne County more than one-half of the farms were smaller than 440 acres although at least 640 acres were considered necessary for profitable operation. In the dry-land section of Goshen County two-fifths of the farms had no more than 460 acres although 640 acres were considered the minimum necessary. Less than 100 acres, however, were considered adequate to provide for a family living in the irrigated section.

In general the operators of the larger farms reported greater increases in net worth for the period they had farmed in the area and greater increases per year of farming than did operators of smaller farms. Farmers on relief tended to be concentrated in areas of small farms, and as a rule relief clients reported farming units considerably smaller than the county average.

In spite of the successive failures of the farmers' staple crops, there had been little change from established to emergency crops during the drought period, 1930–1934. Corn acreage had been reduced, but apparently most of this reduction was due to the crop adjustment program.

In 1934 three-fifths of the farm land in Sherman County was used for crops, according to census figures. In Perkins County nearly three-fourths of the farm land was in crops. For Goshen County as a whole only one-fourth of the farm land was cropland, but the proportion was much higher in the irrigated than in the dry-land farming section. In Cheyenne County only one-third of the farm land was used as cropland.

Livestock numbers had been reduced in all areas by April 1, 1935, the most drastic reductions having been made in hogs and poultry. In nearly all areas feed loans had enabled most farmers to maintain the major portions of their cattle herds. The greatest reduction in cattle had been made in Sherman County where the number of all cattle had been reduced from an average of 22 to 15 per farm.

The farmers were heavily in debt. Real-estate indebtedness was general in all areas and, with the decline of land values after 1930, the ratio of debt to estimated value became high. In some counties a number of farmers were estimated to be carrying an indebtedness approximately equal to, or higher than, the estimated value of their farms.

The feed and seed loans made in 1934–1935 were greater in total and per farm in the livestock-producing section represented by Sherman County than in the other Central Great Plains counties studied. The debt in Sherman County from this source averaged $206 per farm, most of which represented feed loans incurred in an attempt to maintain livestock herds.

Most of the land in the Central Great Plains was held by private individuals. Corporations owned not more than 17 percent of the farm land in any of the selected counties. Nonresident-owned land as reported on production control contracts, however, amounted to from one-fifth to three-fifths of the total land farmed. In Sherman, Perkins, and Cheyenne Counties almost all of this absentee-owned land was operated by tenants.

Tenants made up a disproportionately large part of the farmers on relief rolls. On the average, however, all groups of both tenants and owners interviewed, with the exception of the tenants operating in the nonirrigated section of Goshen County, were solvent in the spring of 1935.

THE SOUTHERN GREAT PLAINS

The Southern Great Plains presents problems of agricultural adjustment considerably different from those in the Central and Northern Great Plains. Precipitation is heavier but there are higher temperatures and more rapid evaporation. A normally mild winter permits winter wheat production, and a long growing season permits the production of grain sorghums.

With the exception of the area represented by Dallam County, the situation in the counties surveyed in the spring of 1935 was less serious in the Southern Great Plains than in the central and western portions of the other areas. Cash receipts in 1934 had been one-third of normal in the row-crop section and one-fourth of normal in the grain section of Dallam County; but they were two-thirds of normal in the row-crop section and about three-fifths of normal in the grain section of Curry County and three-fourths of normal in Hale County.

In 1934 crops remained the most important source of cash receipts in Hale County. In Curry and Dallam Counties, however, farmers were largely dependent for cash receipts on crop production control payments, livestock sales during the Emergency Cattle Purchase Program, and relief work, although normally crop sales made up two-thirds or more of the farmers' receipts in all sections.

In Dallam County 28 percent of the farmers were receiving relief in the spring of 1935. The proportions were much less in the other counties, 15 percent in Curry County and only 12 percent in Hale County.

The farmers in the area represented by Dallam County had been in more serious straits than those in the other areas even before the 1934 drought. In all sections some farmers had been operating at a loss, but only in the wheat-producing sections of Dallam County was the average net worth of all farmers less than when they began farming in the area.

The light sandy soils in the Southern Great Plains, although capable of producing good feed crops, are subject to wind erosion. The sandy loam soils are used for cotton and feed crops in the south and for feed crops in the north. The heavier soils are used for winter wheat production.

Although the growing season is almost always long enough to mature crops, crop production is uncertain, particularly in the northern and western portions of the area, because of high evaporation and the uneven distribution and local character of the rainfall. The period 1931–1934 was one of subnormal rainfall, especially in Dallam County, and it was most serious in 1934. In that year crops were complete failures except in localities where rains occurred at critical times.

The farmers on the light soils in Dallam County reported poor yields or failures of wheat for four-fifths of the years they had been operating. Those on heavier soils reported poor yields or failures for three-fifths of the years. Poor yields or failures were reported for about three-fifths of the years the farmers had been operating in Curry County, and even in Hale County they were reported for almost one-half of the years.

In Dallam County farmers reported low yields or failures of all crops after 1931 and almost complete failures in 1933 and 1934. In Curry County farmers reported short crops in 1933 and failures in 1934. Hale County farmers, however, reported fairly good crops except in 1934 and even in that year wheat yields were good.

Dry weather was the most important cause of crop damage in the Southern Great Plains. Farmers in Dallam County, Tex., reported a high percentage of their cropland seriously damaged and most of their land affected to some extent by wind erosion. Damage by drought had occurred from one-fifth to one-third of the years the farmers had been operating in Dallam County, about two-fifths of the years in Curry County, and about one-half of the years in Hale County.

As in the other areas studied size of farm was associated with the farmers' distress. Farms in Dallam County in both the row-crop and grain sections were usually 320 or 640 acres in size, although farms of about 880 acres in the grain section and 440 acres in the row-crop section were considered necessary for profitable operation.

In Hale County farms of 160 and 320 acres predominated in the groups with cotton and corn-hog contracts. These were considered adequate under normal conditions.

In Curry County the 160-, 320-, and 480-acre farms were most common. The average farm in the wheat section was considered large enough to maintain a family, but an extra 80 acres of pasture was believed necessary for the average farm in the row-crop section.

Although an abnormally large acreage of cropland was idle in 1934, the proportions of crops planted, except for a substitution of sorghums for corn, were much the same as in earlier, more humid years. In Dallam County unfavorable planting and soil conditions had resulted in a high proportion of idle land; nearly two-fifths of the cropland in the row-crop section and one-fourth of that on heavier soil were idle. In the wheat-producing sections of both Dallam and Curry Counties wheat was planted on most farms and occupied on the average one-half or more of the cropland. Other crops were primarily sorghums for feed. In Hale County cotton and sorghums were planted on practically all of the farms.

Livestock numbers were reduced drastically in all sections following the drought. Cattle numbers were little more than one-half of normal on the farms for which records were taken in Dallam County in 1935. The reduction was somewhat less in the other portions of the area, but even there livestock numbers were considerably below normal. Many farmers were left without hogs and a few had no cattle in the spring of 1935. Although livestock numbers in the distressed areas were depleted, most of the farmers had kept as many head as their feed supplies and pastures would carry. Except in Hale County, there had been no opportunity since 1931 in any of the selected counties to create or maintain the feed reserves necessary to carry livestock through a period of drought.

The need for repairs on buildings was reported in all areas. Machinery was generally in poor condition. The estimated cost of necessary machinery repairs on these farms averaged from $41 in the row-crop section of Curry County to $131 in the grain-producing section of Dallam County.

Heavy indebtedness was reported here as in the other areas studied. Thirty-six to forty-four percent of the land was mortgaged in the different counties. The amount of the mortgage per acre varied with land values, but in some sections the land was mortgaged for more than its current value. A large proportion of the first mortgages was held by the Federal Land Bank.

The indebtedness incurred in 1934 and 1935 through emergency crop and feed loans was closely associated with the severity of the drought. It varied from an average of $57 per farm in Hale County to about $400 per farm in Dallam County. The charges for interest on average indebtedness and for taxes on an owner-operated farm of 320 acres in the grain section of Dallam County amounted to more than one-fourth of the average wheat crop of 9 bushels per acre at 75 cents per bushel.

Taxes on some land, especially in the wind-eroded areas, had been unpaid for 4 years or more. Most delinquent taxes, however, had been delinquent for only 1 year.

Nonresident ownership offers further problems in connection with a program of rehabilitation. Title to nearly all land was held by private individuals, but in Dallam County nearly half of this privately owned land was held by nonresidents. Tenancy, associated with nonresident ownership, had been increasing in this area in recent years as in other sections of the Great Plains.

PROSPECTS FOR REHABILITATION OF FARMERS

In almost all of the areas studied permanent rehabilitation of farmers would involve an increase in the size of some of the farms, retirement of some land from crops, an increase in pasture acreage, immediate or eventual replacement of depleted livestock herds, repairs to buildings, and repairs or replacement of machinery. Adjustment of the farmers' debts and loans or advances would often be necessary to effect these changes.

Rehabilitation problems were particularly acute in northwestern North Dakota and northeastern Montana, southwestern North Dakota, central South Dakota, the dry-land farming sections of southeastern Wyoming, the High Plains of eastern Colorado, and the North Plains of Texas. Unless emigration since 1935 has altered the situation, a more equitable distribution of farm land, so as to provide each of the farmers enumerated in the 1935 Census with an acreage recommended as the minimum for providing a farmer and his family a living, would involve the displacement of some farmers in most of the counties surveyed as representative of these areas. In Goshen County, however, the irrigated section could probably absorb the excess farmers from the dry-land section, but new buildings would have to be constructed.

The Red River Valley of North Dakota, typified by Traill County, had no relief problem in the spring of 1935. It is recommended as a

Works Progress Administration.

As the Dust Storm Gathers.

section to which farmers could move from the drought area. A resettlement program of establishing farmers on 160-acre farms could be accomplished by acquiring portions of farms larger than 480 acres. A probable obstacle to such a program, however, is the high value of farm land in this county which might make the cost of resettlement prohibitive.

Changes in land-use policies are advocated for many sections of the Great Plains with a view to withdrawing some of the arable land from cultivation in the interest of soil conservation. In many cases farmers might be encouraged to make this shift by being provided with grass seed, by soil conservation payments, and by tax exemptions during the period of establishing a permanent sod. Where wind erosion has been severe, as in Cheyenne County and parts of the Southern Great Plains, reversion of large acreages to grass is a major need. Grass is also needed on hillsides in Sherman County where water erosion has resulted from tillage on slopes and lack of cover.

In sections in which livestock reductions were drastic, and particularly where insufficient breeding stock was retained, farmers need help in rebuilding their herds. More emphasis on livestock is desirable in some sections in order to make incomes more stable in future years, but this change involves increased pasturage and consequently larger farms in order to prevent overgrazing.

Some farmers need assistance in reconditioning farm buildings to prevent rapid depreciation while others will require additional buildings if they expand livestock production. Repairs or replacements of farm machinery are needed in many sections.

While farms are being reestablished on a productive basis, a supply of working capital for living and operating expenses is needed in some sections. In still others some means of caring for or deferring payments on mortgages, interest, and taxes is necessary if the farm operator is to retain ownership of his land. Adjustment of land values is needed in such an area as that represented by Hyde County.

From this statement of the causes of distress and needed adjustments to alleviate the situation in the Great Plains States, there emerge a number of serious problems which can hardly be met without extensive modifications in the institutional factors influencing long-time adjustments. The problem of enlarging operating units to a size which will permit the operator to survive and to follow an adapted production system, the problem of settling families dislocated in the process of enlargement and of caring for those forced out by failure, and the problem of preventing subdivision of existing economic units or resubdivision of those to be developed are important. Their solution calls for adjustments throughout the region in land tenure, in credit extension, and in tax-assessment and tax-reversion procedures. In extreme situations public land purchase and improvement may be the only feasible way of directing and controlling land use. All of these factors are of vital concern to the Great Plains farmer who undertakes to rehabilitate himself in the region. Yet without reorganization of their operating units many farmers will be unable to build up adequate reserves against future unfavorable years. The agricultural experience of the selected farmers surveyed in the Great Plains indicates that such reorganization will be a long-time process. To be successful it will require governmental assistance on a large scale.

Chapter I

THE NORTHERN GREAT PLAINS

FOLLOWING THE drought of 1934 many farmers in the Northern Great Plains States—the Dakotas and eastern Montana and Wyoming—became dependent on Government assistance. Their crops had been destroyed, depriving them of a source of cash income and of feed for their livestock. Unable to buy feed they had sold much of their livestock to the Government, had added new Government crop and feed loans to their already heavy indebtedness, and had registered for emergency relief grants.

Distress was far more acute in some sections than in others. The six Dakota counties included in this survey of the Northern Great Plains States were selected to represent areas with serious rehabilitation problems and areas where conditions were relatively favorable even in 1934[1] (fig. 1, p. xv). Divide County in northwestern North

[1] The problems in the six counties surveyed may be considered typical of those of other counties in their areas as follows:

County surveyed	Area represented	Other counties in area	
Divide, N. Dak	Northwestern North Dakota and northeastern Montana.	North Dakota:	
		Bottineau	Renville
		Burke	Ward
		McLean	Williams
		Mountrail	
		Montana:	
		Daniels	
		Roosevelt	
		Sheridan	
Hettinger, N. Dak	Southwestern North Dakota	North Dakota:	
		Adams	Slope
		Bowman	Stark
Sheridan, N. Dak	Central North Dakota	North Dakota:	
		Benson	Pierce
		Burleigh	Wells
		Kidder	
Hyde, S. Dak	Central South Dakota	South Dakota:	
		Buffalo	Hughes
		Faulk	Potter
		Hand	Sully
Traill, N. Dak	Red River Valley of eastern North Dakota.	North Dakota:	
		Cass	Pembina
		Grand Forks	Walsh
Moody, S. Dak	Southeastern South Dakota	South Dakota:	
		Bon Homme	Minnehaha
		Clay	Turner
		Lake	Union
		Lincoln	Yankton

Dakota was selected as typical of an area which had suffered a succession of unfavorable crop years since 1929 and where an especially large proportion of farmers was receiving public assistance in 1934. Sheridan County in central North Dakota, Hettinger County in southwestern North Dakota, and Hyde County in central South Dakota were selected for study as representative either of areas marked for permanent retirement of a considerable portion of the land from cultivation or of areas in which the prevailing size of farm has been considered too small for profitable operation.[2] The other two counties, Traill in the Red River Valley of eastern North Dakota and Moody in southeastern South Dakota, were chosen because the sections they represent had been designated as areas which might support a larger farm population and to which farmers might move from such regions as those represented by Divide, Sheridan, Hettinger, and Hyde Counties.[3]

SITUATION OF FARMERS AFTER THE 1934 DROUGHT

Reduction in Incomes

Farmers in all of these sections of the Northern Great Plains were able in the past to average gross cash receipts ranging from nearly $1,400 to more than $2,000 a year. These were the approximate figures reported by selected farmers interviewed in this study based on records covering periods averaging from 13 to 20 years. Farmers in what is known as the Scobey-Plentywood Section of Divide County, N. Dak., reported the lowest average normal gross cash receipts, $1,352 a year, whereas farmers in the North Dakota Black Prairies Section of the same county and in Traill County of eastern North Dakota reported the highest average gross cash receipts, $1,934 and $2,010, respectively. Farmers in Moody County, representing the relatively prosperous southeastern part of the area, reported annual normal gross cash receipts averaging $1,729. In Hyde County the amount reported was $1,686; in Hettinger County, $1,583; and in Sheridan County, $1,489 (appendix table 1).

In 1934 the same farmers in the four central and western counties—Divide, Sheridan, Hettinger, and Hyde—reported gross cash receipts which were far below normal, and most of the income received was from the Federal Government in the form of Agricultural Adjustment Administration benefit payments, payments for livestock purchases, and emergency relief grants (table 1). Including Government payments, average gross cash receipts of these farmers in 1934 were 60 percent of normal in Hyde County, 54 percent of normal in Hettinger

[2] *Maladjustments in Land Use in the United States*, Part VI of the Supplementary Report of the Land Planning Committee to the National Resources Board, Washington, D. C., 1935.

[3] Preliminary classification of land-use consultants, National Resources Board.

County, and 51 percent of normal in Sheridan County. In the Scobey-Plentywood Section of Divide County they were 47 percent of normal but in the Black Prairies Section they were only 32 percent of normal (table 1 and appendix table 1). Average gross cash receipts for 1934 were estimated at $623 in Divide County, $762 in Sheridan County, $855 in Hettinger County, and $1,020 in Hyde County.

Table 1.—Average Gross Receipts per Farm on Selected Farms in Representative Counties in the Northern Great Plains, by Source of Receipts, 1934

Source of receipts	Average receipts per farm						
	Divide						
	North Dakota Black Prairies Section (44 farms)	Scobey-Plenty-wood Section (22 farms)	Het-tinger (63 farms)	Sheri-dan (57 farms)	Hyde (48 farms)	Traill (52 farms)	Moody (86 farms)
Total farm receipts	$786	$792	$1,054	$927	$1,163	$2,169	$1,356
Total cash receipts	617	636	855	762	1,020	1,915	1,159
Crop sales	7	—	46	13	8	1,327	55
Livestock sales	237	287	276	269	600	262	563
Livestock products	76	56	125	218	80	163	183
Agricultural Adjustment Administration contract payments	195	110	317	209	121	153	242
Emergency Relief Administration	68	137	12	11	117	—	53
Other	34	46	79	42	94	10	63
Total products used in home	169	156	199	165	143	254	197
Dairy products	83	81	92	66	71	113	82
Poultry products	24	34	34	34	36	35	26
Meat	60	37	65	57	32	89	75
Crops and garden	2	4	8	8	4	17	14

Augmented by the value of farm products used in the home, the farmers' gross receipts in 1934 ranged from less than $800 in Divide County to less than $1,200 in Hyde County (table 1), and these estimates take no account of the losses suffered through decreased feed, livestock, and equipment inventories.

Because of chattel mortgages and liens on cattle many farmers were able to retain little more than one-third of the purchase price of livestock sold to the Government. If creditors received as large a proportion of the purchase price of all livestock sales as they did of the cattle sold to the Government, farmers' actual cash receipts fell far below the figures stated above. Based on this assumption the estimated average cash receipts in Divide County, for example, were only $460.

Crop sales provided little or no income in the sample counties in central and western North and South Dakota in 1934, although, except in Hyde County, crops were usually the most important source of income (appendix table 1). In Hyde County where 29 percent of the livestock sales were to the Government, two-fifths of the average cash receipts originated in Government expenditures In Divide,

Sheridan, and Hettinger Counties in the central and western Dakotas, the Governm nt purchased the bulk of the livestock sold. As a result, from two-thirds to three-fourths of the cash received by representative farmers was from Government expenditures.

Incomes were much nearer normal in the two eastern counties outside the severe drought area—Traill and Moody—as to both amounts and sources. The average cash receipts in Traill County in 1934 were $1,915, only slightly below normal. In Moody County the 1934 average cash receipts of $1,159 were two-thirds of normal. The sale of crops provided 69 percent of the average 1934 cash receipts in Traill County, which was little below the normal proportion (77 percent), and the sale of livestock and livestock products furnished 22 percent of the 1934 cash receipts, which was the normal proportion. In Moody County the sale of livestock and livestock products provided 64 percent of the average 1934 receipts, which was only slightly less than normal. Crop sales, however, provided an average of only 5 percent of the 1934 cash receipts, whereas they accounted for almost one-third of the average estimated normal cash receipts.

Agricultural Adjustment Administration payments under crop production control contracts made up most of the balance of the 1934 cash receipts in all counties. They provided 37 percent of the 1934 average cash receipts in Hettinger County, about 27 percent in both Sheridan and Divide Counties, and approximately 12 percent in Hyde County. In Moody County corn-hog contracts furnished 21 percent of the receipts, but in Traill County production control contracts accounted for only 8 percent of the total.

Relief grants were relatively most important in Divide County, providing about 15 percent of the 1934 average cash receipts, and in Hyde County where they accounted for 11 percent of the receipts of selected farmers. In the other counties relief grants were relatively unimportant as a part of the total 1934 cash receipts. In Traill County none of the selected farmers received emergency relief grants (table 1).

Insolvency

Relatively more farmers reported themselves insolvent in the four central and western counties of the Northern Great Plains than in the two eastern counties. Large numbers of farmers had failed and left the area, but of those who remained in the central and western counties and were interviewed in this survey, from 11 percent in Sheridan County to 19 percent in Hyde County reported themselves insolvent in the summer of 1935. The proportions were 14 percent in Hettinger County and 16 percent in Divide County.

In Traill County in the Red River Valley, on the other hand, only 1 out of 52 farmers reported himself insolvent in the spring of 1935. In Moody County in southeastern South Dakota, only 10 percent of the selected farmers considered themselves insolvent.

Farmers on Relief Rolls

Reports of the South Dakota Emergency Relief Administration show that over one-half of all farmers in South Dakota were receiving emergency relief on December 31, 1934. The farm relief load was probably equally heavy in North Dakota, judging from reports of the county relief administrations in the selected counties.

In Hyde County representing the Missouri Plateau Area of central South Dakota, a livestock and cash-grain farming area, more than 80 percent of all farmers were on emergency relief rolls in April 1935. In Moody County, however, representing the intensive livestock production area of the southeastern part of the State, and scarcely affected by drought, only 22 percent of the farmers were receiving relief in May 1935, and the proportion declined rapidly throughout the following month. The highest relief intensity rate of any of the six Northern Great Plains counties surveyed was found in Divide County of northwestern North Dakota where 89 percent of all farmers received relief in April 1935. In sharp contrast was Traill County in eastern North Dakota, where it was not considered necessary to set up a county relief administration. The proportions of farmers on relief in Hettinger and Sheridan Counties, 30 and 26 percent, respectively, while much lower than in Divide and Hyde Counties were still higher than the proportions of farmers on relief in the eastern counties.

Table 2.—Date of First Relief to Farm Operators on Relief in April–May 1935 in Representative Counties in the Northern Great Plains

Date of first relief	Number of farm operators				
	Divide	Hettinger	Sheridan	Hyde	Moody
Total[1]	157	187	150	245	99
March 1, 1935, or later	1	7	26	4	—
November 1, 1934–February 28, 1935	7	21	28	90	9
Prior to November 1, 1934	149	159	96	151	90

[1] Number in sample reporting date relief was begun.

In all of the selected counties the relief status of most of the farmers was directly attributable to the 1934 drought, as indicated by the fact that most of those receiving relief had gone on the rolls after it was apparent that their crops were a failure. As a result of near crop failures in 1933, however, many of the relief clients in the central and western counties had received relief as early as the spring of 1934. On the other hand, over one-third of the farmers on relief in Sheridan and Hyde Counties remained off relief rolls until the winter of 1934–35 or later (table 2).

There was no indication that the handicaps of old age, disabilities, or a large number of dependents were responsible for the plight of any appreciable number of the farmers on relief. From 85 to 95 percent of these farmers were not over 60 years of age and from 62

86869°—38——3

to 86 percent were not over 50 years of age (appendix table 2). Four percent was the maximum proportion in any county reporting disabilities that would prevent them from working. Less than one-tenth of the relief clients in Divide, Hyde, and Moody Counties reported more than four children under 16 years of age (appendix table 3), and only between one-fifth and one-fourth of the clients in Hettinger and Sheridan Counties reported more than four children under 16 years of age.

A possible disadvantage in the composition of many of the relief families, however, was the lack of a family labor supply. The majority of the relief clients had no boys 16 years of age or older who were available for farm work.

TYPES OF FARMING

In the two eastern counties, where relief and insolvency rates were lowest and where incomes were nearest to normal in 1934, farming is more nearly suited to climatic conditions than in the four central and western counties. In the region which includes the eastern part of Traill County general, crop-specialty, and dairy farms predominate, according to a classification based on gross income from the 1929 crop, with cash-grain farms of minor importance; in the region which includes the western part of the county most of the farms are cash-grain, but other types of farms are well represented. Likewise the type-of-farming area which includes Moody County, although an intensive livestock production area, has numerous general as well as cash-grain farms.[4]

In contrast are the areas in which Divide, Hettinger, and Sheridan Counties are located, where from 76 to 90 percent of all farms have been classified as cash-grain farms. There is more general farming in the Missouri Plateau Area of central South Dakota, represented by Hyde County, but animal-specialty and cash-grain farms account for 67 percent of the farms in this area.

In general a combination of cash-grain and range livestock production predominates throughout the central and western parts of the Dakotas. Usually where soils are suitable and where the topography permits the use of large-scale equipment, primary emphasis is placed on the production of cash grains; whereas in the rougher sections the emphasis is placed on range livestock production. On the other hand, in eastern North Dakota, represented here by Traill County, and in northeastern South Dakota cash-grain farming is supplemented by other enterprises—potato, dairy, and livestock production. In southeastern South Dakota cash-grain production has been overshadowed by intensive production of beef cattle and hogs.

[4] Elliott, F. F., *Types of Farming in the United States*, U. S. Department of Commerce, Bureau of the Census, Washington, D. C., 1933, table 5.

The differences in farming types between the eastern and the other parts of the area are largely because of differences in topography and climate. A longer growing season and more adequate rainfall enable farmers in the eastern counties to grow a greater variety of crops, produce higher yields, and be successful on smaller acreages than is possible in the regions to the west.

NATURAL FACTORS AFFECTING AGRICULTURE

Topography

Much of the western part of the Dakotas as well as northeastern Wyoming and central and eastern Montana is not suited to crop production because of the rolling to hilly topography. The rougher sections known as the "Bad Lands" border the Little Missouri River in the extreme western part of the Dakotas and the Black Hills in southwestern South Dakota. From this hilly area the land becomes rolling to undulating in the broad area lying between the Missouri River and the Red River Valley and reaches a level plane in the Red River Valley.

Soils

Fertile soils throughout the Northern Great Plains have encouraged a system of cash-grain production, as all major soil types in the area are suited to the production of grains.

The predominant soils belong to two general groups, those east of the Missouri River coming within the classification of Northern Chernozems and most of those west of the river being known as Northern Dark-Browns (fig. 2). Thus, in all of the counties included in this study, except Hettinger, the predominant soils belong to the Northern Chernozem group. The various types of this group appear in widely separated parts of the area, but the nature of the terrain and the effect of the climate naturally affect their productivity in different regions. The lighter types are subject to wind erosion, but in general wind erosion has been a less serious problem in the Northern than in the Southern Great Plains (fig. 3).

In Moody County, in the southeastern part of South Dakota, the predominant soils are the relatively heavy Moody silt loams, occupying a rolling terrain, and the fertile, well-drained Barnes loams and fine sandy loams, occupying an undulating to rolling terrain.[5] Corn, oats, sweet clover, and alfalfa are the principal crops grown on both types of soils in Moody County. The Moody soils are also found in parts of eastern Nebraska and South Dakota.[6]

[5] Bureau of Chemistry and Soils, *Atlas of American Agriculture*, part III, U. S. Department of Agriculture, Washington, D. C., 1935, p. 72.

[6] Watkins, W. I. and Larson, G. A., *Soil Survey of Moody County, South Dakota*, Bulletin 2, Series 1926, U. S. Department of Agriculture, Bureau of Chemistry and Soils, Washington, D. C., 1929, pp. 10–16.

FIG. 2—MAJOR SOIL GROUPS IN THE GREAT PLAINS

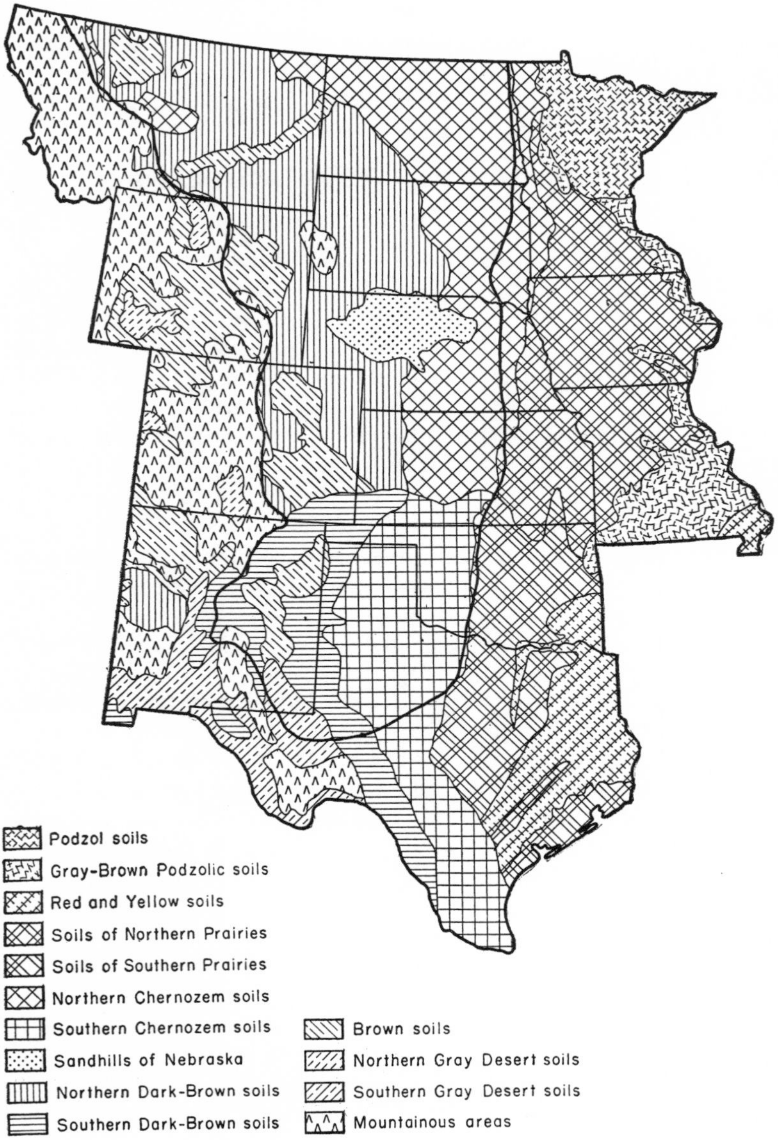

Podzol soils
Gray-Brown Podzolic soils
Red and Yellow soils
Soils of Northern Prairies
Soils of Southern Prairies
Northern Chernozem soils
Southern Chernozem soils
Sandhills of Nebraska
Northern Dark-Brown soils
Southern Dark-Brown soils
Brown soils
Northern Gray Desert soils
Southern Gray Desert soils
Mountainous areas

Note: Irregular line bounds the Great Plains Region as delimited by the Great Plains Committee.

Source: *Atlas of American Agriculture*, Part III, Plate 2, U.S. Department of Agriculture, Bureau of Chemistry and Soils, 1935.

AF-2658, WPA

FIG. 3 - EXTENT OF WIND EROSION IN THE GREAT PLAINS 1934

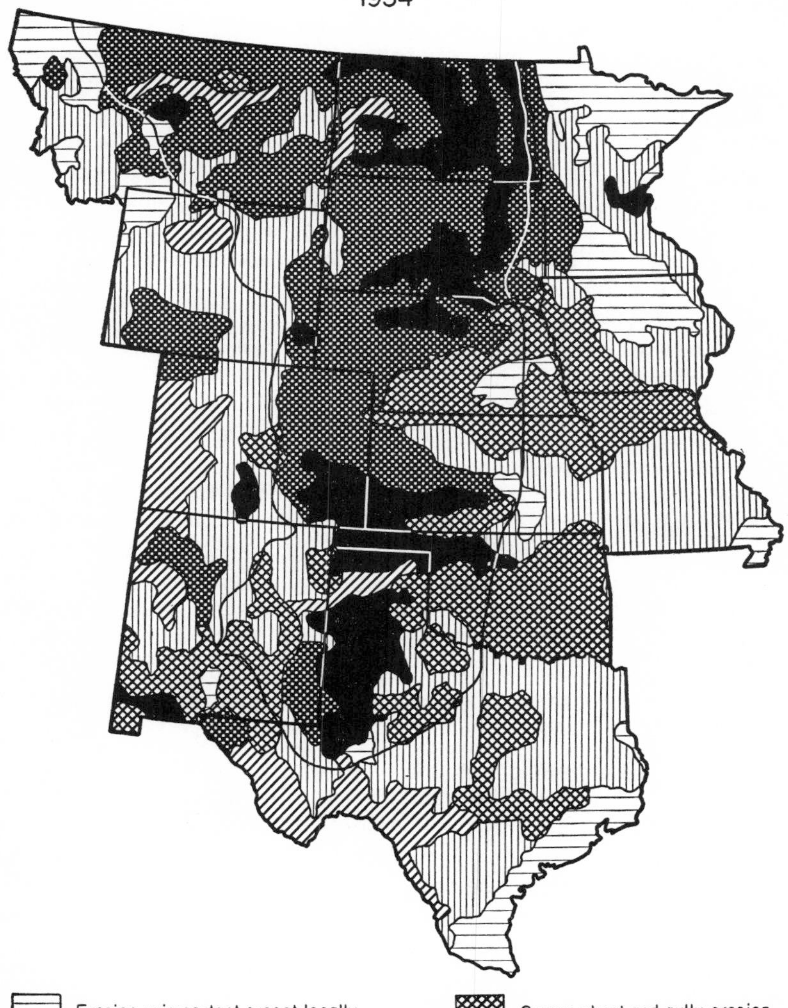

Erosion unimportant except locally

Moderate sheet and gully erosion serious locally

Moderate to severe erosion; includes mesas, mountains, canyons, and badlands

Severe sheet and gully erosion

Slight wind erosion moderate sheet and gully erosion

Moderate to severe wind erosion

Note: Irregular line bounds the Great Plains Region as delimited by the Great Plains Committee.

Source: Adapted from "General Distribution of Erosion," U.S. Department of Agriculture, Soil Conservation Service, August 1936.

AF-2654, WPA

In the other eastern county, Traill County, N. Dak., the highly fertile, generally heavy, but sometimes poorly drained Fargo soils and the lighter textured Bearden soils predominate. The Fargo soils lend themselves to the production of small grains, especially wheat. Bearden soils are adapted to the production of general farm crops, including corn and potatoes.

Sheridan County in central North Dakota is occupied largely by the same type of fertile soil, the Barnes series, which appears in parts of Moody County, S. Dak. The more rolling terrain of the county, however, results in a greater part of the soil being used only for pasture. The Williams soils in the extreme southwestern corner of the county are likewise often used for pasture because of the rolling terrain which they occupy.

Nearly all of Divide County in northwestern North Dakota and Hyde County in the central part of South Dakota are occupied by the Williams soils. The loams and silt loams of this series are adapted to all of the crops grown in the region, but the silty clay loams are used primarily for pasture.[7]

In Hettinger County in southwestern North Dakota, west of the Missouri River, the predominant soils belong to the Rosebud series of the Northern Dark-Brown group. They are lighter in color and texture and generally contain less organic matter than the soils to the east. Sandy loams predominate, occupying a rolling terrain. These soils are capable of producing small grains but, because of their general sandy characteristics, are also adapted to the production of feed crops for livestock.

Climate

Long and severe winters, short but relatively warm summers, and limited and variable rainfall characterize the climate of the entire Northern Great Plains, but the length of the growing season and the annual precipitation are much more favorable in the eastern section than in the other parts of the area. The growing season in the southeastern part of the area averages as much as 150 days in length as compared with less than 100 days in the northwestern part (fig. 4).[8]

Average annual rainfall ranges from less than 12 inches in central Montana to more than 25 inches in southeastern South Dakota. It is less than 20 inches in all but the eastern portions of the area and in the Black Hills section of southwestern South Dakota. A favorable factor is that from one-half to three-fourths of the annual rainfall normally occurs during the growing season.

[7] Machlis, J. A. and Williams, B. H., *Soil Survey of Hyde County, South Dakota*, Bulletin 18, Series 1925, U. S. Department of Agriculture, Bureau of Chemistry and Soils, Washington, D. C., 1930, pp. 11–14.

[8] Bureau of Chemistry and Soils, *Atlas of American Agriculture*, "Climate," Frost and the Growing Season, U. S. Department of Agriculture, Washington, D. C., 1918, pp. 38–39.

FIG. 4 - AVERAGE NUMBER OF DAYS WITHOUT KILLING FROST IN THE GREAT PLAINS

1895 - 1914

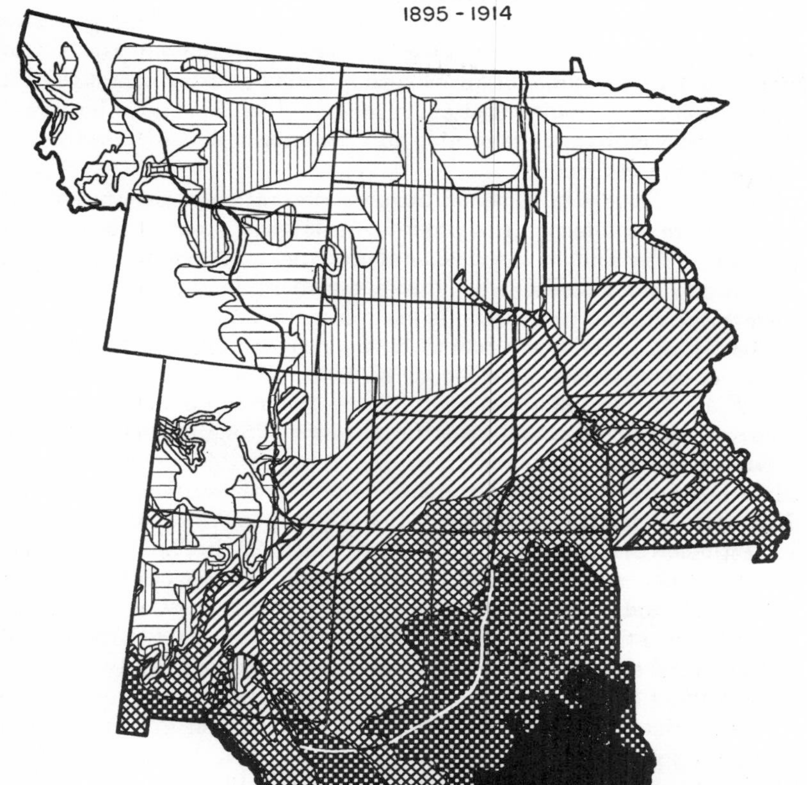

Note: Irregular line bounds the Great Plains Region as delimited by the Great Plains Committee.

Source: Adapted from "Average Number of Days Without Killing Frost," U.S. Department of Agriculture, Weather Bureau, 1916.

AF-2670, WPA

As a result of these climatic conditions, the southeastern portion of the Northern Great Plains States is the only part of the area which normally has adequate rainfall and a sufficiently long growing season to make production of corn for grain reliable. The climate is also well suited to the production of spring grains and legumes for hay. In the Red River Valley section, represented in this study by Traill County, the climate is favorable for the production of potatoes as well as spring grains.

With favorable weather conditions the central and western parts of the area are adapted to the production of spring grains, feed crops, and native hay and to the raising of livestock. Drought conditions, resulting from generally deficient and variable rainfall, occur so often, however, that crop production is hazardous (fig. 5).

The 5-year period from 1930 to 1934 was one of drought throughout the area, and in three of the four central and western counties surveyed, Hettinger, Sheridan, and Hyde, the rainfall deficiency was even greater in 1936 than during the excessive drought of 1934 (fig. 6).

During the 10-year period from 1927 through 1936 precipitation in Divide County was generally deficient during the critical spring and early summer months in 1930, 1931, 1934, and 1936. It was deficient in Hettinger County in 1931, 1933, 1934, and 1936; in Sheridan County in 1928, 1929, 1931, 1934, and 1936; and in Hyde County in 1928, 1931, 1934, and 1936.

In Sheridan County, for the 17-year period 1918–1934, both annual and growing season precipitation were below average in 1919, 1920, 1923, 1926, 1930, 1933, and 1934. In Hyde County records for the 35-year period 1900–1934 show that both annual and growing season precipitation were below average in 1903, 1904, 1907, 1910, 1911, 1912, 1913, 1917, 1922, 1925, 1926, 1928, 1929, 1931, 1933, and 1934.

For the period 1907–1934 both annual and growing season precipitation in Divide County fell below the 28-year average in 1907, 1909, 1913, 1917, 1920, 1929, 1930, 1931, and 1934. During the 5-year drought period from 1930 to 1934 annual precipitation exceeded the 28-year average only in 1932. In Hettinger County both annual and growing season precipitation was below the 28-year average in 1907, 1911, 1913, 1917, 1918, 1921, 1924, 1925, 1926, 1931, 1933, and 1934.

In the eastern counties, on the other hand, droughts have occurred less frequently and have been less severe than in the central and western counties. Precipitation is variable, but the margin between normal precipitation and the minimum required for crop production is much wider than in the central and western counties.

The average annual precipitation recorded in Traill County, N. Dak., during the 24-year period from 1911 through 1934 was 19.88 inches while that during the 5-year period from 1930 through

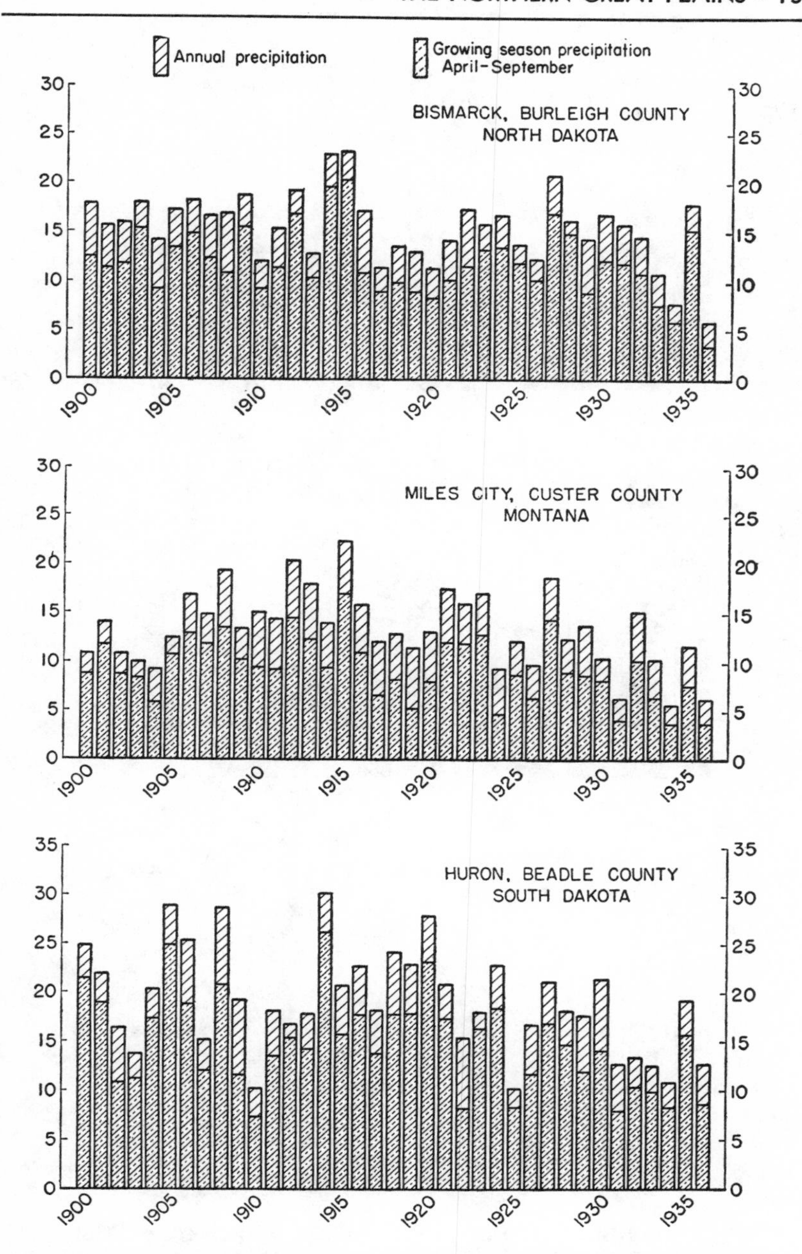

FIG. 5-ANNUAL AND GROWING SEASON PRECIPITATION, SELECTED STATIONS IN THE NORTHERN GREAT PLAINS 1900-1936

Source: U.S. Department of Agriculture, Weather Bureau.

AF-2783, WPA

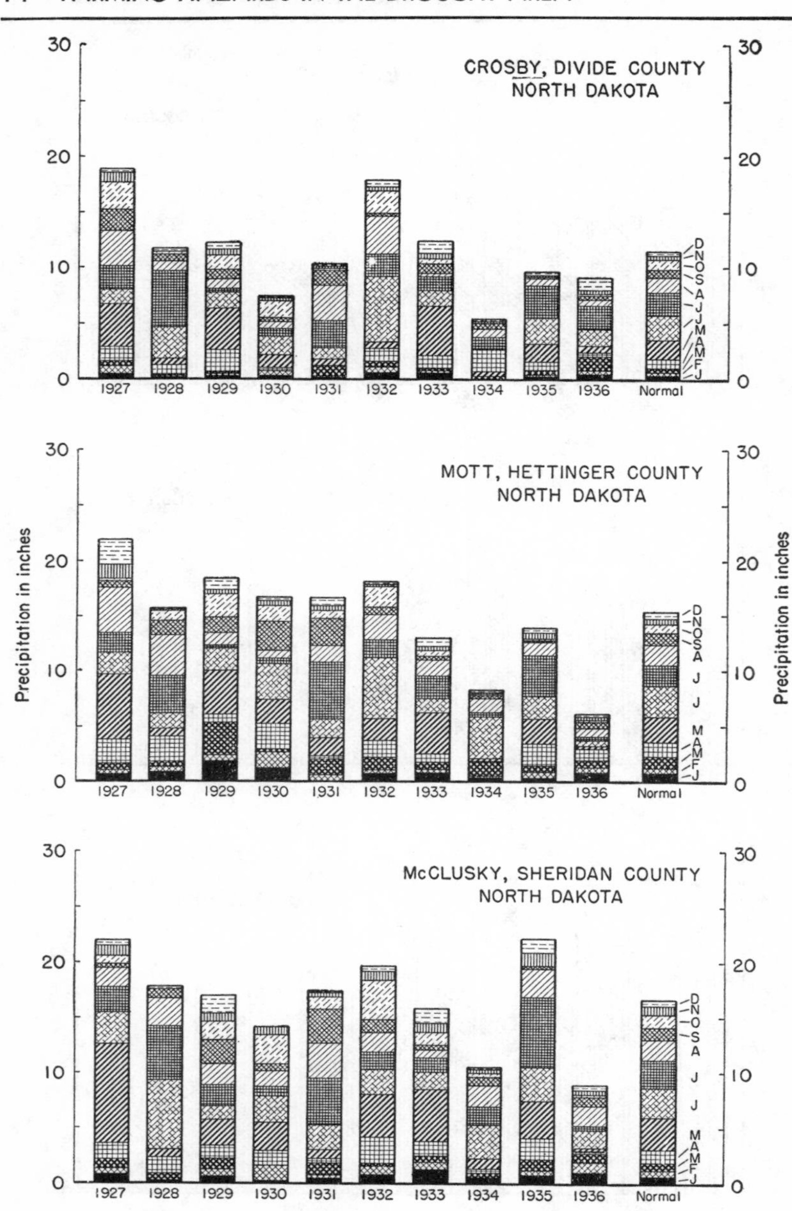

FIG. 6-NORMAL MONTHLY PRECIPITATION AND PRECIPITATION BY MONTHS, SELECTED STATIONS IN THE NORTHERN GREAT PLAINS
1927-1936

Source U S. Department of Agriculture, Weather Bureau.

AF-2775, WPA

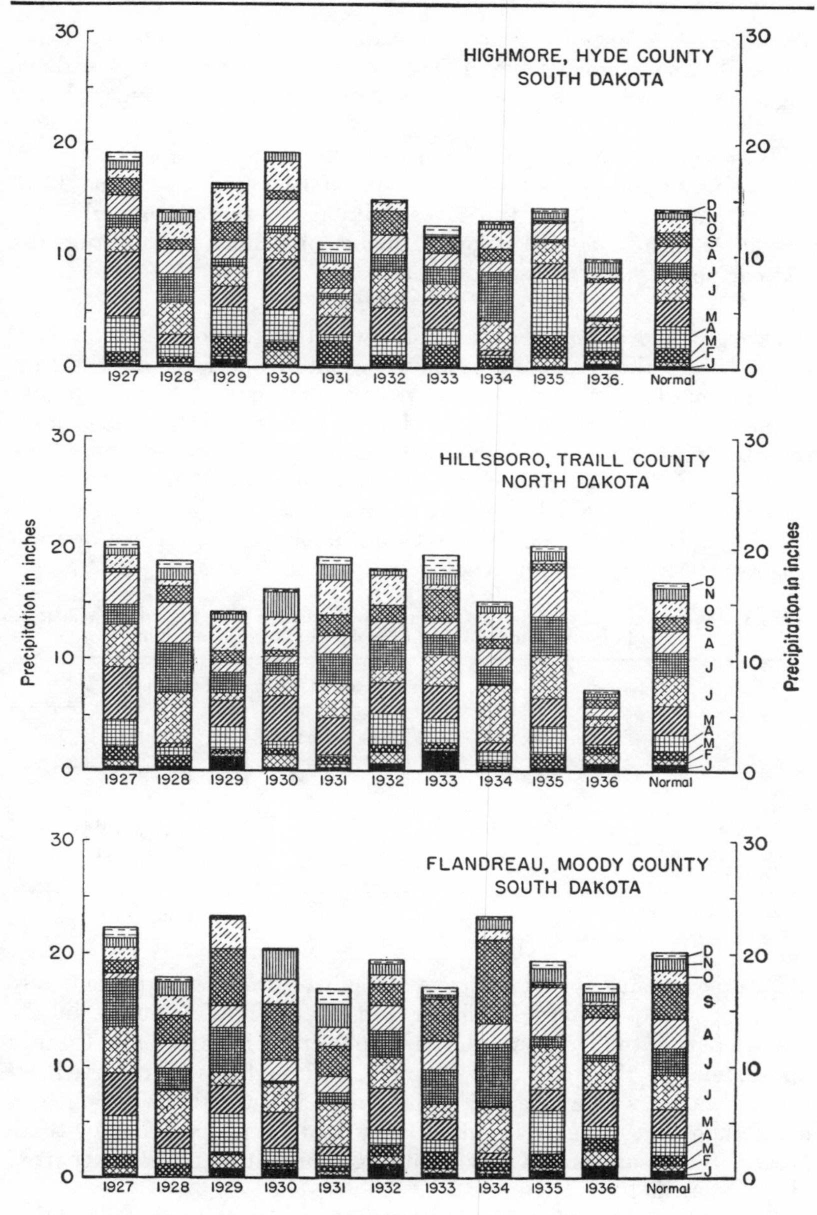

Fig. 6-NORMAL MONTHLY PRECIPITATION AND PRECIPITATION BY MONTHS, SELECTED STATIONS IN THE NORTHERN GREAT PLAINS
1927-1936—Continued

Source: U.S. Department of Agriculture, Weather Bureau.

AF-2777, WPA

1934 was 17.58 inches. Annual precipitation in 1936 was only 7.19 inches, but such a deficiency in Traill County was without precedent, the lowest precipitation previously recorded in this county being 14.14 in 1929.

The average annual precipitation recorded in Moody County, S. Dak., during the 35-year period from 1900 through 1934 was 23.13 inches and that during the 5-year period from 1930 through 1934 was 20.24 inches. It fell below 17 inches only four times during the 35-year period.

Causes of Crop Damage

Drought had damaged crops from two-fifths to more than one-half of the years that selected farmers had been operating in the four sample counties in central and western North and South Dakota (table 3 and appendix table 4). In Hyde County, S. Dak., the farmers reported that some damage was caused by drought 55 percent of the years in which they had operated, and complete damage to crops as a result of drought had occurred more than 1 year out of 6. In Hettinger, Sheridan, and Divide Counties, N. Dak., serious or total loss resulting from drought occurred 1 year in 4.

Table 3.—Percent of Years [1] Different Causes of Crop Damage Were Reported on Selected Farms in Representative Counties in the Northern Great Plains

County	Percent of years damage was reported					
	Drought	Insects	Hail	Soil blowing	Rust	Frost
Divide	40	10	17	2	9	1
Hettinger	43	14	15	3	4	1
Sheridan	41	13	12	3	5	*
Hyde	55	15	13	3	5	4
Traill	26	12	10	3	11	1
Moody	19	3	10	1	1	5

*Less than 0.5 percent.

[1] For length of record see appendix table 4.

Complete failure of all crops as a result of drought had practically never been experienced in either Moody or Traill County in the eastern part of the Dakotas. Even in 1934 crop yields in Traill County approximated the long-time average. Drought was reported by selected farmers as a cause of crop damage in only about one-fifth to one-fourth of the years in which they had been operating in these areas. Total or serious loss resulting from drought had occurred only 1 year in 10 or 15.

The actual amount of crop damage resulting from hail, frost, insects, rust, and soil blowing was difficult to determine since damage because of these causes was associated with other causes which occurred during the same years. In Divide County damage from hail occurred 1 year in 6, and in Sheridan, Hyde, and Hettinger Counties crop damage from this source occurred 1 year in 7 or 8. Damage from insects occurred in Divide County 1 year in 10, but in the other central and western counties and in Traill County it occurred 1 year in 7 or 8. In Moody County it occurred only 1 year in 33 (table 3).

In recent years some damage to the lighter soils throughout the area from soil blowing had been experienced by the farmers interviewed. In 1933 and 1934 wind erosion was common in the central and western counties as a result of insufficient moisture to establish cover crops, but serious damage was generally confined to small areas. Farmers in the Scobey-Plentywood Section of Divide County and those in Hettinger, Sheridan, and Hyde Counties reported an area equivalent to 7 or 8 percent of their cropland as being severely damaged and an area equivalent to 10 to 13 percent of their cropland as being slightly damaged by wind erosion. Farmers in the eastern counties reported that less than 1 percent of their cropland was damaged severely and that about the same proportion was damaged slightly (fig. 3, p. 9).

CROP YIELDS

The natural hazards of the area have made crop yields variable from year to year in all parts of the Northern Great Plains (appendix table 5). Good yields, however, have been reported more frequently in the eastern part of the area and crop failures or near failures more frequently in the central and western parts (appendix tables 6 and 7).

Crop yields of small grains per harvested acre, reported by State agricultural statisticians over a 21-year period ending in 1931, were higher in the eastern than in the western and central counties and were also more reliable from year to year (table 4 and appendix table 5). Likewise, farmers interviewed in the eastern counties reported less frequent poor yields and crop failures since they had begun farming in the area than those in the western and central counties, although the yields which the farmers of the eastern counties classed as poor or failure were considerably higher than those so classified by farmers in the central and western counties (appendix table 7).[9]

Corn for grain was usually a failure or a poor crop in all counties except Moody in southeastern South Dakota, the only section with sufficient rainfall and a long enough growing season to make its production reliable. The average yields reported by the State agricultural statisticians (table 4) do not reflect this tendency since they

[9] The considerable differences between average crop yields reported by the selected farmers (appendix table 7) and by the State statisticians (appendix table 5) are largely explained by the difference in method of calculation, the farmers reporting on a seeded-acre basis and the statisticians on a harvested-acre basis. Thus, the average crop yields of small grains, calculated by the farmers in the central and western counties from their estimates of good and poor yields and their frequency of occurrence, were somewhat lower than those of the State statisticians, owing to the fact that the farmers' estimates included crop failures.

were calculated on a harvested acre basis, and, except in Moody County, most of the corn acreage was cut for fodder and only the best acreage was harvested for grain. Consequently, the harvested yields appeared reasonably good in all counties.

Table 4.—Average Yield per Harvested Acre of Important Crops in Representative Counties in the Northern Great Plains, 1911–1931 [1]

County	Average yield per harvested acre (bushels)				
	Wheat	Barley	Oats	Corn	Flax
Divide	11.7	18.2	24.1	19.4	6.7
Hettinger	8.8	16.8	20.2	19.8	5.8
Sheridan	9.6	17.2	20.6	22.5	6.8
Hyde	9.3	20.2	25.1	19.2	7.0
Traill	12.5	20.6	26.0	25.5	7.9
Moody	12.1	25.8	31.8	29.7	9.2

[1] For years data were not available see appendix table 5.

Sources: Willard, Rex E. and Fuller, O. M., *Type-of-Farming Areas in North Dakota*, Bulletin 212, North Dakota Agricultural Experiment Station, Fargo, N. Dak., July 1927, pp. 254–259; reports of the North Dakota agricultural statistician, Fargo, N. Dak., 1919–1931; and reports of the South Dakota agricultural statistician, Brookings, S. Dak., 1922–1931.

Farmers in the North Dakota Black Prairies Section of Divide County reported good or medium yields of wheat, oats, and barley 3 out of 5 years that they had operated in the area. Yields of wheat and oats were failures about 1 year in 6 or 7, but yields of barley were failures 1 year in 5. Farmers in the Scobey-Plentywood Section of this county reported good yields of wheat and barley only 1 year in 5 and good yields of oats 1 year in 4. Failures of wheat occurred 1 year in 4 or 5 and failures of oats and barley about 1 year in 3. Failures of corn for grain were reported 7 out of every 8 years (appendix table 7).

Farmers in Sheridan County in central North Dakota reported good or medium yields of wheat, oats, and barley 3 years in 5. Failures or near failures of small grains occurred about 1 year in 7 and short crops 1 year in 4. Failures of corn occurred one-third of the time, with good yields reported in about the same proportion. This relatively high frequency of good yields reflects the fact that in the Sheridan County area extensive droughts are not common although years with deficient precipitation occur frequently.

Farmers in Hettinger County in southwestern North Dakota reported good or medium yields of wheat, oats, and barley more than one-half of the time. On the other hand, there were complete failures or poor yields of wheat 2 years in 5 and of oats and barley almost 1 year in 2. Poor yields or failures of corn occurred over one-half of the time.

Farmers in Hyde County in central South Dakota reported good or medium yields of wheat, barley, and oats only one-half of the time. Wheat yields were failures 1 year in 4, and barley and oats failed 1 year in 4 or 5. Corn was a complete failure one-third of the time.

Resettlement Administration (Rothstein).

No Use for This Harvester.

In contrast to these central and western counties were Moody and Traill Counties in the eastern part of the Dakotas, where failures in any crop were relatively rare. Farmers in Traill County reported good or medium yields of all crops 3 years out of 4, and in Moody County yields were good or medium 4 years out of 5. Complete failures of wheat occurred only 1 year in 20 in both counties (appendix table 7).

The disastrous crop failures of 1934 in the four central and western counties were preceded by a series of years in which crops were below average (appendix tables 7 and 8). Crop yields throughout the Northern Great Plains were reasonably good in 1930. In 1931 they were low in Hettinger and Sheridan Counties and almost failures in Divide and Hyde Counties. In 1932 they were fair in all of the counties. In 1933 crop yields were low in all of the central and western counties, and in 1934 they were almost complete failures.

Crop yields in Traill and Moody Counties, on the other hand, were not complete failures at any time during the period. In Traill County they were nearly normal in 1933 and 1934.

ORGANIZATION OF FARMS

In view of the frequent years of crop failures or short crops many of the farms in the central and western sections of the Northern Great Plains have been found too small to provide a sufficient surplus in good years to carry them over the inevitable bad years. Small acreages have also contributed to erosion problems since on the small farms there is a tendency to place too large a proportion of the land in crops, leaving the soil unprotected against wind erosion.

Land-use policies, with the view to increasing the size of many farm operating units and to withdrawing some of the arable land from cultivation in the interest of soil conservation, are advocated for many parts of the central and western Dakotas. Of the counties included in this study, Divide and Hettinger Counties are in areas where an increase in the size of farming units has been recommended. Sheridan County in central North Dakota and Hyde County in central South Dakota are in areas in which permanent withdrawal from cultivation of part of the land now in crops has been advised.[10]

Traill and Moody Counties, on the other hand, are in areas in which it is believed that settlement can be encouraged since the same natural hazards do not exist. Hence, higher crop yields and systems of diversified farming make operations on smaller acreages profitable in these counties.

Data on the financial status of selected farmers in 1935, on their financial progress since beginning operations in the area, and on the farmers receiving relief in 1935 give weight to these recommendations for the counties included in this study (appendix table 9). Small

[10] Preliminary classification of land-use consultants, National Resources Board.

operating units and too much reliance on cash crops appear to be directly related to the rural distress of the central and western counties. Operators of large farms in the counties surveyed were financially stronger than operators of small farms and were less likely to be on relief. In general, farmers primarily dependent on livestock as a source of income had made more financial progress than had those who relied for the most part upon crops.

Size of Operating Unit

The most common size of farm in the central and western counties was 160 to 320 acres. In Hyde County all farms in the county averaged 617 acres in size in 1935,[11] but corn-hog contracts, representing 65 percent of the farms in the county, listed almost 50 percent of the farms as having less than 440 acres with the majority of these having either 160 or 320 acres.

In Divide County in 1935 the average size of all 1,576 farms was 447 acres. Wheat contracts, however, which represented 98 percent of the total farms in the county, showed that 34 percent of the farm holdings were 280 acres or less in size and 29 percent were between 281 and 400 acres in size, with farms of 160 and 320 acres the most common.

In Hettinger County, where there were 1,235 farms in 1935, the average size of all farms was 555 acres. Wheat contracts, representing 99 percent of the farms in the county, indicated that more than 50 percent of the farms were less than 440 acres in size with farms of 160 and 320 acres very common.

Farms in Sheridan County averaged 501 acres in size in 1935. Wheat contracts again showed that farms of 160 and 320 acres were the most common.

Operators of farms under 400 acres had been able as a rule to produce little more than a living. This is shown by estimates made by selected farmers in Divide, Sheridan, Hettinger, and Hyde Counties of their financial progress, as calculated from statements of their assets and liabilities when they began farming in the area, their capital additions to or deductions from the farm business, and their assets and liabilities in 1935 (appendix table 9). In Divide and Sheridan Counties two-fifths of all the selected farmers and one-half of the farmers operating farms of less than 400 acres had operated at a loss since beginning farming in the area. In Hettinger County 30 percent of all selected farmers and 44 percent of those operating farms of 440 acres or less had operated at a loss. In Hyde County 46 percent of all selected farmers and 62 percent of those operating farms of less than 440 acres had operated at a loss.

In all four counties incomes from the farms of less than 281 acres were found to be generally too low to permit the accumulation of

[11] Bureau of the Census, *United States Census of Agriculture: 1935*, U. S. Department of Commerce, Washington, D. C.

reserves. Farmers operating these small farms in the North Dakota Black Prairies Section of Divide County estimated that their incomes were sufficient to accumulate capital in only about 3 out of 10 years. In the Scobey-Plentywood Section of Divide County incomes from small farms of similar size were sufficient to increase capital in only 1 out of 7 or 8 years and in Sheridan County in 3 out of 5 years. In Hyde County only two out of five farmers and in Hettinger County only one out of nine farmers operating farms of less than 280 acres reported that their normal incomes were sufficient to increase their capital (appendix table 1).

In Traill and Moody Counties farms were much smaller on the average than those in the other four sample counties, but even so the farmers in this favorably situated eastern area were able to farm more profitably. The average size of the 1,557 farms in Traill County in 1935 was 343 acres, and the most frequent size of farm had been 320 acres since 1920. Of the Traill County farms with wheat contracts for 1934, 29 percent were less than 200 acres in size, 40 percent were from 200 to 399 acres, and 31 percent were 400 acres or larger. The average size of all 1,358 farms in Moody County in 1935 was 382 acres, and the average size of farms represented by corn-hog contracts was 228 acres. Forty-four percent of the contracting farms were in the 121- to 200-acre group with most of the farms having 160 acres. Twenty-five percent were in the 281- to 360-acre group with most of the farms containing 320 acres.

In Traill County farmers in all size groups had a high net worth in 1935, and it was evident that in this county operation of farms of 160, 240, and 320 acres offered farmers something more than a bare living. Selected farmers in this county reported an average capital gain of $260 per year of farming. Four-fifths of the farmers reported that they had been able to accumulate capital since beginning farming in the area.

In Moody County it appeared that, in most instances, a 160-acre unit was adequate for a farmer to make a living for himself and his family. Farms in the group of less than 121 acres suffered an average yearly loss of $67. Capital accumulated on selected farms of from 121 to 200 acres averaged only $12 a year, but 28 farmers in that group who were operating 160-acre farms accumulated an average of $78 per year. If the record of 1 farmer who suffered abnormally large financial losses were omitted from the group, the remaining 27 operators would show an average accumulation of $184 per year.

Size of Relief Clients' Farms

Inadequacy in size of operating unit was apparently one of the major factors contributing to the inability of farmers on relief rolls to carry themselves through the adverse years of 1933 and 1934. Samples of the farmers' applications for relief indicate that the average

86869°—38——4

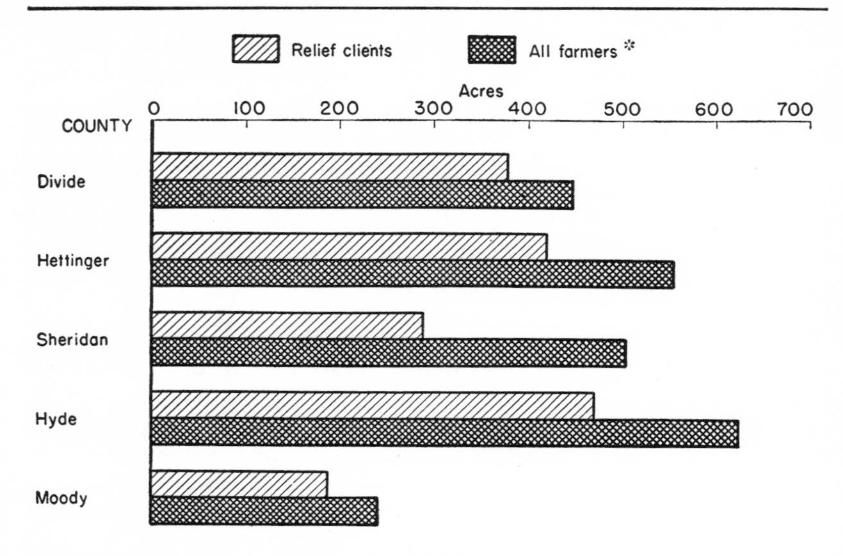

FIG. 7 - AVERAGE SIZE OF FARM OPERATED BY RELIEF CLIENTS AND BY ALL FARMERS IN REPRESENTATIVE COUNTIES IN THE NORTHERN GREAT PLAINS 1935

* *United States Census of Agriculture: 1935.*

AF-2685, WPA

size of farm operated by relief clients was considerably smaller than the county average.

The average size of farm operated by relief clients in Divide County was 373 acres (fig. 7 and appendix table 10), whereas the county average was 447 acres. About three-tenths of the relief clients were operating farms of 280 acres or less and three-fifths were operating farms of 400 acres or less. The average size of farm operated by relief clients in Hyde County was 464 acres as compared with a county average of 617 acres. One-fourth of the relief clients were operating farms of less than 280 acres and almost three-fifths operated farms of less than 440 acres.

In Hettinger County the average size of relief clients' farms was 413 acres as compared with 555 acres, the average size of all farms. About one-fourth of the clients were operating farms of less than 280 acres and almost one-half were operating farms of less than 440 acres.

In Sheridan County the average size of relief clients' farms was 289 acres as compared with a county average of 501 acres. More than one-third of the Sheridan County relief clients were operating farms of less than 240 acres and two-thirds were operating farms of less than 400 acres.

Small farms were also somewhat of a disadvantage in the southeastern part of the area, as indicated by the fact that relief clients in

Moody County were operating smaller farms than the average. The average size of farm reported by relief clients in Moody County was 199 acres, whereas the county average was 238 acres. One-half of the relief clients were operating farms of less than 200 acres.

Use of Land

Cropland use in 1934 was not exactly typical of normal years in the central and western counties. Slightly more acreage had been planted to feed crops or had been left idle than was usually the case. This did not represent a permanent change in the agriculture of the area but was largely the result of drought conditions. Following low yields in 1933, many farmers in the central and western counties were not financially able to seed their usual acreage in 1934 or were unwilling to gamble on a cash crop since experience in the area had taught them that their chances were exceedingly poor when the seedbed was devoid of moisture. The seeding of crops was delayed, and, when it became apparent that cash crops could not be produced, many farmers planted an unusually large proportion of their crop acreage to feed crops in an attempt to produce livestock feed. Most of them left at least part of their cropland idle rather than risk the capital required for seeding.

Table 5.—Utilization of Land on Selected Farms in Representative Counties in the Northern Great Plains, 1934

County	Number of farms reporting	Average number of acres per farm					
		Total	Cropland	Native grass		Former cropland	Farmstead and waste
				Hay	Pasture		
Divide:							
North Dakota Black Prairies Section	44	499	368	23	82	4	22
Scobey-Plentywood Section	22	549	287	7	208	4	43
Hettinger	63	606	371	7	213	2	13
Sheridan	57	547	324	21	184	1	17
Hyde	48	523	217	48	224	22	12
Traill	52	433	393	7	19	1	13
Moody	87	260	211	9	31	—	9

A normal condition, however, is the tendency for operators of small farms to place much higher proportions of their farm land in crops than do operators of larger farms and to practice fallow cultivation to a lesser extent. In the Scobey-Plentywood Section of Divide County selected farmers had an average of only 52 percent of their land in crops in 1934, but on small farms the amount in crops was as high as 73 percent, whereas on farms of more than 800 acres crops occupied only 38 percent of the farm land. In the North Dakota Black Prairies Section of this county, on the other hand, selected farmers on farms of all sizes had 74 percent of the farm land in crops with only a slight proportionate difference between the large and small farms (table 5, fig. 8, and appendix table 11). Spring wheat was the

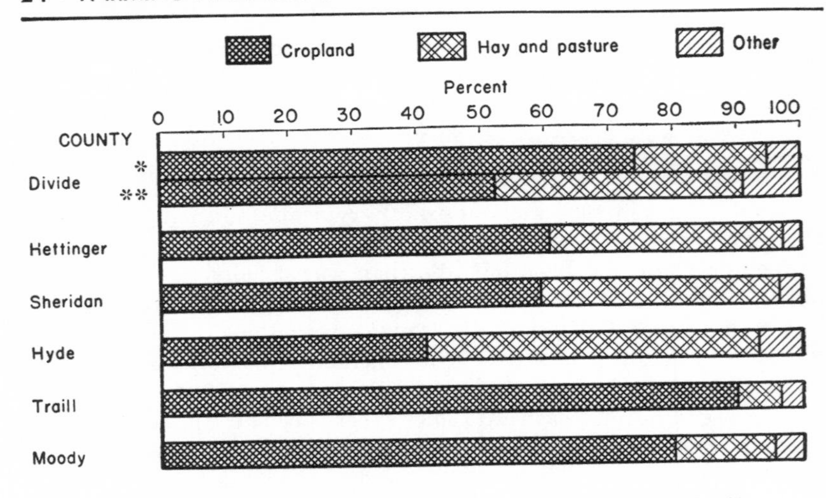

FIG. 8-UTILIZATION OF LAND ON SELECTED FARMS IN REPRESENTATIVE COUNTIES IN THE NORTHERN GREAT PLAINS 1934

* North Dakota Black Prairies Section
** Scobey-Plentywood Section.

AF-2687, WPA

major crop in both sections, occupying 36 percent of the cropland on selected farms in the Black Prairies Section and 38 percent in the Scobey-Plentywood Section (appendix table 12). Oats were second in importance in both sections with corn and barley next in importance in the Black Prairies Section and barley and flax next in importance in the Scobey-Plentywood Section.

In the North Dakota Black Prairies Section 35 percent of the cropland of selected farmers was idle in 1934 and 7 percent was fallow. In the Scobey-Plentywood Section 29 percent was idle and 9 percent was fallow. The fallow land in both sections was limited primarily to the larger farms, the crop acreage on the smaller units being insufficient to justify summer fallow farming.

In Sheridan County 59 percent of the farm land of selected farmers was in crops and 34 percent was in pasture. This proportion was approximately the same on all farms up to 880 acres where the proportion of cropland was smaller and that of pasture land larger than on smaller farms. In 1934 selected farmers reported that 21 percent of the cropland was idle or summer fallowed. Wheat, the major crop, was seeded on 44 percent of the total cropland, corn on 9 percent, oats and barley on 7 percent each, and rye on 5 percent.

Selected farmers in Hettinger County reported 61 percent of the land in crops in 1934, 5 percent of their cropland fallow, and 18 percent idle (appendix table 12). As in Divide County fallow land and wheat planted on fallow land were reported on only the larger farms. The farmers reported that 46 percent of their cropland in 1934 was in wheat, 9 percent in barley, 5 percent in rye, 4 percent in oats, and 8 percent in corn.

In Hyde County the selected farmers had 42 percent of their farm land in crops and 46 percent in pasture. The larger the farm the larger the proportion in pasture and the smaller the proportion in crops. Fallow land was reported by only one farmer, but nearly 38 percent of the cropland of all selected farmers was idle in 1934 because of drought conditions. Wheat and barley were the two major crops seeded in 1934, followed in order of their importance by corn, feed crops, and oats. The acreage of various crops seeded in 1932 and 1933 would indicate that in normal periods the crops in Hyde County in order of their importance are wheat, barley, corn, oats, and rye.

In Traill and Moody Counties much higher proportions of the farm land were in crops than in the central and western counties. The crop acreage in 1934 was about normal, since neither county had suffered much in 1933 and the farmers had had little incentive to vary their crop acreage.

Selected farmers of Traill County reported 91 percent of the farm land in crops and less than 5 percent in native pasture in 1934. In that year 31 percent of the cropland was in wheat, 17 percent in barley, and 10 percent in oats. In 1934 all of the farmers planted wheat and nearly all planted barley, oats, and corn. About one-half planted potatoes. Twelve percent of the cropland of the selected farmers was reported as fallow and less than 6 percent was idle. The relative importance of the various crops had changed little since 1932 (appendix table 13).

In Moody County the selected farmers reported that in 1934, 81 percent of their farm land was in crops and 12 percent in native pasture (appendix table 12). None of the cropland was summer fallowed and only 4 percent was idle. Of the cropland 36 percent was in corn, 24 percent in oats, and 17 percent in barley. From 1932 to 1934 the importance of major crops, as measured by seeded acres, remained approximately the same, but an unusually large proportion of the corn acreage was cut for fodder in 1934.

In all of the selected counties land that was share-rented was used for the most part as cropland, whereas land rented for cash was usually native pasture (appendix table 14). Counties specializing in cash-grain production had a relatively high percentage of share-rented land and comparatively little cash-rented land. Hyde County, which combined livestock with cash-grain production, had a relatively high percentage of cash-rented land. Moody and Traill Counties, with a very small proportion of the farms used for native pasture, had little or no cash-rented land.

Livestock

Cattle production was the most important livestock enterprise in the selected counties of the Northern Great Plains States. Milk cows were important in all but the rougher areas, such as the Scobey-Plentywood Section of Divide County and parts of Hyde County (appendix table 15). Hogs were an important enterprise only in Moody and Hyde Counties. Poultry was produced in small farm flocks in all of the counties.

The acreage of feed crops planted in 1934, the best of which produced very low yields, was insufficient to carry the farmers' livestock. Low cash incomes, depleted cash reserves, and high feed prices limited the importation of livestock feed. This feed shortage, coupled with an urgent need for a supplementary cash income, forced farmers throughout the drought area of the Northern Great Plains to reduce livestock numbers in 1934. Reductions by April 1, 1935, had been most drastic in the central and western counties where the feed shortage was most acute (fig. 9 and appendix table 15).

Hogs were reduced more drastically than any other class of livestock. Numbers of poultry were reduced about one-fourth to two-thirds in the central and western counties and about one-third in Moody County, but they were maintained at near normal levels in Traill County. Work stock numbers were generally maintained at near normal in all of the selected counties.

Cattle numbers were maintained at normal or near normal in the eastern counties, but in the other counties the reduction was severe. Reduction in cattle numbers represents a larger sacrifice than do reductions in other classes of livestock and a larger problem in the rehabilitation of farmers, owing to the greater importance of cattle as a farm enterprise. They were reduced by approximately one-fifth in Hettinger County, one-fourth in Sheridan County, nearly one-half in Hyde County, and two-fifths in the Scobey-Plentywood Section and over one-half in the North Dakota Black Prairies Section of Divide County.

As a general rule, reductions in livestock numbers were more severe proportionately on small than on large farms (appendix table 15). The operators of small farms in the central and western counties of the Northern Great Plains, with limited reserves and limited pasture acreage, were unable to carry their livestock without assistance. Feed loans enabled some to retain a breeding herd as large as their depleted pastures would carry, but many were left with little or no livestock.

In the North Dakota Black Prairies Section of Divide County almost 5 percent of the selected farmers had no milk cows and 95 percent had no beef cows in the spring of 1935 (appendix table 16).

FIG. 9 - PERCENT OF CATTLE PURCHASED UNDER THE EMERGENCY LIVESTOCK PURCHASE PROGRAM OF THE AGRICULTURAL ADJUSTMENT ADMINISTRATION*

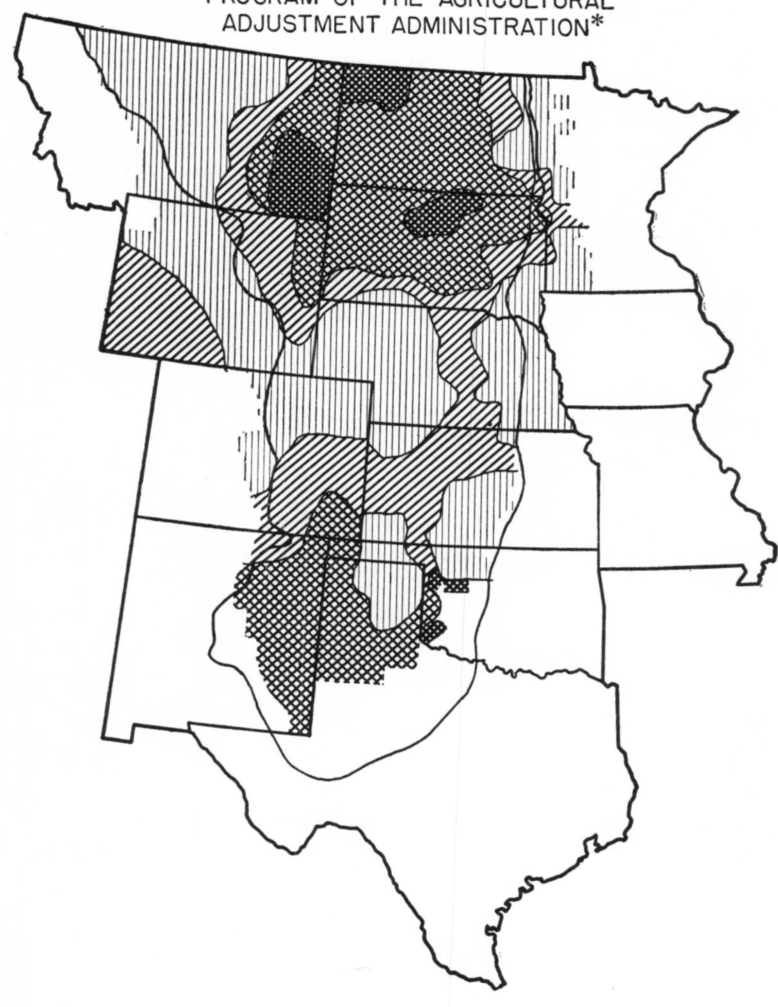

Note: Irregular line bounds the Great Plains Region as delimited by the Great Plains Committee.

* Based on number purchased plus the number reported on farms on January 1, 1935.

Sources: Data from the Agricultural Adjustment Administration and *United States Census of Agriculture: 1935.*

Percent
0-19
20-39
40-59
60-79

AF-2689, WPA

Five percent had no other cattle. No farmers reported more than three brood sows, and one-half had none. Two-thirds had no other hogs, and three-fourths had no more than 50 chickens. In the Scobey-Plentywood Section of Divide County approximately three-fifths of the farmers had no milk cows and two-fifths had no beef cows.

In Hettinger, Sheridan, and Hyde Counties about one-fourth of the farmers had no milk cows and from three-fifths to four-fifths had no beef cows. About one-third of the farmers in Hettinger and Sheridan Counties and two-fifths of those in Hyde County had no brood sows; from two-thirds to seven-tenths had no other hogs; and from three-fifths to four-fifths had no more than 50 chickens.

In most instances the proportions of the farmers in the eastern counties without any of the specified classes of livestock were considerably smaller than those in the western counties. All of the farmers in Traill County had cattle and poultry as did most of those in Moody County. Many of the Traill County farmers had no hogs; but in Moody County, where corn for grain is produced, over three-fourths of the farmers had brood sows and four-fifths had other hogs.

Inadequate livestock enterprises were associated with the need for emergency relief in almost all areas. Numbers of livestock reported by farmers when they went on relief were generally much smaller than those reported by the selected operators in the spring of 1935. In Divide County, where 89 percent of the farmers were on relief, the relief clients reported an average of 6 head of cattle, 2 hogs, 42 chickens, and 3 horses (appendix table 10), whereas the selected farmers had an average of 10 head of cattle, 3 hogs, 48 chickens, and 6 horses (appendix table 15). In Hettinger County the relief clients reported only half as many cattle and chickens as the selected farmers, while in Sheridan County the relief clients reported half as many cattle and three-fourths as many chickens as the selected farmers. Relief clients in Moody County reported approximately three-fifths as many cattle as did the selected farmers. Hyde County was an exception in that relief clients reported about the same number of cattle, more hogs and poultry, and nearly as many horses as did the selected farmers. This situation is probably due to the fact that animal-specialty farms are dominant in this county, and more than 80 percent of the farmers were on relief.

Actually the relief clients' livestock enterprises, as compared with those of the selected farmers, were even smaller than these reports indicate. Since the relief clients' reports were made when they applied for relief, they represented a period which, in the majority of cases, was several months before the selected farmers were interviewed for this study. It was during these intervening months that the drastic reduction of livestock in the area occurred.

Use of Machinery and Labor

On many of the farms throughout the central and western counties surveyed at least a portion of the machinery was old and in need of replacement, but on other farms minor repairs would put it in workable condition. In most instances such replacements were needed on the small tenant-operated farms.

The average estimated value of machinery per farm was $800 or $900 in Divide, Hettinger, and Sheridan Counties, but it was little more than $600 in Hyde County (appendix table 23). The average estimated cost of machinery repairs needed was around $100 per farm in all four counties. The value of machinery per farm was less on tenant-operated farms than on owner-operated farms, and the estimated cost of machinery repairs needed, in proportion to the estimated value of the machinery, was generally somewhat higher on tenant-operated farms.

The usual machinery reported on 320-acre farms in the central and western counties consisted of one 2-bottom gang plow, one 5-section spike-tooth harrow, one 10-foot grain drill, one 1-row cultivator, one grain binder, one mower, one hay rake, and two or three wagons. Additional machinery on 640-acre farms usually consisted of one tractor, one tractor plow, one 8-foot disk harrow, and one grain header.

Farm machinery in the eastern counties was in better condition than that in the central and western counties. Farmers in Traill County were generally able to maintain their own machinery, but some farmers in Moody County needed financial assistance in making machinery repairs. The average estimated cost of machinery repairs needed in Moody County was $84 per farm.

Farms of 160 acres in size in Traill and Moody Counties reported about as much farm machinery as those of 320 acres in the counties in the central and western parts of the Dakotas. The usual machinery reported on 160-acre farms in Traill and Moody Counties consisted of one 2-bottom gang plow, one single disk harrow, one 24-foot spike-tooth harrow, one grain drill, one grain binder, one mowing machine, one hay rake, and two or three wagons. Farmers with 320-acre farms reported, in addition to the above items, one tractor, one tractor plow, one grain drill, two 1-row cultivators or one 2-row cultivator, one 2-row planter, one row binder, and one 1-row corn picker. Each farmer had an automobile and a cream separator.

Combines were not common equipment in the areas surveyed in the Northern Great Plains. In Hettinger County, where they were used more extensively than in any of the other selected counties, they were reported by only 7 of the 63 farmers interviewed.

The value of machinery mounted as the size of farm increased. In the Scobey-Plentywood Section of Divide County machinery on farms of 601–800 acres had an estimated average value 40 percent higher than machinery on farms of 281–400 acres, while in the North Dakota Black Prairies Section machinery on the larger farms was almost twice as valuable as that on the smaller farms. Needed repairs on machinery amounted to 14 percent of the average estimated value of the machinery in the North Dakota Black Prairies Section and to only 7 percent of the value in the Scobey-Plentywood Section. Likewise in Sheridan County equipment on 320-acre farms had an average estimated value of $569 while that on 640-acre farms was valued at $1,323. In Hettinger County machinery on farms of 280–439 acres was valued at $649 while on farms of 560 acres or more machinery was valued at $1,287. Needed repairs amounted to from 12 to 19 percent of the value of machinery.

In Traill and Moody Counties the average value of machinery per farm was much higher than in the central and western counties. Machinery on farms of 160 acres had an estimated average value of $563 in Traill County and $587 in Moody County. Machinery on farms of 320 acres was valued in Traill County at $1,116 and in Moody County at $1,145.

There was some relationship between the size of farms and the amount of labor used. Under the system of agriculture one man without a tractor and without additional help could operate a 400-acre farm including 160 acres of cropland. To operate much more than that, either additional help or power equipment was needed.

In the central and western counties where only one-third to about two-fifths of the smaller farms were operated with tractors, one-half or more of these small farms were operated by only one man. The majority of the larger farms were operated with tractors (appendix table 17), but at the same time from one-half to two-thirds of these larger farms required the labor of more than one man.

A similar situation existed in the eastern counties where the majority of the small farms were operated by only one man without the use of a tractor, while the majority of the large farms were operated with tractors and by more than one man. In many instances, however, the use of large tractors and extensive equipment enabled operators of large farms to work with a labor force that was very little larger than that required on the smaller farms.

The acreage operated in Sheridan County by labor forces of various sizes, with or without tractors (appendix table 18), might be used as an index of labor requirements in the central and western counties, while that operated in Traill County might serve a similar purpose for the eastern counties.

The average size of farm operated with tractors in Sheridan County was 611 acres, including 431 acres of cropland. The average size of farm operated without tractors was 484 acres, including 221 acres of cropland. Farms operated by one man with a tractor averaged 483 acres, which included 312 crop acres, while those operated by one man without a tractor averaged 401 acres, which included 164 crop acres. Crop acreage operated by two men without tractors was approximately the same as that operated by one man with a tractor and nearly twice that operated by one man without a tractor. However, cropland operated per man was less on some of the large farms than it was on some of the small farms, since total acreage as well as crop acreage is a factor determining the size of the labor force and since large farms frequently have a smaller amount of cropland proportionately than do small farms.

The average size of farm operated with tractors in Traill County was 497 acres, with 455 crop acres, and that of farms operated without tractors was 259 acres, with 227 crop acres. The average size of farm operated by one man with a tractor was 455 acres, including 425 acres of cropland, while that operated by one man without a tractor was 234 acres, including 201 crop acres.[12]

Farm Buildings

With the exception of the Scobey-Plentywood Section of Divide County and the smaller farms in Hettinger County, dwellings and other farm buildings of selected farmers in the western and central counties of the Dakotas were adequate although many of them needed paint and repairs. Because livestock need protection in the severe winters common to the area, a material increase in the size of the livestock enterprises would require the construction of new buildings on some farms.

The average cost of needed repairs to farm buildings ranged from $232 to $380 per farm (table 6 and appendix table 19). It was highest on the small farms in Hettinger County, where it amounted to 27 percent of the estimated value of farm buildings, and in the Scobey-Plentywood Section of Divide County, where it amounted to 19 percent of the estimated value of farm buildings. The average estimated value per farm of all farm buildings in the Scobey-Plentywood Section was only $1,204, and on the smaller farms in Hettinger County it was $1,022. In Hyde County needed repairs averaged 12 percent of the value of buildings, and in Sheridan County they amounted to an average of 11 percent. Although under the usual rental agreement the tenant is not responsible for the maintenance of farm buildings, there was no apparent relationship between the tenure of farmers and the estimated cost of repairs needed on their farm buildings.

[12] At least a portion of the additional cropland operated by one man in Traill County, as compared with Sheridan County, is no doubt annual pasture which makes up a considerable proportion of the pasture acreage in the former county. It is counted as cropland because it is rotated with other crops, but annual pasture usually does not require as much work as do other types of crops.

Table 6.—Average Value of Farm Buildings and Estimated Cost of Needed Repairs per Farm on Selected Farms in Representative Counties in the Northern Great Plains, 1935

County	Number of farms reporting	Value of buildings			Cost of needed repairs		
		Total	Dwelling	Other	Total	Dwelling	Other
Divide:							
North Dakota Black Prairies Section	44	$3,084	$1,195	$1,889	$374	$143	$231
Scobey-Plentywood Section	22	1,204	652	552	232	140	92
Hettinger	63	2,321	990	1,331	348	118	230
Sheridan	57	2,299	902	1,397	241	82	159
Hyde	48	2,699	1,153	1,546	336	100	236
Traill	52	3,977	1,665	2,312	301	94	207
Moody	87	3,880	1,395	2,485	380	90	290

Few farmers in the eastern counties needed assistance in the repair or construction of buildings. The average estimated value per farm of all farm buildings was nearly $4,000 in both counties. Available farm buildings in Traill and Moody Counties were occupied, however, and any extensive program tending toward closer settlement in these areas would require the construction of new buildings.

INDEBTEDNESS

Many farmers in the Northern Great Plains were heavily in debt in the spring of 1935. This indebtedness had been accumulating for years in some parts of the area. There were indications that some owner-operators who desired to maintain or increase the productivity of their soils were being forced to mine their farms in order to meet real-estate mortgage payments. Chattel mortgages on machinery and equipment and unpaid feed and seed loans, sometimes dating back several years, added to the farmers' heavy fixed costs in the central and western counties. Tax delinquency was also serious in these sections of the area.

Indebtedness tended to increase with the size of farm (appendix table 9), and owner-operators had a much larger indebtedness than did tenant-operators.

Real-Estate Indebtedness

Real-estate mortgages were reported by 75 to 85 percent of the owner-operators in all of the selected counties and, on the average, represented from 37 to 50 percent of the estimated value of owner-operators' real estate. They represented from 65 to 85 percent of owner-operators' total indebtedness (appendix table 23).

Chattel mortgages were second only to real-estate mortgages as an item of the owners' indebtedness. In the central and western counties they represented from 20 to 27 percent of all of the owners' indebtedness, being of greatest significance in those areas where feed and seed loan indebtedness was heaviest. In the eastern counties, where real-estate indebtedness was heavier than in the other counties, chattel

Resettlement Administration (Rothstein).

A Typical Farm in the Drought Area.

mortgages represented only 5 to 10 percent of the owners' indebtedness.

Chattel mortgages were the only major source of the tenants' indebtedness. They were reported by nearly all tenant-operators and represented from 76 to 92 percent of their indebtedness.

From one-fourth to two-fifths of all land in the selected central and western counties was mortgaged in 1935, and from 1 to 16 percent of the land was carrying more than one mortgage (table 7). The average amount of mortgage indebtedness in these central and western counties ranged from about $10 to more than $12 per acre. In Divide County the average indebtedness of all land per acre was nearly as much as the census valuation of farm land and buildings,[13] and in Hyde County the indebtedness per acre exceeded the census valuation.[14] This excessive indebtedness, as related to the current valuation of farm real estate, was due in part to a decline in real-estate values after many of the mortgages were incurred. But this fact did not alleviate the farmers' need for either a downward adjustment of their indebtedness or assistance in paying carrying charges.

Table 7.—Acreage Mortgaged and Average Indebtedness per Acre, Mortgages of Record in Representative Counties in the Northern Great Plains, 1935

County	Number of acres mortgaged		Percent of all land mortgaged		Average indebtedness per acre
	First mortgage	Other mortgage	First mortgage	Other mortgage	
Divide [1]	113, 420	38, 820	40	14	$12. 69
Hettinger [2]	179, 464	75, 136	38	16	9. 98
Sheridan	253, 709	86, 450	40	14	11. 00
Hyde	143, 252	8, 160	26	1	10. 99
Traill	208, 347	74, 791	38	14	18. 50
Moody	154, 990	30, 214	48	9	37. 00

[1] Based on sample of 13 townships representing 35 percent of land area of county.
[2] Based on sample of 21 townships representing 65 percent of land area of county.

Mortgage indebtedness appeared even heavier in the eastern counties, but farmers in those counties were better able to carry indebtedness. Thirty-eight percent of the land in Traill County and forty-eight percent of the land in Moody County was morgtaged in 1935. The average indebtedness per encumbered acre in Traill County was $18.50. In Moody County the average indebtedness was $37. In the latter county the indebtedness of some farmers was no doubt excessive, but in Traill County the relatively high and stable earning capacity of farms would enable most farmers to meet carrying charges on all indebtedness when due.

[13] Bureau of the Census, *United States Census of Agriculture: 1935*, *op. cit.*

[14] A higher concentration of mortgages on cropland than on pasture land and a higher acre value on cropland than on pasture land were responsible for some cases where the average mortgage indebtedness exceeded the average land value

Foreclosures had been serious in the Missouri Plateau Area of South Dakota, represented by Hyde County. Data pertaining to farm mortgage foreclosures in the region during the 12-year period from 1921 to 1932 indicate that farmers in that area were experiencing financial distress during a period when crop yields were considered satisfactory. From 1921 to 1925 the number of foreclosures in Hyde County and 10 surrounding counties averaged 390 per year.[15] From 1926 to 1930 the average number dropped to 290 a year, but in 1931 and 1932 it increased to 512 annually. During the entire 12-year period 1921–1932, 4,421 farms, or 47 percent of all farms in the 11 counties, changed hands because of mortgage foreclosures. In Hyde County alone 433 farms, or 68 percent of all farms in the county, changed hands through mortgage foreclosures.

A more favorable situation is indicated by similar data pertaining to mortgage foreclosures in southeastern South Dakota. From 1921 to 1925 the number of mortgage foreclosures in Moody and 7 surrounding counties averaged 121 annually and from 1926 to 1930 they averaged 116 annually. In 1931 and 1932 they increased to an average of 313 annually, but during the entire 12-year period only 1,814 farms, or 13 percent of all farms in the 8 counties, changed hands because of mortgage foreclosures.[16]

The Federal Land Bank and the Federal Land Bank Commissioner together held first mortgages on 66 percent of the mortgaged acreage in Divide County in 1935, on 50 percent in Sheridan County, on 66 percent in Hettinger County, and on 59 percent in Traill County (appendix table 20). In Hyde County, where foreclosures had been so high, private individuals held first mortgages on over one-third of the mortgaged acreage, and the Federal Land Bank and Federal Land Bank Commissioner held only 21 percent of the encumbered farm acreage. In Moody County lending corporations were most important, holding first mortgages on 31 percent of the mortgaged acreage; the two Federal agencies held first mortgages on 28 percent; and private individuals, on 27 percent. Lending corporations held only from 2 to 8 percent of the mortgaged acreage in the other counties surveyed.

Crop and Feed Loans

Unpaid feed and seed loans formed a considerable part of farmers' indebtedness in central and western North and South Dakota. The large number of loans made in the early thirties and still outstanding at the end of 1934 were an indication that farmers in the central and

[15] Steele, Harry A., *Farm Mortgage Foreclosures in South Dakota, 1921–1932*, Circular 17, South Dakota Agricultural Experiment Station, Brookings, S. Dak., May 1934.

[16] *Ibid.*

western portions of the Dakotas had been in straightened circumstances even before the recent adverse years.

By December 31, 1934, a total of 544 loans had been made for every 100 farms in Divide County (appendix table 21). Of feed and seed loans made in 1933 or earlier, 78 percent remained unpaid, with an average indebtedness of $542 for every farmer in the county. A further indebtedness of $265 per farm was incurred in 1934, all of which remained outstanding, making a total outstanding debt of $807 per farm in this county.

Three loans had been made for every two farms in Sheridan County. Of feed and seed loans made prior to 1933, 72 percent remained unpaid in December 1934. Counting the 1934 loans, outstanding loans averaged almost $130 per farm.

On December 31, 1934, outstanding indebtedness from feed and seed loans in Hettinger County averaged $192 per farm. Eighty-five percent of the loans contracted in 1932, a year of good crops but low prices, remained unpaid, and practically all loans made after 1932 were still outstanding.

On January 15, 1935, 97 percent of all seed and feed loans contracted in Hyde County in 1932 remained unpaid. Counting additional debts contracted in 1934, indebtedness per farm averaged about $246.

In Traill County, on the other hand, only 908 emergency loans, or an average of approximately 1 loan to every 2 farms, had been made through 1934. Only 533 loans, or about 1 loan to every 3 farms, remained unpaid, the outstanding indebtedness averaging less than $40 per farm.

Federal loans in the other eastern county, Moody, were smaller and were made to a smaller percent of farmers than in any other county surveyed. The outstanding indebtedness per farm, based on the number of loans made and the number outstanding, was about the same as in Traill County, but the indebtedness per loan was somewhat lower.

Tax Delinquencies

During the years from 1930 to 1935 tax delinquencies had increased rapidly in most of the central and western counties. In some of these counties taxes on more than four-fifths of the land were delinquent. Tax delinquency was much less severe in the two eastern counties, Traill and Moody, than in the central and western counties.

Only 11 percent of the farm land in Sheridan County had no delinquent taxes recorded against it during the 5-year period 1928–1932. By May 1935 some of the taxes imposed during those years had been redeemed on 79 percent of the farm land with delinquent taxes for those years, but in most cases the delinquencies for only 1 or 2 years had been redeemed and the remainder was outstanding.

The situation in Divide County from 1928 to 1934 was as bad as that in Sheridan County. In the North Dakota Black Prairies Section 88 percent of the land had been tax delinquent at some time during the 7-year period, and in the Scobey-Plentywood Section 84 percent of the land had been tax delinquent. In May 1935 at least a part, and in some cases all, of the taxes that had become delinquent during that period remained unpaid on 82 percent of the land in the North Dakota Black Prairies Section and on 78 percent of the land in the Scobey-Plentywood Section.

In Hettinger County from 1921 to 1933, taxes on 65 percent of the farm land had become delinquent at some time. Taxes for 1933 became delinquent on 41 percent of the farm land, and in May 1935 only 15 percent of the 1933 delinquencies had been redeemed.

Delinquencies in Hyde County were not a serious problem. Federal loans and crop production contracts had aided farmers materially in making tax payments. Tax sales were held each year, but only 19 percent of all farm land was sold for delinquent 1933 taxes.

Tax delinquencies in Traill and Moody Counties for 1930–1934 were not so extensive as in the central and western counties, and a larger proportion of delinquent taxes had been redeemed than in other areas. Taxes for 1933 in Traill County became delinquent on only 14 percent of the farm land, and by June 1, 1935, over one-third of these had been redeemed. In Moody County taxes for 1933 became delinquent on 28 percent of the farm land, but by June 1935, 91 percent of these had been redeemed.

Relief Clients' Indebtedness

Although the relief clients were operating smaller farms and had fewer assets than the selected farmers, they generally reported almost as much indebtedness. In Divide, Sheridan, and Hyde Counties the relief clients, both owner-operators and tenant-operators, reported only slightly less indebtedness than did the selected farmers of the same tenure (appendix tables 22 and 23). In Hettinger County the owner-operators' and tenant-operators' indebtedness was approximately the same among relief clients as among the selected farmers, and in Moody County it was considerably higher among the relief clients, both owner-operators and tenant-operators.

Real-estate mortgages generally comprised a higher proportion of the indebtedness of owners on relief than they did of the indebtedness of the selected owners. This fact might indicate that the credit of clients was more nearly exhausted when they went on relief than was that of the selected owners when they were interviewed some months later. For small operating units exhausted credit and excessive indebtedness were the inevitable consequences of an adverse period, and they were the final causative factors in the relief clients' need of assistance.

TENURE OF OPERATORS AND OWNERSHIP OF LAND

Tenure of Farm Operators

From two-thirds to four-fifths of all farmers in the sample counties were renting part or all of their operating units in 1935,[17] and from one-fifth to three-fifths of all farm land was being operated under lease. The high degree of farm tenancy is of significance when it is considered in relation to its rate of increase since 1920. The increase was particularly marked in Divide County where the proportion of all farmers who were tenants increased from 14 to 33 percent, whereas the proportion of all farm land operated by tenants increased from 13 to 26 percent (table 8).

Table 8.—Farm Tenancy in Representative Counties in the Northern Great Plains, 1920, 1930, and 1935

County	Percent of farm operators who were tenants			Percent of farm land operated by tenants		
	1920	1930	1935	1920	1930	1935
Divide	14	24	33	13	22	26
Hettinger	19	23	30	16	18	21
Sheridan	28	38	38	24	34	33
Hyde	27	43	52	24	34	45
Traill	36	42	46	35	44	45
Moody	54	56	58	54	57	57

Sources: Bureau of the Census, *Fourteenth Census of the United States: 1920* and *United States Census of Agriculture: 1935*, U. S. Department of Commerce, Washington, D. C.

A high degree of tenancy may lead to soil exhausting practices. This is because under the usual rental agreement the tenant is offered little incentive to maintain or increase the productivity of his operating unit. Secure on his unit usually only for the duration of a yearly lease, the inclination of the tenant is to get all he can from the land during that time. Even with an incentive, he probably could not afford to establish permanent pasture or to plant cover crops on land subject to erosion. In some instances the tenant cannot increase to desirable proportions the size of his livestock enterprise, either because his operating unit does not have land for feed crops or adequate pasturage or because his tenure is insecure.

Tenancy was particularly high in the relatively more prosperous eastern counties, Traill and Moody. The poorer financial position of the tenants in the Northern Great Plains as compared with owners (fig. 10) appeared in many instances to be related to the more recent establishment of the tenant farms and to their smaller size.

In most instances the majority of the farmers who were insolvent were tenant-operators on small farms who had been operating in their

[17] Bureau of the Census, *United States Census of Agriculture: 1935*, *op. cit.*

respective counties less than 10 years. If they had had a more favorable period in which to establish themselves, some of them might have maintained their solvency.

Tenants also comprised a considerably higher proportion of the farmers who had suffered losses than of those who had not. Again this appeared to be due as much to the fact that the tenants were more recent occupants of the area and had smaller farms as to the fact that they were tenants.

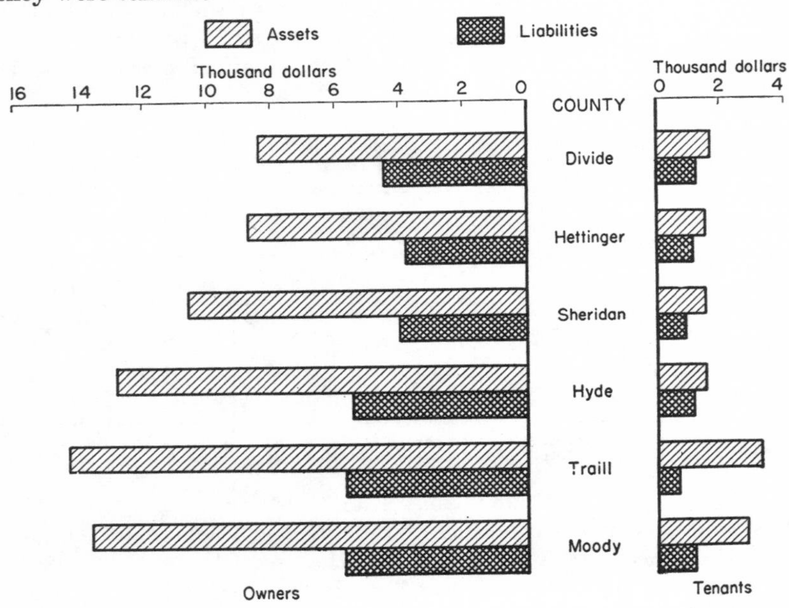

FIG. 10 - AVERAGE VALUE OF FARM ASSETS AND AMOUNT OF LIABILITIES OF SELECTED FARMERS IN REPRESENTATIVE COUNTIES IN THE NORTHERN GREAT PLAINS BY TENURE 1935

AF-2691, WPA

Tenants were relatively more numerous among relief clients than among selected farmers. They comprised 42 percent of the relief clients (appendix table 22) as compared with 30 percent of all farmers [18] in Hettinger County. In Sheridan County they comprised 61 percent of the relief clients and 38 percent of all farmers. In Moody County they comprised 82 percent of the relief clients as compared

[18] Since no data were available, however, for farmers who were forced to give up farming because of financial losses, the financial status represents only that of survivors.

with 58 percent of all farmers. In Hyde and Divide Counties, where more than 80 percent of the farmers were on relief, the extent of tenancy among relief clients was of course not greatly different from that among all farmers in the county.

The average net worth of tenants was much less than that of owners. The greatest disparity was in Hyde County, S. Dak., where the average net worth of selected owners was $7,491 and that of selected tenants was $405. The average net worth of selected Traill County owners was $8,819, whereas that of tenants averaged $2,772. The average net worth of Moody County owners was $7,893, whereas that of tenants was $1,739. Tenancy was especially high in these two relatively prosperous counties.

While tenants suffered from lack of opportunity to accumulate reserves because of their recent arrival in the area, owners suffered from depreciated land values. In Moody County, for instance, six of the seven farmers who reported themselves insolvent in 1935 were tenant-operators, five of whom had been in the area less than 10 years. Seven of the eleven selected farmers who had not been able to accumulate capital were owner-operators whose losses, in most instances, were incurred through the depreciation of real-estate values, and two of the four tenants who had suffered losses had been in the area less than 10 years.

Ownership of Land

Corporation holdings should not present a problem in the development of a rehabilitation program in the Northern Great Plains. Although foreclosures in recent years had transferred ownership of some land to corporate lending agencies, in 1935 corporations owned not more than 7 percent of the land in any of the central and western counties and not more than 12 percent in either of the eastern counties. Private individuals owned 79 percent of the land in Divide County, 91 percent in Sheridan County, 85 percent in Hettinger County, 74 percent in Hyde County, 91 percent in Traill County, and 87 percent in Moody County (table 9).

Table 9.—Percent of Land Owned by Different Types of Owners in Representative Counties in the Northern Great Plains, 1935

Type of owner	Percent of land owned					
	Divide	Hettinger	Sheridan	Hyde	Traill	Moody
Total	100.0	100.0	100.0	100.0	100.0	100.0
Private	79.2	85.0	90.9	74.1	91.2	87.2
Corporate	7.0	5.3	3.8	5.5	7.5	11.6
State and county	4.5	1.1	1.5	10.6	0.9	0.8
Federal Land Bank	2.3	0.3	0.4	0.3	*	0.4
Other	7.0	8.3	3.4	9.5	0.4	—

*Less than 0.05 percent.

Sources: Agricultural Adjustment Administration contracts and records in offices of county tax assessors.

Absentee ownership, on the other hand, is an important factor to consider. Much of the land in this area was owned by nonresidents in 1934 and 1935 although not to so great an extent as in some portions of the Central and Southern Great Plains.

Records taken from the county registration books in the various counties in 1935 showed that nonresidents owned 33 percent of the land in Divide County, 27 percent in Hettinger County, 51 percent in Sheridan County, and 29 percent in Traill County. Data taken from production control contracts of the Agricultural Adjustment Administration showed that in 1934 nonresidents owned 29 percent of the farm land in Hyde County and 18 percent in Moody County. The ownership of such large proportions of the land by nonresident landlords creates a problem since such landlords are often less interested in cooperating in a program for conserving the land and building a balanced farm economy than they are in collecting immediate returns.

Chapter II

THE CENTRAL GREAT PLAINS

THE DROUGHTS of 1931–34 were less severe and agricultural conditions during the period were less acute in most of the Central Great Plains—western Nebraska and Kansas and eastern Wyoming and Colorado—than in most of the Northern Great Plains. The western part of the Central Great Plains experienced considerable distress, but in none of the counties surveyed were conditions as serious as in some of the Dakota counties.

The major portion of the winter wheat area of the United States lies within the Central Great Plains States, but livestock production predominates in central Nebraska and north central Kansas, and in some of the western sections, where range livestock predominates. Intensive production of such crops as sugar beets and alfalfa predominates in those parts of the area where irrigation is practiced.

The counties selected for this study represent all of these types of farming as well as different types of problems, different degrees of farm distress, and different rehabilitation needs of farmers in the various sections of the region[1] (fig. 1, p. xv). Sherman County, Nebr., was selected for study because it was representative of the Loess Hills Area of central Nebraska where a larger part of the farm population was receiving emergency relief in 1935 than in any other

[1] The counties surveyed are typical of other counties in their areas as follows:

County surveyed	Area represented	Other counties in area	
Sherman, Nebr.	Loess Hills of central Nebraska	Nebraska:	
		Custer	Loup
		Dawson	Valley
		Garfield	Wheeler
		Greeley	
Perkins, Nebr.	Southwestern Wheat Area of Nebraska	Nebraska:	
		Chase	Deuel
		Cheyenne	Keith
Goshen, Wyo.	Southeastern Wyoming	Wyoming:	
		Laramie	
		Platte	
		Nebraska:	
		Scotts Bluff	
Cheyenne, Colo.	High Plains of eastern Colorado	Colorado:	
		Kiowa	Washington
		Kit Carson	

large area of the State. Cheyenne County, Colo., and Goshen County, Wyo., were selected for study as representative of the High Plains of eastern Colorado and southeastern Wyoming where drought and unfavorable conditions had prevailed for a number of years prior to 1935. These areas were considered to be in need of a comprehensive rehabilitation program. In Goshen County wind erosion had damaged a large proportion of the cropland, and most of the eroded acreage was marked for retirement from cultivation.

Since Goshen County includes both irrigated and nonirrigated farm land, however, the choice of this county for study affords an opportunity to examine differences in farm prosperity between an irrigated and a nonirrigated section. By several indices farms in the irrigated section of this county were in a more favorable position in 1935 than were farms in other sections.

Perkins County, Nebr., was chosen for study as representative of the cash-grain areas of southwestern Nebraska. Financial conditions of farmers throughout Perkins County were relatively favorable in 1935 as compared with other sections of Nebraska.

SITUATION OF FARMERS AFTER THE 1934 DROUGHT

Reductions in incomes and in livestock inventories, changes in sources of income, and the proportions of farmers on relief or rehabilitation rolls show the effects of the 1934 drought on farmers who were still operating in the Central Great Plains in the spring of 1935. No data are available concerning those farmers who had completely lost out and left the area.

Reduction in Incomes

Largely because of crop failures, gross cash receipts in 1934, including relief and other Government benefits, had been reduced to one-third of normal in Sherman County and cut in half in Perkins and Cheyenne Counties and in the nonirrigated section of Goshen County (table 10 and appendix table 24). Cash receipts were nearest to normal in the irrigated section of Goshen County where the reduction from normal was less than one-third. Except in this irrigated area, most of the 1934 gross cash receipts reported by selected farmers, as in the Northern Great Plains, came from direct or indirect Government expenditures.

Most of these Government expenditures were in the form of Agricultural Adjustment Administration benefits or payments for livestock. None of the selected farmers in the irrigated section of Goshen County and the loam section of Perkins County reported cash receipts from emergency relief payments in 1934. In Sherman and Cheyenne Counties, the sandy loam section of Perkins County, and the nonirrigated section of Goshen County, less than 4 percent of the gross cash receipts was derived from emergency relief. Work off the farm, which was often under Government auspices, likewise accounted for a very small proportion of the gross cash receipts, averaging less than 7 percent in any county.

Selected farmers in Sherman County reported that their average cash receipts in 1934 were only $502 as compared with $1,534 in normal years. Almost all of this amount in 1934 was derived from Government funds. Crop sales, normally supplying about one-third of the gross cash receipts in this county, were practically nonexistent in 1934. More than 90 percent of the cash receipts of selected farmers in Sherman County in 1934 came from the sale of livestock and livestock products or from Agricultural Adjustment Administration contract payments.

In Cheyenne County farmers reported that their gross cash receipts had dropped to $938 in 1934 from an average of $1,798. Normally nearly one-half of their average gross cash receipts was derived from crop sales, but in 1934 the proportion from this source dropped to 11 percent. About 60 percent of the cash receipts came from livestock sales, mostly to the Government, and from Agricultural Adjustment Administration benefit payments.

Table 10.—Average Gross Receipts per Farm on Selected Farms in Representative Counties in the Central Great Plains, by Source of Receipts, 1934

Source of receipts	Average receipts per farm					
		Perkins		Goshen		
	Sherman (57 farms)	Loam section (36 farms)	Sandy loam section (37 farms)	Irrigated section (29 farms)	Nonirrigated section (43 farms)	Cheyenne (56 farms)
Total farm receipts	$614	$2, 544	$1, 906	$3, 595	$1, 506	$1, 084
Total cash receipts	502	2, 319	1, 749	3, 421	1, 336	938
Crop sales	2	552	224	1, 774	382	100
Livestock sales	161	661	695	875	367	447
Livestock products	125	230	167	211	168	166
Work off the farm	22	36	37	73	48	62
Agricultural Adjustment Administration contract payments	174	784	577	433	342	113
Emergency Relief Administration	14	—	2	—	3	32
Other	4	56	47	55	26	18
Total products used in home	112	225	157	174	170	146
Dairy products	43	90	57	68	68	59
Poultry products	34	79	57	55	55	49
Meat	34	52	40	40	34	37
Crops and garden	1	4	3	11	13	1

Crop sales normally provided from 70 to 77 percent of the gross cash receipts in Perkins and Goshen Counties, livestock sales providing only from 22 to 26 percent. In 1934, however, the relative importance of the two products was largely reversed in all but the irrigated section of Goshen County. Crop sales provided only 13 percent of the cash receipts in the sandy loam section and 24 percent in the loam section of Perkins County, and 29 percent in the nonirrigated section of Goshen County. Livestock and livestock products sales furnished about 40 to 50 percent of the gross cash receipts in all three sections and Agricultural Adjustment Administration benefits provided most of the balance. Most of the livestock sales were made to the Government (fig. 9, p. 27) except in Perkins County, where most of the cattle sales were made through the regular market. Average gross cash receipts were reduced in 1934 to $2,319 from a norm of $4,536 in the loam section of Perkins County; to $1,749 from a norm of $3,647 in the sandy loam section of the same county; and to $1,336 from a norm of $2,534 in the nonirrigated section of Goshen County.

Crops were still the most important source of income in the irrigated section of Goshen County in 1934, but their share of the total cash receipts had been reduced from 77 percent to 52 percent, while receipts from livestock and livestock products had increased in importance from 22 to 31 percent of the total. Agricultural Adjustment Administration contracts were relatively unimportant, accounting for only one-eighth of the gross cash receipts. Total cash receipts in 1934 averaged $3,421 as compared with a norm of $4,972.

The average value of farm products used in the home in 1934 ranged from $112 in Sherman County to $225 in the loam section of Perkins County. When these amounts are added to the cash receipts, the average receipts per farm ranged from $614 in Sherman County to $3,595 in the irrigated section of Goshen County, but these figures do not reflect the losses suffered by farmers as a result of decreased livestock, feed, and equipment inventories.

Farmers on Relief and Rehabilitation Rolls

Nowhere in the representative counties of the Central Great Plains did the proportions of farmers receiving emergency relief or rehabilitation loans in the spring of 1935 equal the proportions in most of the Northern Great Plains counties. About one-third of all farmers in Cheyenne County and one-fifth in Goshen and Sherman Counties were on emergency relief or rehabilitation rolls. In Perkins County, Nebr., only 7 percent of the farmers received relief, either human or drought relief.

Not all farmers on relief rolls actually received relief, as some had been placed on the rolls to make them eligible for rehabilitation loans. In Cheyenne County, for instance, in May 1935, county relief officials reported that 16 percent of all farmers in the county (in addition to the 32 percent listed as relief clients) had registered on the relief rolls in order to become eligible for rehabilitation loans. These farmers had barely made a living in 1934, and their reserves were nearly exhausted.

The 1934 drought was not the only cause of the farmers' distress. A number of factors combined to bring farmers to dependency. A series of dry years prior to 1934 in some parts of the area, wind and water erosion in other parts, and faulty organization of farms in some sections, with too much land in crops and too little dependence on livestock, are some of these factors.

Reduction of livestock inventories was forced by a series of dry years preceding 1934 in all but Sherman County and the irrigated section of Goshen County. Crop yields were low in these sections from 1931 through 1933. Hence, when crops failed in 1934 feed reserves to take care of the emergency had been exhausted. Incomes from cash crops had likewise been reduced in the preceding years so that the farmers were unable to purchase feed.

Many of the farmers who were forced to accept relief grants or rehabilitation loans were apparently farmers who had not been established in the area long enough and in a favorable enough period to build up reserves with which to cope with the natural hazards of the region. Nearly one-third of the relief clients in Sherman County and over two-fifths of those in Perkins County had been in their respective areas for less than 5 years. If these individuals had had more time and a more favorable period in which to establish themselves and accumulate reserves, it is possible that at least some of them could have remained self-supporting.

As it was, the resources of the farmers on relief and rehabilitation were very low as compared with those of selected farmers interviewed. In Goshen County the rehabilitation applicants who were owner-operators reported an average net worth of $1,046 as compared with from $5,000 to more than $7,000 reported by selected farmers in the county. Those who were tenant-operators had an average net worth of only $176 as compared with about $1,600 reported by tenant-operators among the selected farmers. Of the relief clients in Perkins County the owner-operators had an average net worth of only $603 as compared with about $10,000 to $14,000 reported by selected owner-operators. Similarly the tenant-operators on relief in this county reported an average net worth of $273 as compared with $582 and $1,202 reported by selected tenant-operators in the county (appendix table 47).

The relief needs of farmers in Sherman County appear to have been more recent than in the other counties. Seven-eighths of the farmers on relief in the spring of 1935 had come on the rolls since the preceding November (table 11). In Cheyenne County, on the other hand, farm distress was of longer standing, as indicated by the fact that most of the farmers on relief had come on the rolls prior to November 1934. Most of the small number of relief clients in Perkins County had come on relief since November 1, 1934.

It is evident that physical disabilities and the handicap of large families had little to do with the farmers' distress. Most of the relief clients in the counties studied were in the active age groups (appendix table 25), and the few who did report physical disabilities may have had family labor to supplement their own. The usual number of children per family was only one to four (appendix table 26), and in none of the selected counties did more than one-fifth of the relief clients have more than four children who were under 16 years of age.

Analysis of the natural conditions in the region, of the organization of farms, and of such factors as land ownership and tenancy help to throw further light on reasons for the farmers' distress. These factors must be related, of course, to types of farming in the area.

Table 11.—Date of First Relief to Farm Operators on Relief in April–May 1935 in Representative Counties in the Central Great Plains

Date of first relief	Number of farm operators [1]		
	Sherman	Perkins	Cheyenne
Total [2]	258	27	186
March 1, 1935, or later	119	—	1
November 1, 1934–February 28, 1935	107	15	17
Prior to November 1, 1934	32	12	168

[1] Comparable data not available for Goshen County.
[2] Number in sample reporting date relief was begun.

TYPES OF FARMING

The natural factors affecting agriculture and the response of various crops to those factors have largely determined the type of farming developed in the Central Great Plains States. In the eastern section—central Nebraska and north central Kansas—where the soils and climate have favored the production of corn and alfalfa hay, primary emphasis has been placed on livestock production with cash grains a supplementary enterprise. In the tillable portions of the High Plains Section where wheat is favored, cash-grain production is predominant. In the sand hills and in other areas not suited for cultivation range-livestock production predominates. The intensive production of such crops as sugar beets and alfalfa hay predominates in the irrigated sections, with minor emphasis placed on the production of livestock.

Sherman County, a portion of the central Nebraska Loess Hills, has a type of farming characterized as "livestock, some cash-grain." In a classification based on gross income in 1929, 50 percent of the farms in the area were classed as animal-specialty farms, and 54 percent of the gross income for all farms in the area was derived from the sale of meat animals. General farms were second in importance, accounting for 23 percent of the farms, followed by cash-grain farms (17 percent).[2]

[2] Elliott, F. F., *Types of Farming in the United States*, U. S. Department of Commerce, Bureau of the Census, Washington, D. C., 1933, table 5.

Perkins County, in the Platte High Plains, has a cash-grain and livestock type of farming. Of the farms in 1929, 77 percent were classed as cash-grain, and of the 1929 gross income for all farms in the area 67 percent was from the sale of cash grains.

Cheyenne County, Colo., also part of the High Plains Area, is characterized by range-livestock, cash-grain production. Of the income of farms in the area in 1929, 40 percent was derived from the sale of meat animals and 38 percent from cash grains. Although livestock is more important than cash grains as a source of income, cash-grain production accounts for the predominant group of farms, 38 percent of the total. Animal-specialty farms and stock ranches together account for 23 percent of the farms, and general farms account for 20 percent.

Goshen County, Wyo., with both irrigated and nonirrigated land, shows interesting contrasts in types of farming. Three different type-of-farming areas are found in the county. The irrigated portion, part of the Scotts Bluff Basin, is characterized by the production of sugar beets, livestock, and potatoes. Nearly three-fourths of the farms in the Scotts Bluff Basin area were classed as crop-specialty farms in 1929, and 37 percent of the 1929 gross income for all farms was derived from the sale of sugar beets. About one-half of the farm land in this section was irrigated. The northern portion, part of the Niobrara Plains, is characterized by the production of range-livestock, and the southern part of the county, in the Platte Piedmont, is part of a larger area characterized as "cash-grain, livestock." [3]

Hard winter wheat is the principal crop throughout the nonirrigated portions of the Central Great Plains with the exception of central Nebraska and north central Kansas. In the latter areas corn is the most important crop, followed in order of their importance by oats, hay (primarily alfalfa), wheat, and barley. In the northwestern portion of the Central Great Plains wheat is the most important crop on nonirrigated land, followed in importance by corn, oats, and barley. On the irrigated land sugar beets and alfalfa hay are the principal crops, followed in importance by barley, oats, and potatoes. In the western and southern portions of the area wheat, sorghums, barley, and corn are the major crops.

NATURAL FACTORS AFFECTING AGRICULTURE

Topography

Gradually sloping from the High Plains in the west to the Missouri Valley Prairies in the east, the Central Great Plains are generally undulating to rolling. The High Plains Section comprises the major portion of the region. Across this broad upland plain the Arkansas

[3] *Ibid.*

River in the south and the Platte River in the north flow from the Rocky Mountains in a general easterly direction, each occupying a broad, leisurely-descending valley.[4] Other indentations in the surface of the High Plains are caused by smaller drainage channels. Some of these are not large enough to cause any material interruption in the general terrain. Others form deep box-like canyons bordered by a rough terrain.

Deposits of wind-blown sand in the form of dunes or small rounded hills and ridges of moderate height appear on the generally smooth plains in some sections. These areas of sand hills are extremely susceptible to wind erosion unless covered with native vegetation, and when the vegetation is destroyed by overgrazing, burning, or cultivation, they become a waste of shifting dunes. The most extensive sand-hills area of the Central Great Plains is that of north central Nebraska, but smaller areas are located in southeastern Wyoming, eastern Colorado, and southwestern Nebraska.

Within the sand hills surplus water drains into irregular basins or flats which have no surface outlet. Some of these basins, particularly those located in the northern part of the area, are occupied by lakes or marshes during years of normal or excessive rainfall. Others are dry the greater part of the year.

In southeastern Wyoming the High Plains consist of broad flat uplands broken by extensive escarpments and isolated buttes. The valley of the North Platte River and the Goshen Hole, a low plain formed by the erosion of the river and its tributaries, interrupt the upland features in this section.

The topography of the Missouri Valley Prairies to the east is more varied than that of the High Plains, ranging from level plains to rolling hills dissected by numerous drainage channels. The Platte River, as in the High Plains, flows through a wide, relatively shallow valley. In general, however, the main streams flow through this section in narrow valleys bordered by rough land similar to that of the "Bad Lands" in the Northern Great Plains.

Soils

The soils of the Central Great Plains, as in the Northern Great Plains, are subhumid and arid.[5] They include the Chernozems or Black soils, which are also found in the Northern Great Plains east of the Missouri River, and the Northern Dark-Brown soils, also found in the Northern Great Plains west of the Missouri River. In addition there are two other major groups in the Central Great Plains—the Brown soils and the sand hills of Nebraska (fig. 2, p. 8).

---

[4] Johnson, W. D., *The High Plains and Its Utilization*, 21st and 22d Reports, U. S. Geological Survey, Washington, D. C., 1899–1900.

[5] Bureau of Chemistry and Soils, *Atlas of American Agriculture*, Part III, U. S. Department of Agriculture, Washington, D. C., 1935, p. 72.

In this area the Chernozems are found in the prairie sections of central Kansas and Nebraska. The Northern Dark-Brown soils occupy all of the High Plains Section lying within the Central Great Plains with the exception of the sand-hills area of north central Nebraska and a portion of south central and central Colorado occupied by the Brown soils.

Of the counties included in this survey, Sherman County, Nebr., is the only one occupied by the Black soils which predominate in the counties studied in the Northern Great Plains. Colby silt loam is the dominant type in this county.

Because of severe erosion the surface layer of the Colby soils in this region is shallow. Much of the terrain occupied by Colby silt loam is too rough for cultivation. It is used for pasture and supports a good growth of nutritious grasses. The cultivated areas are used for hay and feed crops, chiefly corn, alfalfa, and sweet clover.[6] The Holdrege soils, occupying much of south central Nebraska and north central Kansas, also occur in this county. They are upland soils, generally appearing in areas of level topography. In Sherman County they are used for all crops which are commonly grown in the area.[7]

In the dry-land areas of Goshen County, Wyo., the southeastern portion of Perkins County, Nebr., and the eastern and north central portions of Cheyenne County, Colo., the predominant soils are the Rosebud series of the Dark-Brown group. Rosebud loam occupies a level to rolling topography in Perkins County, the rolling portions being used for pasture and hay production and the more level portions for corn and wheat.[8] Rosebud silt loams and very fine sandy loams in Goshen County occupy level to undulating topography. The lighter type is best adapted to wheat production although barley and potatoes are grown with a fair degree of success. Under proper dry-land farming methods good yields of all the common dry-land crops have been obtained on the silt loams, but under irrigation it is probable that this soil would be a little more difficult to handle than the fine sandy loam or fine sand types, such as are at present under irrigation in this area.[9]

Another body of soils classed as the Dawes series is also located in Perkins County, generally occupying a flat to gently undulating

[6] Brown, L. A., Gemmell, R. L., and Hayes, F. A., *Soil Survey of Sherman County, Nebraska,* Series 1931, No. 5, U. S. Department of Agriculture, Bureau of Chemistry and Soils, Washington, D. C., 1934, pp. 19–21.

[7] *Ibid.,* pp. 17–18.

[8] Wolfanger, Louis A., Russom, V. M., and Strieter, E. H., *Soil Survey of Perkins County, Nebraska,* U. S. Department of Agriculture, Bureau of Soils, Washington, D. C., 1924, pp. 899–906.

[9] Veatch, J. O. and McClure, R. W., *Soil Survey of the Fort Laramie Area, Wyoming–Nebraska,* U. S. Department of Agriculture, Bureau of Soils, Washington, D. C., 1921, pp. 23–29.

terrain. The dominant type is a loam which is used both for pasture and for the production of wheat and corn. The smaller areas of sandy loams are used primarily for the production of corn and sorghums.[10]

The Laurel series, usually sandy loams and fine sandy loams underlain by a bed of gravel, predominates in the valleys of the main drainage channels throughout the Dark-Brown soils belt. In the Fort Laramie area of Goshen County, Wyo., and the adjoining Scotts Bluff County, Nebr., these soils are generally irrigated and are used for the production of alfalfa, potatoes, sugar beets, and sweet clover.[11]

Climate

The climate of the Central Great Plains is characterized by wide extremes of temperature, great variations in precipitation from season to season and from year to year, much sunshine, dry air, and considerable wind movement. Precipitation increases from west to east, with the result that the climate of the western sections is usually described as semiarid, whereas that of the Prairies Section is described as dry subhumid. The climate of the entire area can be said to vary from year to year between arid and humid, with the arid years occurring more frequently in the High Plains Section than in the Prairies Section.

The length of growing season increases from the northwest to the southeast (fig. 4, p. 11). At Fort Laramie, Wyo., in the northwestern portion of the area, the average frost-free season is 124 days. At Dodge City, Kans., in the southern part of the area the average frost-free season is 186 days.

Climatic conditions in the Loess Hills Area of central Nebraska are favorable to the production of grain and hay and the raising of livestock. Cool moist spring weather favors the growth of small grains. Summers are long with temperature sufficiently high to favor the growth of corn. Annual precipitation averages about 25 inches, with 81 percent occurring during the period from April through September. Moisture is usually sufficient for crop production during the critical spring and early summer months although short dry periods sometimes occur in July and August.

In the western section, as typified by Goshen County in southeastern Wyoming, Perkins County in southwestern Nebraska, and Cheyenne County in eastern Colorado, precipitation is less abundant and more irregular than in the eastern section. In Goshen County, Wyo., in the northwestern portion of the High Plains Section, annual precipitation averages little more than 13 inches. About 75 percent of that amount normally occurs during the period from April through

[10] Wolfanger, Louis A., Russom, V. M., and Strieter, E. H., *op. cit.*, pp. 907–911.
[11] Veatch, J. O. and McClure, R. W., *op. cit.*, pp. 44–46.

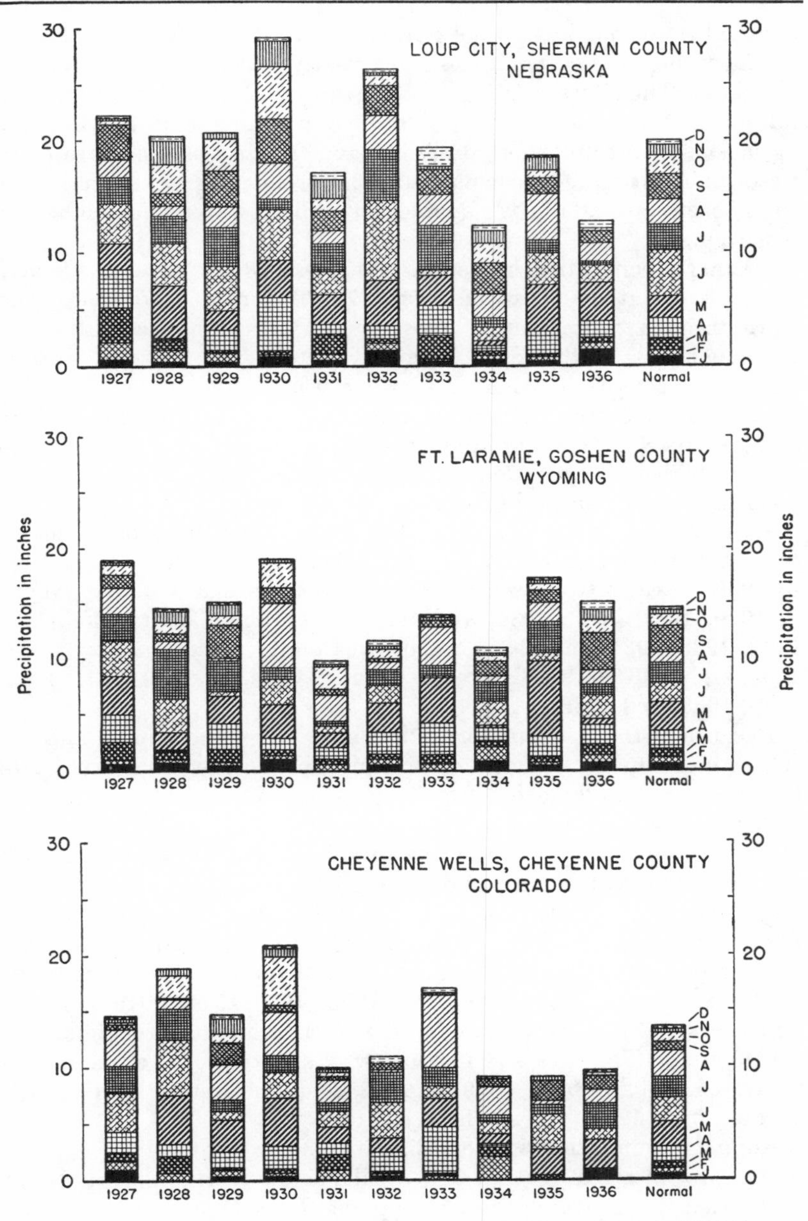

FIG. 11-NORMAL MONTHLY PRECIPITATION AND PRECIPITATION BY MONTHS, SELECTED STATIONS IN THE CENTRAL GREAT PLAINS 1927-1936

Source: U.S. Department of Agriculture, Weather Bureau.

AF-2781, WPA

September so that in years of normal precipitation the production of small grains and drought-resistant, early-maturing feed crops is possible. The short growing season restricts the production of corn for grain. Because of the low annual amounts and the extreme variations in precipitation, only dry-land farming methods are practiced on nonirrigated benchlands. The production of such crops as sugar beets and alfalfa is possible only where water is available for irrigation.

Annual precipitation in Perkins County and in Cheyenne County averages about 17–18 inches, with 78–79 percent occurring from April through September. Crops favored by climatic conditions in these portions of the High Plains are similar to those in Goshen County, except that a longer growing season gives corn and other feed crops a better chance to mature. Crop production is more stable in Perkins County than in Goshen County, but in Cheyenne County higher precipitation is offset by higher temperature, a greater wind movement, and a higher rate of evaporation.

Rainfall has frequently been deficient during the critical spring and early summer months (fig. 11). During the period from 1927 to 1936 it seems to have been deficient in Sherman County, Nebr., in 1929, 1931, 1933, 1934, and 1936; in Perkins County, Nebr., in 1931, 1933, 1934, and 1936; in Goshen County, Wyo., in 1928, 1931, 1934, and 1936; and in Cheyenne County, Colo., in 1929, 1931, 1932, 1934, 1935, and 1936.

Because of the frequent torrential character of the rainfall and the subsequent runoff, amounts of precipitation do not always indicate the moisture available for crops. However, precipitation and crop yields show a high degree of correlation.

The period 1931–1934 was one of subnormal rainfall throughout the Central Great Plains, and in many regions the lack of rainfall was more serious in 1934 than in any other year from 1924 through 1936. Such periods of drought were not without precedent, however. Early reports and precipitation records indicate that the years 1860–1863, 1874–1876, 1887–1890, 1893–1895, 1910–1914, 1916–1918, as well as 1931–1936, were periods of general drought throughout the entire area. The western portion was affected by an additional period of drought from 1879 to 1882, and the eastern portion was affected from 1924 to 1926 (fig. 12).

Annual precipitation was less than in 1934 in 14 of the 62 years for which precipitation records are available at North Platte, Nebr. (1875–1936); and during the 4-year period from 1893 to 1896 annual precipitation averaged less than during the 4-year period from 1931 to 1934. At Cheyenne, Wyo., annual precipitation was less than in 1934 in 14 of the years from 1871 to 1936 for which records are available. During the 4-year period from 1886 to 1889 annual precipita-

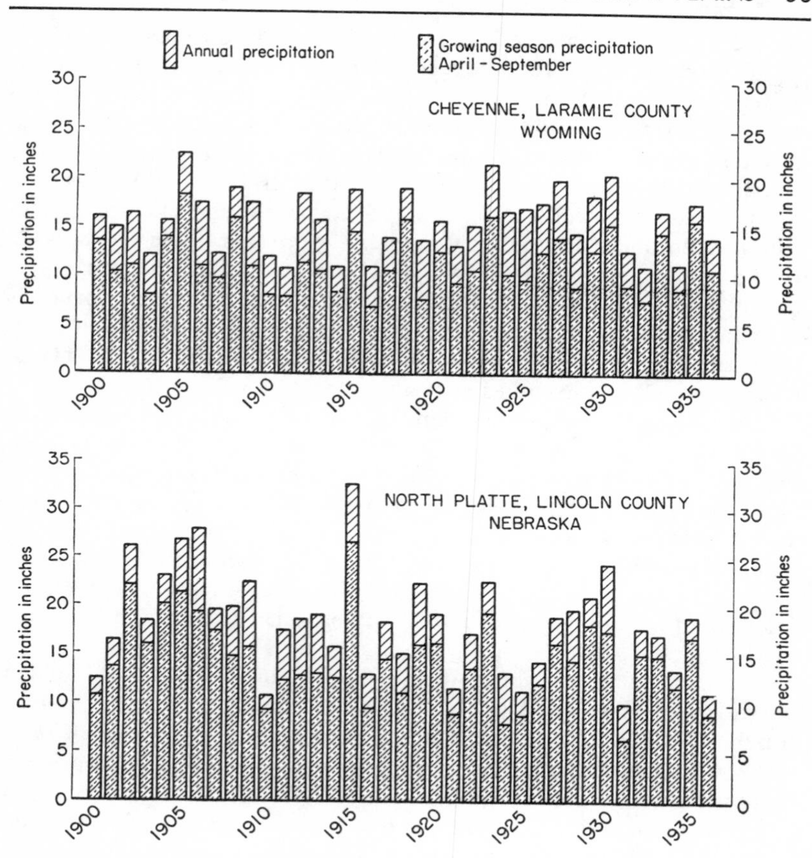

FIG. 12-ANNUAL AND GROWING SEASON PRECIPITATION, SELECTED STATIONS IN THE CENTRAL GREAT PLAINS 1900-1936

Source: U. S. Department of Agriculture, Weather Bureau. AF-2785, WPA

tion at Fort Laramie, Goshen County, Wyo., averaged only 65 percent of that from 1931 to 1934. At Dodge City, Kans., average annual precipitation during the 4-year period 1916–1919 was less than that from 1931 to 1934. Annual precipitation was less than in 1934, however, in only 3 of the 62 years for which records are available (1875–1936).

Population Movements as Affected by Precipitation

Precipitation, or lack of it, has caused frequent mass movements of farmers in and out of the area. At the time of the original settlement of the Central Great Plains, information about the climate was limited. The first wave that really populated the area was at its height from 1883 to 1886, a period of above normal precipitation throughout most of the area. Misled by the popular belief in the migration of rainfall and encouraged by the Government, the press, railroads, land companies, and various financial interests, settlers moved into the area to stake out homestead tracts of 160 acres provided by the Government. Soon the farmers found that precipitation was normally limited and variable, and that their homesteads were too small to provide a living. Many of the farmers moved out of the area. The next period of ample rainfall, however, brought other farmers into the region, only to go through the same experience. Thus, the history of the occupation of the Central Great Plains is one of alternating advance and recession.[12]

After 1895, however, emigration during droughts was less noticeable than during earlier periods. As the requirements of the area became apparent, the value of larger holdings was realized, and the Government in its later Homestead Acts provided for 320- and 640-acre tracts. Moreover, precipitation from 1895 to 1909 was relatively high and reasonably stable so that during that period the settlers had an opportunity not only to adapt their farm organization to the area but also to acquire reserves and to prepare themselves for less productive periods.

Ford County, Kans., illustrates the history of the occupation of the Central Great Plains. During a relatively humid period the population increased from an average of 0.77 person per square mile in 1883 to 8.86 persons per square mile in 1887, while the farm population [13] increased from an average of 2.80 persons per square mile in 1885 to 5.32 persons in 1887. During the dry period from 1887 to 1890 the farm population declined to an average of 2.98 persons per square mile in 1891 and increased in 1892 and 1893 after the drought was broken. From 1893 to 1895, another period of drought, the farm population declined to a point slightly less than that of 1885. After 1895 the farm population of Ford County increased more uniformly than in the preceding decade although periods of drought were usually accompanied, or immediately followed, either by a decline in population or by a period in which the increase in population was retarded. Each year from 1895 to 1932 that the annual precipitation at Dodge City fell below 17 inches, the farm population of Ford County remained stationary for a year or declined. In all other years it increased, the average annual increase during the 37-year period being 0.14 person per square mile.

[12] See Taeuber, Conrad and Taylor, Carl C., *The People of the Drought States*, Research Bulletin Series V, No. 2, Division of Social Research, Works Progress Administration, Washington, D. C., 1937.

[13] County population, less that of villages and towns. *Biennial Reports*, Kansas State Board of Agriculture, Topeka, Kans.

Causes of Crop Damage

Drought was reported as the most frequent cause of crop damage throughout the Central Great Plains in the experience of the farmers interviewed (table 12 and appendix table 27). Because of the inclusion of reports from farmers whose experience does not extend prior to the recent period of drought, however, it is probable that in most of the selected counties the importance of drought as a cause of crop damage was overemphasized.

Table 12.—Percent of Years [1] Different Causes of Crop Damage Were Reported on Selected Farms in Representative Counties in the Central Great Plains

County	Percent of years damage was reported						
	Drought	Hail	Soil blowing	Rust	Insects	Frost	Excessive precipitation
Sherman	45	9	6	5	2	2	2
Perkins:							
Loam section	47	21	12	6	17	6	3
Sandy loam section	38	15	10	4	9	8	—
Goshen:							
Irrigated section	14	15	8	2	20	9	2
Nonirrigated section	27	11	15	6	5	4	1
Cheyenne	52	21	7	7	9	3	6

[1] For length of record see appendix table 27.

Selected farmers in Sherman County, Nebr., estimated that their crops had been damaged by drought more than 3 years out of 7, the damage being slight 1 year in 5, serious 1 year in 6 or 7, and total 1 year in 12. Farmers in the loam section of Perkins County, Nebr., reported a more serious situation. They estimated that crop damage by drought had occurred almost one-half of the years. Those in the sandy loam section of the county estimated that it had occurred about 2 years out of 5. In both the loam and the sandy loam sections total damage to crops by drought occurred about 1 year in 7 or 8.

Crop damage by drought was reported as having occurred about 1 year in 7 in the irrigated section of Goshen County, Wyo., and 1 year in 3 or 4 in the nonirrigated section. Damage in the irrigated section of Goshen County was due partly to inadequate supplies of irrigation water [14] and partly to the operation of some nonirrigated cropland in the irrigated section. In Cheyenne County, Colo., crop damage by drought was reported as occurring in more than one-half of the years.

[14] Reports from managers of the various irrigation projects in Goshen County show that the supply of irrigation water in the Horse Creek and Torrington Districts was maintained at normal or near normal levels in 1934. But in the Goshen District in the western part of the irrigated section, the supply of water available for irrigating some 45,000 acres of land had declined from an average of about 3.0 feet per acre during the 11-year period 1922–1932 to 2.0 feet in 1933 and to 0.6 foot in 1934. About one-third of the relief clients and rehabilitation applicants in Goshen County in 1935 were located in the irrigated portion where supplies of irrigation water were low in 1934.

Hail was second only to drought as a cause of crop damage in all of the areas surveyed with the exception of Goshen County. Serious damage from hail was not the general rule, however, since destructive hailstorms are usually confined to rather narrow belts. Some damage to crops as a result of hail occurred 1 year in 5 in Cheyenne County and in the loam section of Perkins County and 1 year in 6 or 7 in the sandy loam section of Perkins County and in the irrigated section of Goshen County.

Damage to crops from soil blowing occurred only about 1 year in 17 in Sherman County, but at the other extreme it was reported about 1 year in 6 or 7 in the nonirrigated section of Goshen County. In limited areas, such as the western portion of Goshen County, erosion is so severe that land is being retired from crop production (fig. 3, p. 9). Farmers on relief in the nonirrigated section of the county in 1935 were concentrated in areas where it had been recommended that at least part of the farm land be retired from cultivation.

Insects, primarily grasshoppers, were another major cause of crop damage in the loam section of Perkins County and in the irrigated section of Goshen County, but in the other selected areas damage from this source occurred less than 1 year in 10.

Frost was most destructive in the northwestern part of the area where the growing season is shortest. Because of the adaptation of crops to the area, however, damage by frost was infrequent, occurring less than 1 year in 10 in the irrigated section of Goshen County and in the sandy loam section of Perkins County, the two areas in which it was most important as a cause of crop damage.

Occasional damage to small grains by rust, and to other crops by excessive precipitation, was reported throughout the area.

CROP YIELDS

Precipitation, more than any other factor, has controlled crop production in the Central Great Plains. Average crop yields decrease with precipitation from east to west; but variable precipitation, combined with other factors affecting plant growth, has frequently caused wide departures from average yields (table 13 and appendix table 28).

County yields of important crops have closely approximated those in the type-of-farming area in which each representative county is located. Corn has yielded the highest quantity of feed per acre in central and southwestern Nebraska, represented by Sherman County, and its yields have varied little more than those of other crops. In the nonirrigated sections of southeastern Wyoming, represented by Goshen County, wheat yields have been more stable than those of corn. In the irrigated sections both corn and wheat yields have been high as well as relatively stable, but these crops have been largely

Resettlement Administration (Rothstein).

Twenty Bushels From Thirty-eight Acres!

replaced by sugar beets and alfalfa. In western Kansas and eastern Colorado, represented by Cheyenne County, corn yields have been higher than wheat yields, but the corn yields have been more variable (appendix table 29).

Table 13.—Average Yield per Harvested Acre of Important Crops in Representative Counties in the Central Great Plains, 1910–1932 [1]

County	Average yield per harvested acre (bushels)			
	Wheat	Barley	Oats	Corn
Sherman	14.3	22.2	25.7	22.4
Perkins	13.0	22.0	23.0	20.3
Goshen	13.6	17.1	26.7	19.3
Cheyenne	9.1	12.7	15.7	13.0

[1] For years data were not available see appendix table 28.

Sources: *Annual Reports*, Nebraska State Board of Agriculture, Lincoln, Nebr., 1913–1922; *Nebraska Agricultural Statistics*, Department of Agriculture, Lincoln, Nebr., 1923–1932; *Wyoming Agricultural Statistics*, State Department of Agriculture, Cheyenne, Wyo., 1923–1932; and *Yearbooks of the State of Colorado*, State Board of Immigration, Denver, Colo., 1918–1933.

Estimates of farmers [15] interviewed in this study show that crop failures and poor yields have occurred less frequently in the eastern than in the western part of the area. In Sherman County, Nebr., for example, the farmers estimated that failures of wheat, corn, and oats had occurred only 1 year in 8 or 9 and poor yields only 1 year in every 5, whereas the farmers in Cheyenne County, Colo., estimated that wheat failures had occurred more than 3 years out of 7, corn failures more than 3 years out of 10, and oats failures more than one-half of the years (appendix table 30).

During the period of subnormal rainfall from 1931 to 1933 crop yields reported by selected farmers failed to approximate the long-time average in any of the counties studied except Sherman County, Nebr., and the irrigated section of Goshen County, Wyo. (appendix table 31). Together with the cumulative effects of this period, the deficiencies in precipitation and the abnormally high temperatures in 1934 brought crop yields in that year to new lows.

[15] The farmers tended to report higher crop yields than were reported by the State agricultural statisticians, but average yields calculated from the farmers' estimates of good and poor yields and their frequency of occurrence corresponded rather closely with the county averages (table 13 and appendix table 30). The most notable exception to this was the farmers' estimates in Cheyenne County, Colo., which indicated yields of wheat and oats considerably smaller than the county average. However, their estimates showed failures or poor yields of both wheat and oats three-fifths of the years. In all other instances the farmers' estimates of yields were actually higher than the State statisticians' reports since the latter were on a harvested-acre basis while the former were more nearly on a seeded-acre basis.

ORGANIZATION OF FARMS

As in the Northern Great Plains, the organization of many farms in the Central Great Plains is not well adapted to the natural conditions of the area. Many farms are too small, too much acreage has been placed in cash crops, and livestock numbers are sometimes inadequate. The 1934 drought, following several years of deficient rainfall, furthered these weaknesses by forcing farmers to reduce their livestock inventories.

Size of Operating Unit

In the Central Great Plains, particularly in the High Plains Section, areas have been classified by State land use consultants as containing many farms too small for profitable operation. The 160-acre farm, the size of the original homestead tracts, is the most frequent size in Sherman County, Nebr., and in the irrigated section of Goshen County, Wyo. In the nonirrigated section of Goshen County, Wyo., and in Cheyenne County, Colo., the 320-acre farm is the most frequent size. In Perkins County, Nebr., much of which was settled during the operation of the Kincaid Act,[16] the 640-acre farm is the most prevalent size.

In this study it was found that selected farmers on the smaller farms had usually been operating at a loss, as indicated by their estimates of assets and liabilities when they began farming in the area, by additions to or deductions from their business, and by their assets and liabilities in 1935 (appendix table 32). Exceptions were found only in the sandy loam section of Perkins County and the irrigated section of Goshen County. It must be remembered, however, that the records indicate the brighter side of the picture, as they represent only survivors. An unknown number of farmers had given up farming and had left the area.

The records of selected farmers indicate that in Sherman County a farm of 360 acres is necessary for profitable operation. On the average, only the farmers operating farms of this size reported that they had been able to increase their capital since they began farming in the area (appendix table 32). Yet data secured from corn-hog contracts representing 1,097 farms (appendix table 34) and from 57 selected farms, averaging about the same size as all farms in the county,[17] indicate that about one-half of the farms in Sherman County in 1934 were less than 200 acres in size and that only one-fourth to one-third of the farms were 280 acres or larger.

In Perkins County the consensus of the 73 farmers interviewed was that a 400-acre farm was the minimum usually necessary to provide an

[16] The Kincaid Act of 1904 provided for homesteads of 640 acres in western Nebraska.

[17] The 1935 Census of Agriculture reported 1,444 farms in Sherman County with an average size of 242 acres; the average size of the farms represented by corn-hog contracts was 248 acres and that of the selected farms was 241 acres.

adequate family income. In the sandy loam section farmers on all sizes of farms had been able on the average to increase their capital since farming in the area, but in the loam section the operation of less than 400 acres was unprofitable (appendix table 32). Yet data from corn-hog contracts representing 798 farms, averaging about the same size as those enumerated in the census,[18] showed that 22 percent of the farms were less than 281 acres in size and 24 percent were between 281 and 440 acres (appendix table 34).

In Goshen County many of the farmers in the irrigated section were of the opinion that 80 or 90 acres were sufficient to provide an adequate family living, but the consensus among farmers in the nonirrigated section was that 640 acres should be the minimum size of an operating unit. Farmers on acreages of all sizes in the irrigated section had been able on the average to increase their capital since they began farming in the area. In the nonirrigated section the operation of less than 281 acres was unprofitable on the average (appendix table 32). Of the farms with corn-hog contracts, 41 percent in this section were 460 acres or smaller in size (appendix table 34). In the irrigated section 23 percent of the farms with corn-hog contracts had only 100 acres or less, while 58 percent were between 101 and 280 acres in size.

In Cheyenne County almost all of the selected farmers estimated that 640 acres were necessary to afford profitable operation. On second-grade land only the group operating 720 acres or more had been able to show capital increases, and on the third-grade land the operation of less than 400 acres, exclusive of free range utilized, was unprofitable. Production control contract data show that 54 percent of the corn-hog contract farms were 440 acres or smaller in size and of the 56 selected farms 24 were less than 560 acres in size.[19]

On the other hand, the largest farms in all areas reported that their normal incomes were sufficient to meet expenses. More large than small farms in most sections normally earned incomes sufficient

[18] The 1935 Census of Agriculture reported 958 farms in Perkins County, Nebr., with an average size of 566 acres; the farms with corn-hog contracts averaged 577 acres each.

[19] In both Goshen and Cheyenne Counties the average size of the production control contract farms and of the selected farms is not comparable to that of all farms enumerated by the 1935 Census of Agriculture, owing to the fact that these data exclude large ranches which are included in the census data. The census reported 1,538 farms in Goshen County, averaging 770 acres in size; the production control data represented 175 farms in the irrigated section of the county, averaging 201 acres, and 395 farms in the nonirrigated section, averaging 724 acres; of the 72 selected farms, those in the irrigated section averaged 276 acres and those in the nonirrigated section averaged 959 acres. In Cheyenne County the census reported 671 farms, averaging 764 acres, whereas the average size of 397 corn-hog contract farms was 548 acres and that of 56 selected farms was 666 acres.

to increase their capital (appendix table 24). They had experienced fewer years when their incomes were not sufficient to meet their expenses or to reduce their indebtedness.

Size of Relief Clients' Farms

The average size of farm operated by the relief clients in all of the selected counties was smaller than that operated by the selected farmers.

The average size of farm operated by the relief clients in Perkins County was only 212 acres as compared with a county average of 566 acres. The majority of the relief clients were operating 180 acres or less. In Goshen County the relief farmers were concentrated in

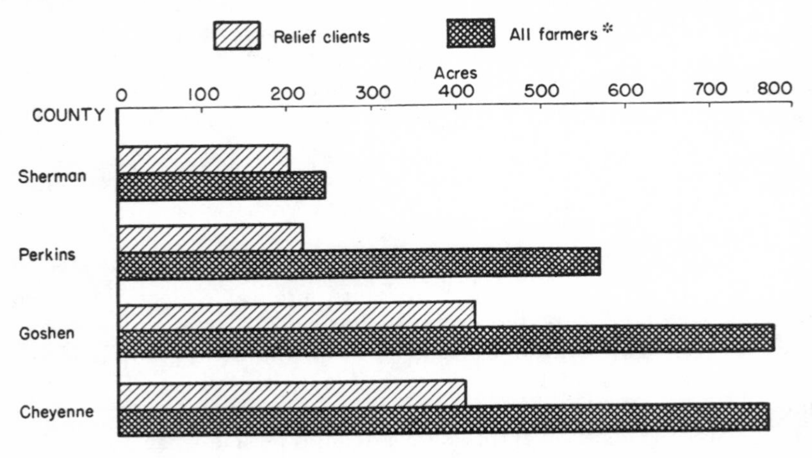

FIG. 13 - AVERAGE SIZE OF FARM OPERATED BY RELIEF CLIENTS AND BY ALL FARMERS IN REPRESENTATIVE COUNTIES IN THE CENTRAL GREAT PLAINS
1935

* *United States Census of Agriculture: 1935.* AF-2697, WPA

localities where small farms predominated. In Cheyenne County the farms operated by relief clients averaged only 403 acres as compared with a county average of 764 acres.

In Sherman County the difference was not great, the average size of farm operated by the relief clients being 200 acres as compared with a county average of 241 acres (fig. 13 and appendix table 33). Two-thirds of the relief clients, however, were operating farms of 180 acres or less.

Use of Land

Throughout the Central Great Plains, where soils and topography are at all suitable for crop production, the land is generally utilized as cropland. Where the topography is too rough for the convenient use of machinery, or where the soils are not adapted to crop production either because of their nature or because of damage by erosion, the land is commonly utilized for grazing.

Much of the acreage in cropland should, in the interest of soil conservation, be shifted to permanent pasture. This is true on many farms, both large and small, but particularly on the small operating units where the proportion of the farm land that is used as cropland is usually higher than on the large operating units.

The proportion of farm land devoted to crops in 1934 amounted to 73 percent in Perkins County and 60 percent in Sherman County, according to census figures,[20] but only 34 percent cf the farm land in Cheyenne County and only 25 percent of that in Goshen County was used for crops. A preponderance of rolling land and limited precipitation restricted the possibilities for crop production in the latter county. In the northern part of the county, for instance, 73 percent of the land area was in farms and 90 percent of the farm land was in pasture. In the irrigated section, however, the major portion of the land was in crops, as indicated by corn-hog contracts representing 175 farms in the central or irrigated section. They show that in 1934, 60 percent of the farm land in that section was used as cropland and 32 percent as native pasture. In the nonirrigated or dry-farming section in the southern part of the county, however, only 37 percent of the farm land was used as cropland and 60 percent was used as pasture (appendix table 34).

Data from the representative farmers in the irrigated section of Goshen County indicate a somewhat smaller proportion of the farm land used as cropland and a larger proportion used as pasture than that shown by the corn-hog contracts. In the nonirrigated section they reported a slightly higher proportion of the farm land used as cropland and a slightly lower proportion used as pasture than that shown by the corn-hog contracts (appendix table 35).

In Goshen County 52 percent of the land farmed by selected farmers in the irrigated section was owned by the operators, 28 percent was share-rented, and 20 percent was cash-rented. In the nonirrigated section 58 percent of the land operated was owned by the operators, 21 percent was share-rented, and 21 percent was cash-rented. In both sections the major portion of the share-rented land was used as cropland, while the major portion of the cash-rented land was used as pasture. The proportion of the owned land that was used as pasture was higher in the nonirrigated than in the irrigated section (fig. 14 and appendix table 36).

In Sherman County data from 57 selected farmers and from corn-hog contracts representing 1,097 farms (table 14 and appendix tables

[20] Bureau of the Census, *United States Census of Agriculture: 1935*, U. S. Department of Commerce, Washington, D. C.

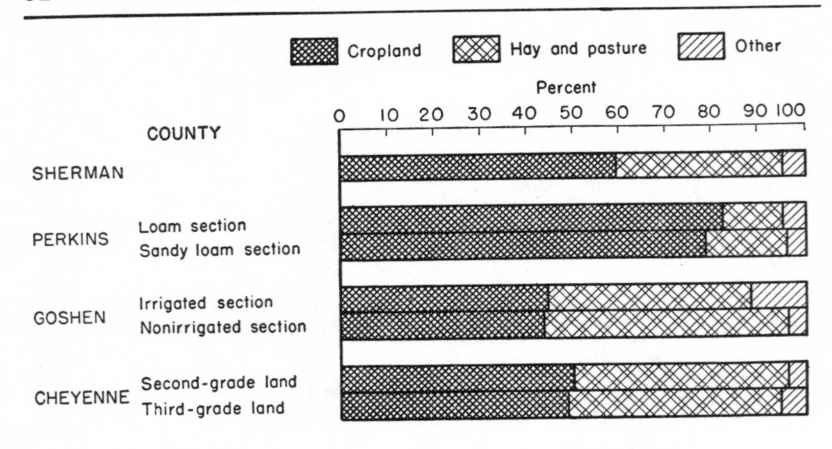

FIG. 14-UTILIZATION OF LAND ON SELECTED FARMS IN REPRESENTATIVE COUNTIES IN THE CENTRAL GREAT PLAINS 1934

AF-2699, WPA

34 and 35) indicate that in 1934, 58 or 59 percent of the farm land was cropland, 30 or 31 percent was native pasture, and 6 or 7 percent was native hay. Of the land operated, less than one-fourth was owned by the operator, one-fourth was cash-rented, and over one-half was share-rented (fig. 14 and appendix table 36). Approximately two-thirds of the land owned by the operator, seven-tenths of the share-rented land, and three-tenths of the cash-rented land were used as cropland.

Table 14.—Utilization of Land on Selected Farms in Representative Counties in the Central Great Plains, 1934

County	Number of farms reporting	Average number of acres per farm					
		Total	Crop-land	Native grass		Former crop-land	Farm-stead and waste
				Hay	Pasture		
Sherman	57	241	144	15	74	—	8
Perkins:							
Loam section	36	714	588	1	94	—	31
Sandy loam section	37	619	465	3	126	10	15
Goshen:							
Irrigated section	29	276	122	3	120	7	24
Nonirrigated section	43	959	410	1	505	17	26
Cheyenne	56	666	327	—	310	7	22

In Cheyenne County corn-hog contracts representing 397 farms indicate that even in the farming sections of the county little more than one-half of the farm land was used as cropland and most of the remainder as pasture. Use of farm land by selected farmers was similar to that shown by the corn-hog contracts (appendix table 34). The proportion of the total land used by them as cropland ranged from 60 percent on farms of less than 400 acres to 46 percent on farms of 720 acres or more, and averaged 49 percent for all farms. The proportion used as pasture ranged from 35 percent on the smaller farms to 51 percent on those of 720 acres or more and averaged 47 percent for all farms. On both the second- and third-grade land approximately two-fifths of the land operated was owned by the operators, more than one-half was share-rented, and less than one-tenth was cash-rented. The use of both the owned and the share-rented land was rather evenly distributed between cropland and hay and pasture land. Most of the cash-rented land was used as pasture.

In Perkins County, Nebr., data from corn-hog contracts representing 798 farms indicate that in 1934, 74 percent of the farm land was used as cropland, 1 percent as native hay, and 19 percent as native pasture. The proportion of the farm in cropland and in native hay or pasture was nearly the same for groups of different sized farms up to 880 acres, but on the larger farms the proportion of the farm land in pasture was greater than on the smaller farms. The selected farmers in the grain-producing section in the northwestern part of Perkins County had more cropland and less pasture than did those in the sandy loam section of the southeast. In both sections more than two-fifths of the land operated was owned by the operator, one-half was share-rented, and one-tenth was cash-rented. Most of the owned and share-rented land was used as cropland, but nearly one-half of the cash-rented land in the loam section and seven-tenths of the cash-rented land in the sandy loam section were used as pasture (appendix table 36).

Corn occupied the highest percentage of the cropland on the selected farms in 1934 in Sherman and Cheyenne Counties and in the sandy loam section of Perkins County (appendix table 37). Wheat occupied the highest percentage of the cropland in the loam section of Perkins County and in the nonirrigated section of Goshen County, while sugar beets and alfalfa were the most important crops, as measured by the acreage occupied, in the irrigated section of Goshen County.

In Sherman County corn was grown on all of the selected farms in 1934, oats on nearly all, and wheat and barley on about one-half of the farms. Alfalfa was reported on nearly all of the large farms. Corn occupied a higher percentage of the cropland on the small than on the large farms.

In Perkins County corn was grown on all of the selected farms in the sandy loam section and on nearly all of the selected farms in the loam section, but it occupied a higher percentage of the cropland in the former section. The opposite was true of wheat, which was grown on nearly all farms in both sections but occupied a higher percentage of the cropland in the loam section. Feed crops were grown on most of the farms in both sections. Barley and oats were grown on most of the farms in the loam section but on less than one-half of the farms in the sandy loam section. Summer fallow was the usual practice in the loam section, but it was limited primarily to the larger farms in the sandy loam section.

In the nonirrigated section of Goshen County both corn and wheat were grown on three-fourths of the selected farms in 1934. Wheat, however, occupied 37 percent of the cropland, whereas corn occupied only 12 percent. Barley and oats were grown on less than one-half and sorghums on less than one-fifth of the farms. Summer fallow practices were followed on about one-half of the farms, primarily the larger units. About one-fourth of all cropland was fallowed in 1934.

In the irrigated section of Goshen County both sugar beets and alfalfa hay were grown on nearly all of the farms in 1934, each occupying more than one-fourth of the cropland. Barley was grown on more than two-thirds of the farms and oats and potatoes on nearly three-fifths. Corn was grown only on the smaller farms.

In Cheyenne County corn and sorghums for feed were grown on nearly all and barley on about two-fifths of the farms. Only 2 of the 56 selected farmers had wheat and only 2 had land that was being summer fallowed.

The drought of 1934 had not greatly affected the proportion of acres seeded to different crops in the selected counties of the Central Great Plains. Except for a reduction in corn acreage in 1934, no marked departure from established to emergency crops had been made during the period 1930–1934 (appendix table 38). It is probable that much of the corn acreage reduction was due to the crop adjustment program of the Agricultural Adjustment Administration.

Livestock

As in the Northern Great Plains, cattle was normally the most important livestock enterprise in the Central Great Plains (appendix table 39). Range livestock was of particular importance in the sandy loam section of Perkins County and in Cheyenne County. Hogs were an important enterprise only in Sherman and Perkins Counties. Poultry flocks, normally averaging 100 birds or more, were reported by most of the farmers interviewed.

In the Central Great Plains as a whole reductions from normal as a result of drought were more drastic for hogs than for any other class of livestock (appendix table 39). The total number of hogs was reduced two-thirds or more in all of the selected areas except the irrigated section of Goshen County. The number of brood sows was reduced as drastically as the number of all hogs in the representative counties with the exception of Sherman County.

In general, feed loans had enabled most farmers to maintain the major portion of their cattle herds, including a nucleus for breeding operations. Milk cows were maintained at normal levels in both sections of Perkins County and in the irrigated section of Goshen County. They had been reduced only slightly in Cheyenne County. The greatest reduction in cattle had been made in Sherman County where the number of milk cows had been reduced from an average of 10 to 7 per farm, and the number of all cattle from an average of 22 to 15 per farm.

Reduction of beef herds was generally greater than that of milk herds. In the areas where cattle herds were an important enterprise, however, the numbers of beef cows or of other cattle maintained were usually sufficient to rebuild the herds in a relatively short time.

Numbers of poultry reported on April 1, 1935, were generally about one-fifth to one-third lower than normal. Sheep production was not an important enterprise in any of the selected areas, but in all counties where sheep were reported, the numbers on April 1, 1935, were normal or above. Work stock had not been reduced materially in any of the counties.

Although sufficient stock remained in the counties as a whole to rebuild the various classes of livestock to normal numbers, individual farmers needed assistance in restoring livestock. In all of the selected areas some farmers had disposed of nearly all of their livestock by April 1, 1935 (appendix table 40). In Sherman County 12 of the 57 selected farmers had no brood sows and 22 had no other hogs; 2 farmers had no milk cows, 3 had no chickens, and 1 farmer had no work stock. More than one-third of the farmers had less than 6 milk cows, two-fifths had 10 or less head of all classes of cattle, more than one-half had 3 or less brood sows, and three-tenths had 50 or less chickens. In the other counties more largely dependent on crops, the proportions of farmers without milk cows or brood sows were somewhat larger. From 1 in 18 to 1 in 5 had no milk cows, and from 2 out of 3 to 2 out of 5 had no brood sows.

Except in Sherman County relief clients had much smaller numbers of livestock than did the selected farmers (appendix tables 33 and 39). The differences were especially marked in Perkins and Goshen Counties.

Use of Labor and Machinery

Lack of labor was not in general an important factor in limiting the size of farms in the Central Great Plains (appendix table 41). The smaller farms were using about the same amount of labor as some of the larger farms. In Cheyenne County, for example, the amount of labor regularly employed on the 320-acre farms was approximately the same as that used on the 480-acre farms, and in Sherman County the amount of labor regularly used on the 160-acre farms was approximately the same as that used on the 240-acre farms. In all areas the larger farms required more extra harvest labor in years of good crop yields than did the smaller farms, but with the use of larger equipment general on the larger farms, such a difference was usually not great.

In the irrigated section of Goshen County, however, where intensive farming is practiced, the 160-acre farms were using approximately one-sixth more regularly employed labor and a great deal more extra hired labor than were the 80-acre farms. In most of the selected areas in the Central Great Plains one man could operate a 160-acre farm without help and a 320-acre farm with some help during the seeding and harvesting seasons. A 160-acre farm in the irrigated section of Goshen County, however, would require the labor of two men, plus extra hired labor during the beet and haying seasons.

The average estimated value of machinery ranged from $249 on tenant-operated farms in the nonirrigated section of Goshen County to $1,815 on owner-operated farms in the loam section of Perkins County. In general, the average investment in machinery was lowest in the corn producing areas and highest in the small grain areas (appendix table 47).

Farm Buildings

Farm buildings in Perkins and Sherman Counties and in the irrigated section of Goshen County were generally adequate. Minor building repairs were needed on many farms, but rehabilitation of most farmers would not require a large cash expenditure for farm improvements. Where expansion of livestock enterprises was desirable, however, some additional farm buildings might be necessary.

The average estimated value of all farm buildings in these counties ranged from $2,583 per farm in the irrigated section of Goshen County to $4,142 per farm in the loam section of Perkins County. The average estimated cost per farm of all building repairs needed ranged from $51 in the irrigated section of Goshen County to $270 in Sherman County (table 15 and appendix table 42).

Table 15.—Average Value of Farm Buildings and Estimated Cost of Needed Repairs per Farm on Selected Farms in Representative Counties in the Central Great Plains, 1935

County	Number of farms reporting	Value of buildings			Cost of needed repairs		
		Total	Dwelling	Other	Total	Dwelling	Other
Sherman	57	$2,592	$1,314	$1,278	$270	$117	$153
Perkins:							
Loam section	36	4,142	1,643	2,499	89	36	53
Sandy loam section	37	3,070	1,305	1,765	172	102	70
Goshen:							
Irrigated section	29	2,583	1,199	1,384	51	37	14
Nonirrigated section	43	1,604	655	949	141	96	45
Cheyenne	56	2,043	752	1,291	104	52	52

Works Progress Administration.

A Typical Barnyard.

On the other hand, farm buildings were inadequate in Cheyenne County and in some portions of the nonirrigated section of Goshen County. The average estimated value in 1935 of all farm buildings was only $1,604 per farm in the nonirrigated section of Goshen County and only $2,043 in Cheyenne County. Moreover, approximately two-fifths of the total value of farm buildings in both sections was represented by dwellings. The average estimated cost per farm of all building repairs needed was $141 in the nonirrigated section of Goshen County and $104 in Cheyenne County.

INDEBTEDNESS

Real-estate mortgages and taxes place a heavy burden on the farm owners of the Central Great Plains (appendix table 47). A few of the owners in the counties studied reported no real-estate indebtedness but, in general, real-estate mortgages, averaging from more than one-third to more than one-half of the estimated value of all owner-operated farms, represented the chief source of owners' indebtedness. Chattel mortgages, the tenant-operators' largest source of indebtedness, were reported by most of the tenants and by most of the owner-operators as well. Indebtedness for crop and feed loans was not so serious in this region as in other parts of the drought area in 1935.

The meaning of mortgages and taxation to the farmers in the Central Great Plains may be exemplified by a hypothetical case. A 160-acre farm in Sherman County, Nebr., with a nominal mortgage of $5,000 and assessed at the usual rates would have an annual fixed charge of $300 for interest and $60 for taxes. An average corn yield of 22 bushels, if worth only 50 cents a bushel, would provide a gross return of $11 an acre. At that rate 33 acres of the crop, or half that normally produced on the usual 160-acre farm, would be required to meet these fixed charges. In 1934 the entire cash income received on the average 160-acre farm, including that received from the various governmental agencies, was little more than enough to meet these fixed charges.

Real-Estate Indebtedness

From 26 to 41 percent of all land in the representative counties of the Central Great Plains was mortgaged in 1935, according to mortgages of record taken from the county registration books. From 3 to 9 percent of the land carried more than one mortgage.

The average indebtedness per acre ranged from $4.43 in Cheyenne County, where a little more than one-fourth of the land was mortgaged, to $29.10 in Sherman County, where two-fifths of the acreage was mortgaged (table 16).

Because of depreciation in land values the ratio of indebtedness to valuation had nearly doubled between 1930 and 1935, although indebtedness per acre in 1935 was slightly lower than that reported by the census for all full owner-operators in 1930.[21] In some of the counties in 1935 a number of the farmers must have been carrying an indebtedness approximately equal to, or higher than, the estimated value of their farms.

Table 16.—Acreage Mortgaged and Average Indebtedness per Acre, Mortgages of Record in Representative Counties in the Central Great Plains, 1935

County	Number of acres mortgaged		Percent of all land mortgaged		Average indebtedness per acre
	First mortgage	Other mortgage	First mortgage	Other mortgage	
Sherman	150, 694	26, 210	41	7	$29. 10
Perkins	192, 478	49, 815	34	9	14. 65
Goshen	474, 516	89, 593	35	7	5. 44
Cheyenne	293, 522	29, 427	26	3	4. 43

Private individuals, corporations, and the Federal Land Bank held most of the first mortgages (appendix table 43). The Federal Land Bank Commissioner held most of the second mortgages. In Perkins and Cheyenne Counties, where many former private and corporate loans had been refinanced, the Federal Land Bank held almost two-fifths of the first mortgages. The usual interest rate on mortgages was between 5 and 6 percent.

Crop and Feed Loans

On December 31, 1934, the unpaid balance of 1934 crop and feed loans ranged from $6,790 in Cheyenne County to $57,623 in Goshen County (appendix table 44). On February 28, 1935, the unpaid balance of 1934–1935 feed loans ranged from $26,446 in Perkins County to $290,128 in Sherman County. Combined, these outstanding loans averaged from $39 per farm in Perkins County to $206 per farm in Sherman County.

Although not so extensive as in many parts of the Great Plains drought area, these loans represent a financial burden which must be considered in any attempt to rehabilitate the farmers.

Taxation and Tax Delinquencies

Taxes remained delinquent in May 1935 on 17 percent of the land area in Perkins County and on 28 percent of the land area in Cheyenne County. In some instances they had been delinquent for 4 years or more. Taxes for the year 1933 became delinquent on approximately one-fourth of the land area in Sherman County and on more than two-fifths of the land area in Goshen County. Most of these delinquencies had been paid by 1935. The payment of taxes did not always mean that the farmer was in a relatively strong financial position since

[21] Bureau of the Census, *Fifteenth Census of the United States: 1930*, Agriculture Vol. II, U. S. Department of Commerce, Washington, D. C., 1932.

in many cases delinquent taxes had been redeemed by holders of mortgages on the land. The redemption of taxes by the mortgage holder meant an increase in the farmer's indebtedness and financial burden even though it might not necessarily imply an impending foreclosure.

The rate of taxation varied among counties throughout the area and among school districts within each county. The assessed valuation varied within each county, depending on soil, use of land, location, and improvements. The usual real-estate tax in 1934 was approximately $60 for a 160-acre farm in Sherman County. It was $135 for a 640-acre farm in Perkins County, $60 for a 320-acre farm in Cheyenne County, and $45 for a 320-acre farm in the dry-farming section of Goshen County. The usual tax in Goshen County on a 160-acre irrigated farm with 100 acres of irrigated land and 60 acres of dry-farming land was approximately $110.

Relief Clients' Indebtedness

In all of the counties studied the average indebtedness reported by both the owner-operators and the tenant-operators who were receiving relief was smaller than that reported by the selected farmers (appendix tables 45 and 47). Indebtedness of owner-operators, and to a lesser degree that of tenant-operators, corresponded to the size of farm operated. Real-estate mortgages usually represented a smaller proportion, and chattel mortgages and other debts a larger proportion, of the indebtedness of owner-operators on relief than of those selected for study. Chattel mortgages usually represented a smaller proportion of the indebtedness of tenant-operators on relief than of those selected for study.

Statements of assets and net worth for farmers who received drought relief in Perkins County, and for those who applied for rehabilitation loans in Goshen County,[22] show that their small indebtedness, as compared with that of the selected farmers, was due to the fact that their assets were proportionately limited. Even with their smaller indebtedness, the relief clients' equity in their property was more nearly exhausted than was that of the selected farmers.

OWNERSHIP OF LAND AND TENURE OF OPERATORS

In 1935 the great majority of the land in the selected counties of the Central Great Plains was owned by private individuals. They owned about 80 percent in Sherman and Cheyenne Counties and the irrigated section of Goshen County and 96 to 100 percent in Perkins County and the nonirrigated section of Goshen County (table 17). Although foreclosures during recent years had transferred ownership to lending

[22] Such statements were not available for relief clients in Sherman and Cheyenne Counties.

agencies on a large scale in some of the counties, not more than 17 percent of the land in any of the selected counties was owned by corporations, including all loan, mortgage, and insurance companies, as well as joint stock land banks.

Table 17.—Percent of Land Owned by Different Types of Owners in Representative Counties in the Central Great Plains, 1935

Type of owner	Percent of land owned				
	Sherman	Perkins	Goshen		Cheyenne
			Irrigated section	Nonirrigated section	
Total	100	100	100	100	100
Private	80	96	81	100	80
Corporate	16	2	17	*	11
Public	*	1	2	—	5
Quasi-public	*	*	—	—	*
Unknown	4	*	—	—	4

*Less than 0.5 percent.

Sources: Agricultural Adjustment Administration contracts and records in offices of county tax assessors

Private ownership is not an indication of owner-operation, and land operated by tenants may be subjected to exploitative practices whether privately or corporately owned. Under the usual rental agreement a tenant is offered no incentive to conserve soil productivity, and he is likely to exploit the soil unless some supervision or restriction is exercised by the owner.

Residents of the county owned from three- to four-fifths of the farm land in all counties studied with the exception of the irrigated part of Goshen County, Wyo. Here nonresidents owned 58 percent of the land in striking contrast with the nonirrigated section of the county where only 22 percent of the land was owned by nonresidents of the county (appendix table 46). These data represent only the farms with production control contracts, however, and consequently do not show fully the tendency toward absentee-ownership in such areas as Cheyenne County, Colo., where grazing lands predominate.

Tenants operated most of the land in Sherman and Perkins Counties, Nebr., owner-operators being found on only 38 and 30 percent of the land, respectively. All of the farm land owned by nonresidents of these counties was operated by tenants. In Cheyenne County, Colo., three-fifths of the land was owner-operated. Few resident owners in this county rented farms to tenants, but practically all of the nonresident owners had turned over the operation of their land to tenants.

From 1920 to 1930 farm tenancy had increased steadily in the Central Great Plains. In Sherman County the proportion of all farm operators who were tenants increased from 38 to 52 percent and in Perkins County the proportion increased from 35 to 49 percent.

In both Goshen and Cheyenne Counties the proportion of tenant-operators trebled from 1920 to 1935 (table 18).

Table 18.—Farm Tenancy in Representative Counties in the Central Great Plains, 1920, 1930, and 1935

County	Percent of farm operators who were tenants			Percent of farm land operated by tenants		
	1920	1930	1935	1920	1930	1935
Sherman	38	46	52	37	45	50
Perkins	35	44	49	29	37	40
Goshen	13	33	39	9	16	20
Cheyenne	14	40	45	10	29	32

Sources: Bureau of the Census, *Fourteenth Census of the United States: 1920* and *United States Census of Agriculture: 1935*, U. S. Department of Commerce, Washington, D. C.

In spite of a larger indebtedness owner-operators in all of the selected areas were in a much stronger position financially than were tenant-operators in 1935 (fig. 15 and appendix table 47). The tenant-

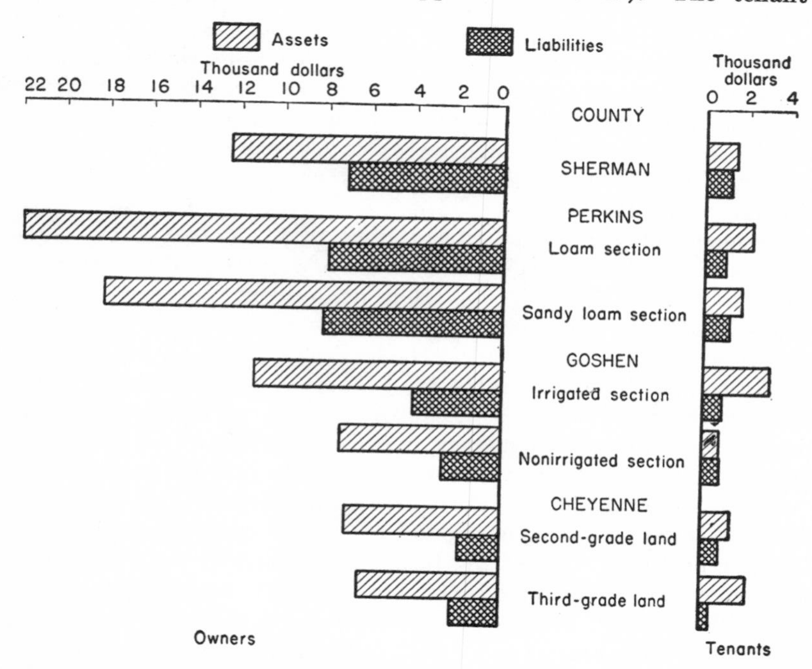

FIG. 15-AVERAGE VALUE OF FARM ASSETS AND AMOUNT OF LIABILITIES OF SELECTED FARMERS IN REPRESENTATIVE COUNTIES IN THE CENTRAL GREAT PLAINS BY TENURE 1935

AF-2701, WPA.

operators' reserves usually were not sufficient to carry them through a series of adverse years. On the average, however, all groups of owner-operators and all groups of tenant-operators, with the exception of the tenants operating in the nonirrigated section of Goshen County, were solvent.

The average net worth of owners ranged from $4,347 on third-grade land in Cheyenne County to $14,060 in the loam section of Perkins County. The greatest disparity between the average net worth of owners and tenants occurred in the nonirrigated portion of Goshen County, where owners had an average net worth of $4,989 and tenants were insolvent.

The weak financial position of tenants as compared with owners is indicated by the larger proportions of tenants among relief clients as compared with all farmers (table 18 and appendix table 45). In Sherman County over three-fourths of the relief clients as compared with one-half of all farmers were tenant-operators, and in Perkins County the proportion was four-fifths as compared with one-half. In Goshen County almost three-fifths of the relief farmers were tenants as compared with two-fifths of all farmers. Less than one-half of all farmers in Cheyenne County were tenants, whereas two-thirds of the relief farmers were tenants.

Chapter III

THE SOUTHERN GREAT PLAINS

THE SOUTHERN Great Plains presents problems of agricultural adjustment different from those in the Central and Northern Great Plains because of higher temperature, more rapid evaporation, and longer frost-free periods. Marked contrasts in farm conditions appear within the region.

Winter wheat production has dominated farming in part of the area. In other sections row feed crops, such as sorghums, have assumed greater importance. Corn is an alternate crop in some sections. Cotton production has been developed on large acreages in the southern portions of the area. In the rough and sandy sections range livestock production is maintained.

Within the limits of the Southern Great Plains are sections in which farming has been definitely successful. These sections, adjacent to or near the so-called Dust Bowl, have received scant attention. Publicity has been directed toward the wind-eroded areas where farming on light soil with long-continued drought has produced a situation favorable to soil blowing.

Three counties were surveyed as illustrative of different agricultural conditions in the Southern Great Plains [1] (fig. 1, p. xv). Economic and financial conditions in Dallam County, Tex., were considered rep-

[1] The counties surveyed and the areas they represent were as follows:

County surveyed	Area represented	Other counties in area
Dallam, Tex.	North Plains of Texas	Texas: Hartley New Mexico: Union
Hale, Tex.	South Plains of Texas Panhandle	Texas: Armstrong, Floyd Bailey, Hall Briscoe, Lamb Carson, Parmer Castro, Randall Deaf Smith, Swisher
Curry, N. Mex.	Upper South Plains of Texas Panhandle and High Plains of eastern New Mexico.	Texas (same counties as above) New Mexico: Quay Roosevelt

resentative of the Canadian-Cimarron High Plains of Texas and northeastern New Mexico. Here wind erosion had aggravated the drought situation and rural distress was acute. Curry County, N. Mex., represented an area whose low mean annual precipitation and frequent droughts had subjected it to emigration and to adjustment in the type of agricultural production. Hale County, Tex., was selected as typical of the South Plains area since its crop production and farm practices are representative of the small grain-producing counties to the north and also of the cotton-growing counties to the south.

SITUATION OF FARMERS AFTER THE 1934 DROUGHT

Reduction in Incomes

Incomes of farmers of the Southern Great Plains were sharply curtailed in 1934. Farmers' estimates of normal cash receipts show that 1934 cash receipts were one-third of normal in the row-crop section and one-fourth of normal in the grain section of Dallam County, two-thirds of normal in the row-crop section and about three-fifths of normal in the grain section of Curry County, and three-fourths of normal in Hale County (table 19 and appendix table 48).

Table 19.—Average Gross Receipts per Farm on Selected Farms in Representative Counties in the Southern Great Plains, by Source of Receipts, 1934

Source of receipts	Average receipts per farm				
	Dallam		Hale (156 farms)	Curry	
	Row-crop section (43 farms)	Grain section (37 farms)		Row-crop section (63 farms)	Grain section (47 farms)
Total farm receipts	$1, 128	$1, 081	$2, 037	$1, 334	$1, 479
Total cash receipts	978	962	1, 861	1, 181	1, 309
Crop sales	19	28	1, 065	437	379
Livestock sales	499	227	220	227	313
Livestock products	74	90	195	195	185
Agricultural Adjustment Administration contract payments	306	414	276	133	355
Emergency Relief Administration	24	39	1	17	44
Other	56	164	104	172	33
Total products used in home	150	119	176	153	170
Dairy products	53	40	58	56	53
Poultry products	44	41	45	48	46
Meat	40	32	41	37	44
Crops and garden	13	6	32	12	27

Normally from two-thirds to more than four-fifths of the farmers' receipts came from crop production. Even in the row-crop sections, definitely better adapted to feed than to grain crops, normal receipts from crops were reported to be double those from livestock, although livestock sales were more important there than in the other sections studied.

In 1934, however, the principal sources of cash receipts in Dallam County were livestock sales, made largely to the Government during the Emergency Livestock Purchase Program, Agricultural Adjustment Administration contract payments, and, on the smaller farms, grants from the Federal Emergency Relief Administration. Income from these same sources was important in Hale and Curry Counties but not so important as receipts from crop sales.

Receipts from crop sales were closely related to the severity of drought, increasing in amount toward the South and East. They were negligible in Dallam County (2 or 3 percent of the total), but in Curry County they accounted for 29 percent of the total cash receipts in the grain section and 37 percent in the row-crop section. Crop sales remained the most important source of the gross cash receipts in Hale County in the southernmost part of the area, accounting for 57 percent of the total.

Livestock sales were the source of about one-half of the cash receipts in the row-crop section of Dallam County, one-fourth in the grain sections of both Dallam and Curry Counties, one-fifth in the row-crop section of Curry County, and one-eighth in Hale County. Crop production control payments and relief grants were the source of nearly one-half of the cash receipts in the grain section of Dallam County, about one-third in the row-crop section of Dallam County and in the grain section of Curry County, and about one-seventh in the row-crop section of Curry County and in Hale County.

The average cash receipts received by the selected farmers in 1934, including Government benefits, were slightly under $1,000 in Dallam County as compared with normal receipts of about $3,300. They were about $1,200 in the row-crop section of Curry County as compared with $1,800 normally, and $1,300 in the grain section of Curry County as compared with $2,300. In Hale County the 1934 gross cash receipts were about $1,900 as compared with about $2,500 normally (table 19 and appendix table 48). The value of farm products used in the home added from $119 to $176 to the annual farm income in each area surveyed.

These estimates make no allowance for losses because of decreases in livestock, feed, and equipment inventories, or for the portion of the reported cash receipts which may have been attached through liens and chattel mortgages. In Dallam County, for example, the farmers actually received only 36 percent of the total payment for all cattle purchased in the county by the Government during the Emergency Livestock Purchase Program; 64 percent of the payment went directly to those holding liens and chattel mortgages on the cattle.

The inadequacy of the farmers' incomes in 1934 in the various selected areas is shown by reports of individual farmers. About one-half of the farmers interviewed in Dallam County reported that their receipts in 1934, including all Government benefits, were not sufficient to meet their expenses. Only 1 farmer in 10 in the row-crop section and 1 in 20 in the grain section reported receipts greater than expenses. In Curry County almost one-third of the farmers in the grain section and one-sixth of those in the row-crop section reported that their 1934 receipts were not sufficient to meet expenses, while only one in five in the row-crop section and one in eight in the grain section reported that they were able to increase capital. On the other hand, almost four-fifths of the farmers in Hale County reported receipts equal to or greater than operating expenses.

The precariousness of the farmers' situation in the Southern Great Plains is shown not only by their losses in 1934 but also by the large number that had sustained financial losses since they began farming in the area. The proportions of the selected farmers who had been operating at a loss since beginning farming in the area were 67 percent in the grain section and 42 percent in the row-crop section of Dallam County, 30 percent in Hale County, and 17 percent in the row-crop section and 6 percent in the grain section of Curry County.

Farmers on Relief and Rehabilitation Rolls

Reports of the State relief administrators in the Southern Great Plains indicate that from one-eighth to two-fifths of the farm families in most of the Texas Panhandle counties and over one-half of the farm families in the extreme southeastern Colorado counties were receiving relief in March 1935. In the extreme southwestern portion of Kansas the rural case load in March 1935 was equivalent to one-third to one-half of the number of farmers in the different counties. Similar reports for Oklahoma and New Mexico counties were not obtained.

In May 1935 the County Relief Administrator in Dallam County, Tex., reported that 199 farmers, or 28 percent of all farmers in the county, were receiving relief. Fifty-eight of these had been accepted as rural rehabilitation clients. In Hale County 219 farmers, or 12 percent of all farmers in the county, were receiving relief in April 1935. Only 46 of these had received rehabilitation loans by July 1935. In Curry County 220 farmers, or 15 percent of all farmers in the county, were on the relief rolls in May 1935, and 94 of these had been accepted as rural rehabilitation clients.[2] Only 135 farmers had actually received relief, the other clients having applied for relief solely to become eligible for rehabilitation loans.

The fact that three out of five relief clients in Curry County began receiving relief after June 1, 1934, when it became apparent that the

[2] The usual amount of relief received by Curry County clients was between $15 and $25 per month, and the average amount received by all clients was $23 per month. The 94 farmers who had been accepted as rehabilitation clients had received no rehabilitation loans at the time of this study but their budgets called for loans averaging $536.

crops in 1934 were a failure, reflects their dependence on crops. Of the 135 relief recipients in Curry County, 20 began receiving relief prior to January 1934, 33 between January and May, 35 between June and October, and 47 after October. In both Hale and Curry Counties farmers on relief rolls had an unusually high proportion of their land devoted to crops.

Tenancy and dependency appeared related. The proportion of relief clients who were tenants was much greater than that among the selected farmers, and in all of the areas studied owner-operators were stronger financially than tenant-operators. However, another factor may have been the recent arrival of these farmers in the area and the small resources which they had been able to accumulate in that time. Many of the farmers who were in the worst straits had been in the area a relatively short time. In Curry County about half of the relief clients had been farming in the area not more than 10 years.

It is unlikely that physical disabilities or an unusually large number of dependents contributed to the need for assistance of many of the relief clients. More than four-fifths of the relief clients in the selected counties were 55 years of age or younger, and in none of the selected counties were more than one-twelfth over 60 years of age (appendix table 49). In Dallam County only 5 percent of the relief clients reported disabilities that incapacitated them for work. None of the relief clients in Hale County who had been approved for rehabilitation, and only 2 percent of all relief clients in Curry County were unable to work. Most of the relief clients had children, but in Dallam County only one out of eight and in Curry County only one out of six had more than three children under 16 years of age (appendix table 50). In Hale County only one out of five of the relief clients who had been approved for rehabilitation had more than three children under 12 years of age.

TYPES OF FARMING

Variations in natural factors, and their effects on crop production, give rise to different systems of farming in different sections of the Southern Plains. The northern portion of the area, where the topography and climatic conditions favor the production of crops, is a cash-grain area. Primary emphasis is placed on the production of winter wheat on the heavier soils and grain sorghums on the lighter soils.[3] A large proportion of the area immediately south of the cash-grain area (along the Canadian River) is too rugged for crop production and is used predominantly for range livestock. Further south, where the higher temperatures and the long growing season permit its production, cotton is the principal cash crop.

[3] Carter, William T., Jr., *The Soils of Texas*, Bulletin 431, Texas Agricultural Experiment Station, College Station, Tex., 1931, p. 145.

Dallam County, Tex., is located in the cash-grain area. In the southern and western sections of the county grain sorghums are the principal cash crop, whereas in the northern and eastern portions of the county winter wheat predominates. Hence, in this report the two sections are referred to as the row-crop and the grain sections. In the type-of-farming area which includes the grain section of Dallam County, according to a classification of farms based on the gross income from the 1929 crop,[4] 76 percent of the farms were cash-grain farms, 7 percent crop-specialty farms, 6 percent general farms, and only 7 percent animal-specialty or dairy farms or stock ranches. In the type-of-farming area which includes the southern and western sections of Dallam County, 48 percent of the farms were classed as cash-grain farms, 3 percent as crop-specialty farms, 5 percent as general farms, and only 12 percent as animal-specialty farms or stock ranches.

Hale County, Tex., and Curry County, N. Mex., are located south of the Canadian River in an area where some cotton is produced. Little cotton is produced in Curry County, however, since its high altitude and low temperature make the production of cotton hazardous. In Hale County cotton production is an important enterprise in the southern part. In a classification of farms in the area in which both Hale County and Curry County are located,[5] 60 percent of the farms were classed as cash-grain farms and 23 percent as cotton farms.

NATURAL FACTORS AFFECTING AGRICULTURE

The 1934 drought was not solely responsible for the distress of farmers in the Southern Great Plains in the spring of 1935. Study of the natural conditions of the region shows that agriculture is normally hazardous.

Topography

The topography of the Southern Great Plains is similar to that of the Central Great Plains. The area in general is a high plain sloping in a southeasterly direction from an elevation of approximately 6,000 feet in northeastern New Mexico to an elevation of approximately 2,000 feet at the southeastern corner of the Texas Panhandle. The High Plains Section to the west is generally level to undulating, interspersed with rough areas along the drainage channels. The eastern portion of the area is irregularly undulating. The principal drainage channels consist of the Cimarron River and its tributaries in southern Kansas and the Oklahoma Panhandle, the Canadian River and its tributaries in the northern and central portion of the Texas Panhandle, and the head waters of the Red and Brazos Rivers in the southern portion of the Texas Panhandle.

[4] Elliott, F. F., *Types of Farming in the United States*, U. S. Department of Commerce, Bureau of the Census, Washington, D. C., 1933, table 5.

[5] *Ibid.*

The continuity of the Plains is further broken by sand dunes or low rounded hills and ridges in localities where the soils are nearly pure sand. Such regions are extremely susceptible to wind erosion unless protected by a vegetative cover. In the southern portions of the area there are numerous small depressions or lake beds, which seem to have been caused by the sinking of the surface or by the removal of soil material by wind. These basins range in size from a few acres to 50 acres or more. They have no surface outlets but often remain dry for several years, containing water only during seasons of heavy rainfall.[6]

Soils

The Southern Great Plains has three soil groups—the Chernozem or Black soils and the Brown soils, which occur in other sections of the Great Plains, and the Southern Dark-Brown soils (fig. 2, p. 8).[7]

Soils in the western and southwestern portions of Dallam County, Tex., are of the Otero series of the Brown group, which generally occupy a rolling area that is subject to erosion. Those in all other portions of the county are of the Springer series of the Dark-Brown group. The fine sandy loam of the Springer series is used for crop production, while the loamy fine sand and fine sand are used almost exclusively as range land for livestock.[8] Because of their sandy characteristics, the soils in the southwestern and south central portions of the county are best adapted to the production of sorghums and other row crops. The heavier soils in the other portions of the county are adapted to the production of small grains.

Soils in Hale County, Tex., are Amarillo loams, clay loams, and sandy loams. They are adapted to the production of small grains and sorghums, and in the southern part of the county, where the growing season is longer, they are adapted to the production of cotton.

Soils in Curry County, N. Mex., are of the Springer series, ranging from sandy loams and sands in the southern and western portions of the county to heavier or "tight" soils in the rest of the county. The heavy soils are adapted to the production of small grains, while the light sandy soils are adapted to the production of sorghums and other row crops.

Climate

The climate of the Southern Great Plains is characterized by rather severe winters, considerable wind movement during the spring and early summer months, and warm summer days with comparatively

[6] Carter, William T., Jr. and Others, *Reconnaissance Soil Survey of Northwest Texas*, Department of Agriculture, Bureau of Soils, Washington, D. C., 1922, p. 3.

[7] Bureau of Chemistry and Soils, *Atlas of American Agriculture*, part III, U. S. Department of Agriculture, Washington, D. C., 1935, p. 74.

[8] Sweet, A. T. and Poulson, E. N., *Soil Survey of the Fort Sumner Area, New Mexico*, Series 1930, Bulletin No. 1, U. S. Department of Agriculture, Bureau of Chemistry and Soils, Washington, D. C., 1933, pp. 9–11.

cool nights. Dry periods, accompanied by hot winds, are not uncommon during the summer months. Local hailstorms occur frequently during the late spring and early summer. The climate may be classified as varying from year to year between arid and subhumid.

As in the other Great Plains areas the average length of the frost-free season increases from northwest to southeast, ranging from approximately 170 days in southeastern Colorado to over 210 days in the southeastern portion of the Texas Panhandle [9] (fig. 4, p. 11). It has been from 2 to 3 weeks shorter than average in about one-fifth of the years for which records are available.

As in the other Great Plains areas the average annual precipitation in the Southern Great Plains increases from west to east. The average annual precipitation ranges from as low as 12 inches in southeastern Colorado to approximately 25 inches in the eastern part of the area. Approximately three-fourths of the annual precipitation normally occurs during the warm growing season from April through September.

More precipitation is required for plant growth in the southern than in the other portions of the Great Plains, owing to a high rate of evaporation caused by high temperatures throughout the summer, much sunshine,[10] low humidity, and high wind movements. During the summer months, June through August, average monthly temperatures range from about 70 to 80 degrees. Precipitation during the summer is often local in character with the result that crops in one locality may produce fair yields, whereas those in an adjacent locality may be complete failures.

Precipitation in the selected counties is usually adequate for plant growth (fig. 16), but the frequent departures from normal make the production of crops hazardous. This is particularly true in the northern and western portions of the area represented by Dallam County, Tex., and Curry County, N. Mex., although the production of crops adapted to the climate and soils is usually possible. Hard winter wheat and sorghums are best adapted to the climate in these regions. The length of growing season is almost always adequate for the maturing of sorghums unless their seeding has been delayed because of moisture deficiency in the spring.

Hard winter wheat, barley, and sorghums are also adapted to the climatic conditions in Hale County, Tex. In the southern part of the county, as in other counties lying immediately south, the production of cotton is possible because of the long growing season and the high summer temperatures.

---

[9] Bureau of Chemistry and Soils, *Atlas of American Agriculture*, "Climate," Frost and the Growing Season, U. S. Department of Agriculture, Washington, D. C., 1918, pp. 38–39.

[10] Bureau of Chemistry and Soils, *Atlas of American Agriculture*, "Climate," Temperature, Sunshine and Wind, U. S. Department of Agriculture, Washington, D. C., 1928, pp. 32–33.

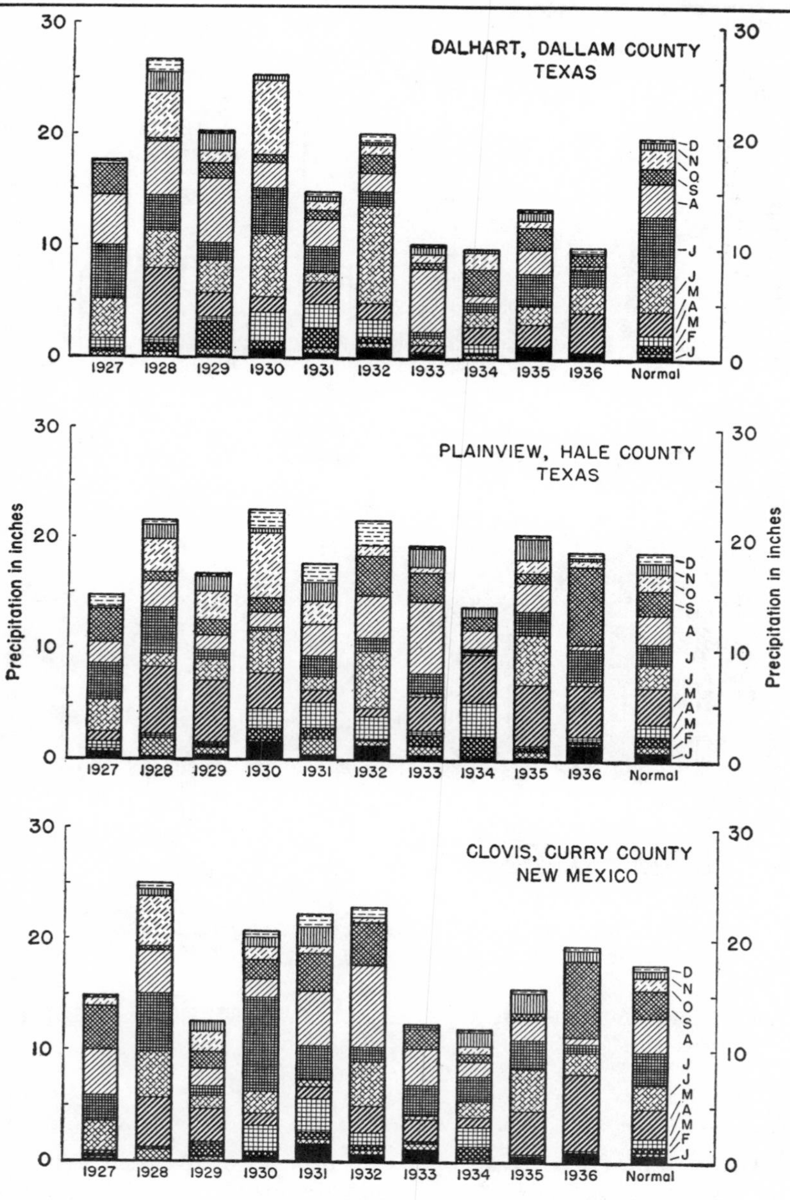

FIG. 16–NORMAL MONTHLY PRECIPITATION AND PRECIPITATION BY MONTHS, SELECTED STATIONS IN THE SOUTHERN GREAT PLAINS
1927–1936

Source: U.S. Department of Agriculture, Weather Bureau.

AF-2779, WPA

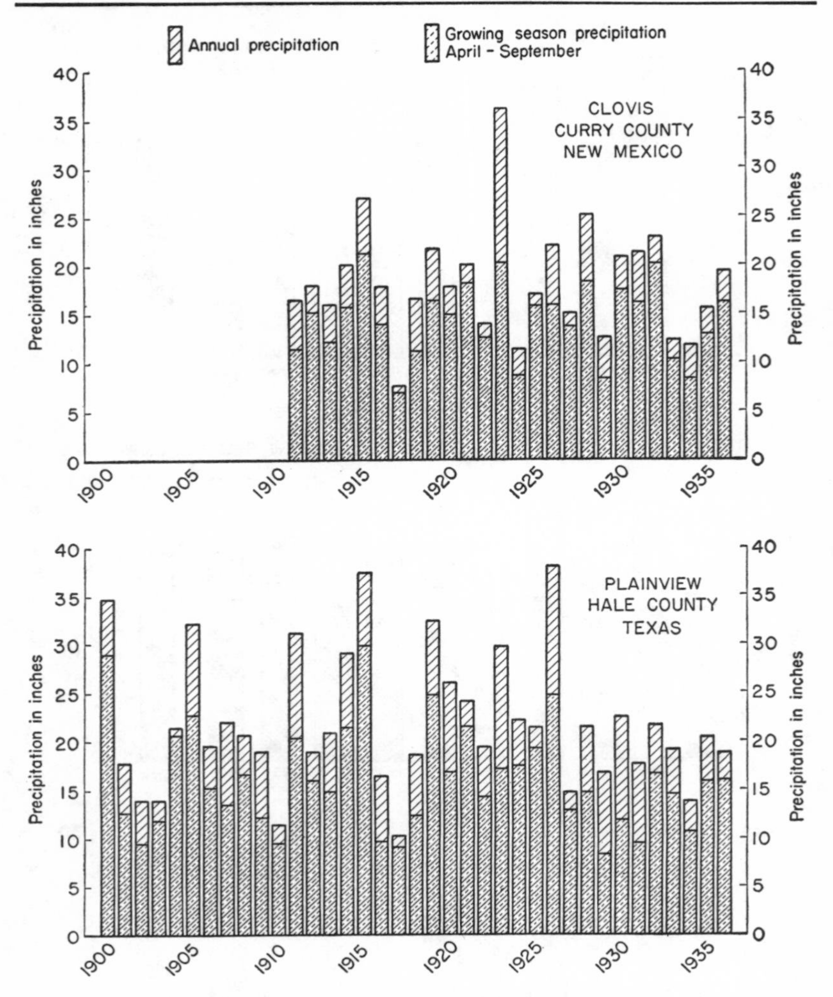

FIG. 17 - ANNUAL AND GROWING SEASON PRECIPITATION, SELECTED STATIONS IN THE SOUTHERN GREAT PLAINS 1900-1936

Source: U.S. Department of Agriculture, Weather Bureau. AF-2787, WPA

Although for the area as a whole the drought of 1933 and 1934 was the worst on record (fig. 17), years of extremely low rainfall and long periods of subnormal rainfall are common in the area. Records of precipitation available since 1900 indicate that 1901–1903, 1910, 1916–1918, and 1931–1934 were general periods of subnormal rainfall in the area, and that 1924 and 1927 were additional years in which precipitation was generally deficient.

During the period 1927–1936 rainfall during the critical spring and early summer months seems to have been deficient in Dallam County, Tex., in 5 years; in Hale County, Tex., in 4 years; and in Curry County, N. Mex., in 6 years. The lack of rainfall was more serious in 1934 than in any of the previous years.

The period 1931–1934 was one of subnormal precipitation throughout the Southern Great Plains but only the 2 years, 1933 and 1934, comprised a period of abnormal drought. The 9.78 inches of precipitation recorded in Dallam County, Tex., in 1934 was the lowest on record. In Hale County, Tex., however, precipitation in both 1910 and 1917 was less than the 13.75 inches recorded in 1934, and in Curry County, N. Mex., precipitation recorded in 1917 and in 1924 was less than the 11.77 inches recorded in 1934.

Causes of Crop Damage

Most of the damage to crops in the Southern Great Plains is due to drought, soil blowing (fig. 3, p. 9), and hail. When damage to crops by drought and soil blowing occurs, it is usually general throughout the area although it is frequently more severe in the northwestern portion. Damage by hail is usually confined to small localities.

Estimates of selected farmers indicate that damage to crops by drought has occurred from approximately one-fifth to one-third of the years in Dallam County, approximately two-fifths of the years in Curry County, and almost one-half of the years in Hale County (table 20 and appendix table 51). Soil blowing has damaged crops less frequently than drought, but soil blowing and drought combined have caused serious damage to, or total loss of, crops approximately 1 year in 3 in all of the selected counties except in the grain section of Dallam County, where this damage has occurred 1 year in 4.

Table 20.—Percent of Years [1] Different Causes of Crop Damage Were Reported on Selected Farms in Representative Counties in the Southern Great Plains

County	Percent of years damage was reported						
	Drought	Hail	Soil blowing	Smut and rust	Insects	Frost	Excessive precipitation
Dallam:							
Row-crop section	35	7	12	1	5	5	2
Grain section	22	9	14	4	4	1	11
Hale	49	33	3	1	4	4	2
Curry:							
Row-crop section	40	14	7	1	12	6	4
Grain section	44	17	6	2	1	1	—

[1] For length of record see appendix table 51.

Damage from hail has occurred less than 1 year in 10 in Dallam County, 1 year in 6 in Curry County, and 1 year in 3 in Hale County. Severe damage to crops by hail has been infrequent except in Hale County, where serious damage to, or total loss of, crops from this cause has occurred about 1 year in 6. Other causes of crop damage reported by the selected farmers included smut and rust, insects, frost, and excessive precipitation, but their occurrence was infrequent and the damage caused by them was usually slight.

Excessive periods of drought have not only destroyed crops but also have augmented wind erosion to such an extent that the productivity of the land has been greatly impaired. Considerable cropland and, in some localities, entire farms have been abandoned because of wind erosion. Small farms have suffered particularly because of their high proportion of land in crops. Such damage has been most extensive in the northern portion of the area and, of the three representative counties, in Dallam County. In that county most of the farmers receiving relief or rehabilitation advances in the spring of 1935 were concentrated in the sandy sections most affected by wind erosion.

Farmers in the grain section of Dallam County estimated that an area equivalent to 31 percent of their cropland had been damaged severely and an area equivalent to 50 percent had been damaged slightly by wind erosion. Farmers in the row-crop section estimated that an area equivalent to 46 percent of their cropland had been damaged severely and an area equivalent to 45 percent of their cropland had been damaged slightly. Farmers in Curry County reported that an area equivalent to 6 to 8 percent of their cropland had been damaged severely and an area equivalent to 38 percent of their cropland had been damaged slightly. Farmers in Hale County reported little damage to their land by wind erosion. Some damage to permanent pastures by wind erosion was found where the sod adjacent to cropland was covered by drifting soil.

CROP YIELDS

As in the Northern and Central Great Plains precipitation is the most important factor controlling crop production in the Southern Great Plains, but the timeliness and character of precipitation are more important here than in the other Great Plains areas. Because of variations in character as well as amounts of precipitation, crop yields vary widely from year to year as well as from one locality to another within the same year, and crop failures have been common.

Amounts of precipitation do not always indicate the availability of moisture for crops. In 1931, for example, when precipitation in the two Texas counties was limited, crop yields were well above average because of soil and subsoil moisture following abundant rainfall during the preceding year. On the other hand, after the dry year of 1931, precipitation in 1932 approximated or exceeded normal in all of the selected counties. Yields of all crops in Dallam and Curry Counties and those of small grains and cotton in Hale County, however, were decidedly below average because even normal amounts of

Works Progress Administration.

After the Dust Storm.

rainfall were not sufficient to offset the depleted supplies of soil moisture. Yields of row crops were reasonably good in Hale County but only because these crops were planted late and because the long growing season permitted the utilization of the abundant rainfall which occurred during the summer months.

In 1933 and 1934 amounts of precipitation were more directly related to crop yields than in the 2 preceding years. Coincident with the deficiencies in precipitation, crop yields were extremely low in 1933 throughout the entire area. In 1934 they were almost complete failures in all but a few local areas where precipitation occurred at a critical time.

Crop yields over a long period of years are not available for any of the selected counties or for the central and southern portions of the area. Crop yields available for southwestern Kansas, however, might serve as an index of crop production possibilities in the northern areas. Because of similarities in soils as well as climatic conditions, crop yields reported for Baca County, Colo., may be considered generally representative of those portions of the area typified by Dallam County, Tex. (appendix table 52).

The variability of crop yields per harvested acre is illustrated best by the yields reported in southwestern Kansas. Here yields of winter wheat were usually between 3 and 17 bushels per harvested acre but ranged from complete failure to 24 bushels per acre. Yields of corn and barley were as variable as those of wheat. Grain sorghums yields were more stable, and no complete failures were reported during the period 1915–1932.

Yields per seeded acre were, of course, lower than were yields per harvested acre, and they were also more variable. From 1911 to 1931 the average yield of wheat per seeded acre was only 9.2 bushels. One-fourth of the crop yields per seeded acre reported during that period were 2 bushels or less; one-third were 4 bushels or less; and more than three-fifths exceeded or fell short of the average by 5 or more bushels.

The especially low yields of crops from 1930 to 1934 (appendix table 53) help to explain the relative degrees of distress throughout the area in 1935. Crop yields were almost a complete failure in Dallam County in 1933 and 1934 and in Curry County in 1934. With the exception of those obtained in Hale County in 1934, wheat yields had not approximated the long-time average in any of the selected areas since 1931, and in Dallam County they had been almost a complete failure since that time. Corn yields had not approximated the long-time average yield in Dallam County since 1931 and in Curry County since 1932. Yields of sorghums had been generally higher than those of other crops during the drought years, but even sorghums had produced low yields since 1931 in Dallam and Curry Counties.

Yields reported by selected farmers in the counties studied show how yields vary from one section to another (appendix table 54). Farmers reported higher yields of wheat and less frequent failures in the grain section than in the row-crop section of both Dallam and Curry Counties. Calculated yields of corn and the frequency of poor yields or failures were about the same in the two sections of each county. Yields of grain sorghums were slightly higher and poor yields and failures were less frequent in the row-crop than in the grain section of Dallam County; but in the row-crop section of Curry County yields were lower and poor yields or failures more frequent than in the grain section. Yields of feed sorghums [11] were about the same in the grain and row-crop sections of both Dallam and Curry Counties.

Cotton yields were reported by farmers in Hale County. They averaged 182 pounds per seeded acre, with poor yields or failures occurring 2 years in 5.

These farmers' estimates emphasize the precarious position of any farmer in the Southern Great Plains. They indicate that poor yields or failures of wheat had occurred from nearly one-half of the time in Hale County to four-fifths of the time in the row-crop section of Dallam County. Poor yields or failures of corn had occurred from two-fifths to one-half of the time; and poor yields or failures of grain sorghums had occurred from three-tenths to over one-half of the time (table 21 and appendix table 54).

Table 21.—Percent of Years [1] Poor Yields or Failures of Important Crops Were Reported by Selected Farmers in Representative Counties in the Southern Great Plains

County	Percent of years reported							
	Wheat		Corn		Grain sorghums		Feed sorghums	
	Poor yield	Failure	Poor yield	Failure	Poor yield	Failure	Poor yield	Failure
Dallam:								
Row-crop section	4	77	17	23	13	18	17	33
Grain section	16	44	14	24	20	22	20	28
Hale	21	24	—	—	23	21	24	19
Curry:								
Row-crop section	29	37	26	24	29	23	16	21
Grain section	27	33	35	16	23	17	23	18

[1] For number of crops reported see appendix table 54.

ORGANIZATION OF FARMS

As in the other sections of the Great Plains, size of farm, amount of cropland and pasture, crops grown, and number and kinds of livestock were significant factors to be considered in analyzing the plight of farmers in 1934 and 1935 and the possibilities for their rehabilitation.

[11] Grain sorghums yields as reported may be high because farmers tended to report yields only when grain was produced and not to report sorghums which were cut for forage.

Too much dependence on crops and too little dependence on livestock in a region of frequent crop failures seemed to contribute to the distress of the farmers. Livestock farmers had made more financial progress than crop farmers in Dallam and Curry Counties. This was particularly true of the row-crop section in Dallam County where most of the crop farmers had suffered heavy losses while most of the livestock farmers had accumulated some capital since they began farming in the area.

On the other hand, in Hale County in the southeastern part of the Southern Great Plains a major livestock enterprise is apparently not so essential to a successful farm economy. A somewhat higher proportion of the crop farmers in this county were able to make financial progress, and their average annual accumulation of capital was larger than that of the livestock farmers. In part, of course, this may have been due to larger farms and larger acreages of cropland on the crop farms.

Moreover, length of residence in the area was an important factor in relation to financial progress. Of those who had suffered financial losses in the row-crop section of Dallam County, 83 percent, and of those in the grain section, 72 percent, had been operating 10 years or less in the area. Of those who had suffered losses in the other areas, all in the row-crop section and two-thirds in the grain section of Curry County and over two-fifths in Hale County had been operating 10 years or less in the area. Had these farmers been in the area for a longer time, it is possible that some of those who were operating large farms might have been able to make some financial progress. But, with so much dependence placed on crop sales for income and with crop failures common in the area, it is not likely that many who were operating small farms could have prevented financial losses (appendix table 55).

Size of Operating Unit

Because cash-grain production is adapted to large-scale farming, the cash-grain farmers in the northern part of the Southern Great Plains generally operate larger acreages than do the cotton farmers in the southern part. For the same reason farms located in the wheat-producing sections of the cash-grain area are generally larger than those in the row-crop sections. Stock ranches in either section are larger than grain or cotton farms.

According to the 1935 Census of Agriculture the average size of farm in Dallam County was 1,107 acres. In Curry County it was 606 acres, and in Hale County it was 318 acres. A tendency in the past to adjust the size of farm to the production possibilities of the area was apparent only in Curry County. From 1920 to 1935 the number of farms in Dallam and Hale Counties had increased materially, whereas the average size of farms had decreased. In Curry County the number of farms had increased between 1925 and 1935 but the average size of farm had also increased.[12]

Data from corn-hog production control contracts representing 71 percent of all farms in the county indicate that farms of 160, 320, and 640 acres were the most common in Dallam County in 1934 (appendix table 56). The average size of the 80 farms in Dallam County for which farm records were taken was 974 acres, those in the row-crop section averaging 904 acres and those in the grain section averaging 1,056 acres (appendix table 57). In both the row-crop and the grain sections the 320- and 640-acre farms predominated.

In Hale County data pertaining to the size of farms in 1934 were secured from farmers with cotton as well as corn-hog production control contracts. Farms represented by the cotton contracts (appendix table 58) were generally somewhat smaller than those represented by the corn-hog contracts, but the 160- and 320-acre farms were most common in both groups. The average size of corn-hog contract farms was 325 acres, whereas that of the cotton farms was 282 acres. The 160- and 320-acre farms were also most common among the 156 selected farms for which records were taken. The average size of these farms was 387 acres, one-third of them being 200 acres or smaller, and about two-thirds being 400 acres or smaller (appendix table 57).

The 160-, 320-, and 480-acre farms were most common in Curry County. The 491 farms represented by corn-hog production control contracts averaged 557 acres in size. The 110 selected farms averaged 591 acres, those in the row-crop section averaging 511 acres and those in the grain section averaging 699 acres. About two-thirds of the farms in the row-crop section and nearly one-half of the farms in the grain section were less than 560 acres in size.

In Dallam County many farms were too small for economic operation. In the grain section of Dallam County only farms of 881 acres or more reported capital increases on the average since beginning operations in the area (appendix table 55). On the average, in the row-crop section of the county operators of less than 441 acres had not made expenses. A small operating unit was characteristic of the farmers on relief rolls. The average size of farm operated by the 46 relief clients in Hale County who had been approved for rehabilitation loans was only 71 acres as compared with an average of 282 acres for all farms with cotton contracts, an average of 325 acres for all farms with corn-hog contracts, and an average of 318 acres for all farms in the county. Approximately two-thirds of the clients who had been approved for rehabilitation were operating farms of 60 acres or less and all but three were operating farms of 160 acres or less (appendix table 59).

[12] Bureau of the Census, *United States Census of Agriculture: 1935*, U. S. Department of Commerce, Washington, D. C.

In Curry County the average size of farm operated by relief clients was 284 acres as compared with an average of 557 acres for all farms represented by corn-hog contracts and an average of 606 acres for all farms in the county. Forty-four percent of the farms operated by relief clients, as compared with only twenty-seven percent of those represented by corn-hog contracts, were less than 280 acres in size, and about three-fourths of them, as compared with about one-half of the corn-hog contract farms, were less than 380 acres in size.

Data pertaining to the acreage operated by relief clients in Dallam County were not available.

Use of Land

In 1935 crops occupied 45 percent of the farm land in Dallam County, 53 percent in Curry County, and 78 percent in Hale County.[13] Information from production control contracts and from selected farmers (fig. 18, table 22, and appendix tables 56, 57, and 58) in Dallam and Curry Counties indicates a somewhat higher percentage of the farm land utilized as cropland than that reported by the census. Presumably, this was because a large proportion of the farms in Dallam and Curry Counties were ranches with a high proportion of land in pasture, and such farms were not generally included among either the farms surveyed or those with production control contracts. Information from contracts and from selected farmers in Hale County was similar to that reported by the census. There were few ranches in Hale County, and a larger proportion of all farms was represented in the samples than in the other two counties.

Table 22.—Utilization of Land on Selected Farms in Representative Counties in the Southern Great Plains, 1934

County	Number of farms reporting	Average number of acres per farm				
		Total	Cropland	Pasture	Former cropland	Farm-stead and waste
Dallam:						
Row-crop section	43	904	534	352	5	13
Grain section	37	1,056	768	267	4	17
Hale	156	387	318	56	—	13
Curry:						
Row-crop section	63	511	353	135	8	15
Grain section	47	699	482	201	3	13

The proportion of the farm land that was used as cropland was generally higher on the small farms than on the large farms. The difference in land use by small and large farms was most pronounced in Dallam and Curry Counties, where the proportion of land in crops on the small farms was generally higher than the average in crops for all farms. This explains why small farms, especially in Dallam County, suffered more from wind erosion than did the large farms.

[13] *Ibid.*

Most of the land operated by the selected farmers was either owned by the operators or share-rented. Land that was rented for cash represented less than 2 percent of the total land operated in Hale County, 4 percent in Dallam County, and 6 percent in the grain section and 8 percent in the row-crop section of Curry County (appendix table 60). About three-tenths of the land operated in Curry County, two-fifths in Dallam County, and one-half in Hale County were share-rented, while from one-half of the land operated in Hale County to nearly two-thirds of that operated in Curry County was owned by the operator. Most of the cash-rented land was used for hay or pasture, and most of the share-rented land was used as cropland.

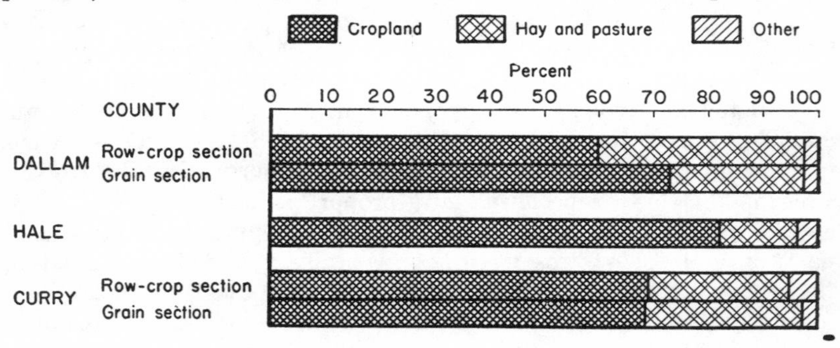

FIG. 18 - UTILIZATION OF LAND ON SELECTED FARMS IN REPRESENTATIVE COUNTIES IN THE SOUTHERN GREAT PLAINS 1934

AF-2705, WPA

In 1934 wheat occupied one-half or more of the cropland on the farms in the grain sections of Dallam and Curry Counties, about one-third of the crop acreage in Hale County and the row-crop section of Curry County, and less than one-fifth in the row-crop section of Dallam County (appendix table 61). It was planted on three-fourths of the farms in Hale County; on more than four-fifths of the farms in the grain section of Curry County; on about one-half of the farms in the grain section of Dallam County and the row-crop section of Curry County; and on less than one-fourth of the farms, principally the larger units, in the row-crop section of Dallam County.

Wheat seeded on fallow land was limited primarily to the grain sections of Dallam and Curry Counties although some wheat on fallow was reported in Hale County on a few of the larger farms and in the row-crop section of Curry County. In the grain section of Dallam County less than one-fourth of the farms and in the grain section of Curry County only three-tenths of the farms had wheat planted on fallow. Primarily these were the larger units in both counties.

Sorghums were the principal forage crop planted in both Dallam and Curry Counties, and in Hale County they were second only to wheat in acreage occupied. In the grain section of Dallam County and in Hale County they were planted on practically all farms, and in the row-crop sections of both Dallam and Curry Counties they were planted on all farms. Most of the farmers in the grain section of Curry County also planted sorghums.

Corn was planted on two-thirds of the farms in the row-crop section of Dallam County, on almost four-fifths in the row-crop section and on more than one-half in the grain section of Curry County, and on one-third in the grain section of Dallam County.

Cotton occupied approximately one-seventh of the cropland in Hale County and was planted on almost all of the farms.

In the grain section of Dallam County fallow land was reported on none of the small farms and on only one-sixth of all farms, but idle cropland was reported on three-fourths of all farms. In the row-crop section fallow land was limited to a few of the larger farms, but more than four-fifths of the farmers reported idle cropland.

In Hale County fallow land was reported on more than one-half of the larger farms and on more than two-fifths of all farms. Idle cropland was reported on about three-tenths of the farms and was not limited to farms of any particular size.

In the grain section of Curry County a smaller proportion of the cropland was left idle than in the grain section of Dallam County. Almost one-half of the farmers reported fallow land, but little more than one-fourth of them reported idle cropland. In the row-crop section both fallow land and idle cropland were reported on about one-fifth of the farms, the fallow land being limited to the larger farms and the idle cropland being distributed among farms of all sizes.

The large proportion of Dallam County cropland that was left idle in 1934 indicates that the acreage seeded to various crops in that year was not normal. Reports of the acreage seeded from 1930 to 1934 (appendix table 62) show that in Dallam County the acreage seeded to each of the important crops in 1934, and to a lesser degree the acreage seeded in 1933, was less than that seeded in the 3 preceding years. However, the proportion of the cropland seeded to the various crops had not changed materially except for corn, which had become relatively less important. Acreages seeded in 1933 and 1934 might in general be considered representative of conditions in the county during dry years, while acreages seeded in 1930 and 1931 might be considered representative of conditions in the more moist periods.

In Hale County, where drought had not been so severe, crop acreages were more stable than in Dallam County. The acreage seeded to wheat had declined only gradually from 1930 to 1934, but the decline probably resulted from the crop reduction program as much as from unfavorable seeding conditions. The acreage seeded to sorghums was increased slightly in 1934 and to that extent may have represented a substitution of sorghums for other crops.

In both the row-crop section and the grain section of Curry County drought conditions had resulted in a substitution of drought-resistant sorghums for corn and wheat. The acreage seeded to wheat in 1930 was less than that seeded from 1931 to 1934 but that seeded in 1933 and 1934 was less than that seeded in the 2 preceding years. The acreage seeded to corn declined materially in 1933 and 1934, but the acreage planted to sorghums in 1934 was slightly higher than in any of the preceding 4 years.

Livestock

In April 1935 cattle comprised the one important livestock enterprise in all of the selected areas (appendix table 63). On most farms the hog enterprise provided meat for home consumption only. In none of the areas studied did the selected farmers have an average of more than one brood sow per farm in April 1935, and many of the farmers had none. Poultry was raised on most of the farms. Sheep were reported only on a few of the larger farms in Hale County.

In Dallam County farmers in the row-crop section normally had more cattle than did the farmers in the grain section. In April 1935 this superiority of numbers still held although reductions had been more drastic in the row-crop section than in the grain section on many of the farms. On the other hand, farmers in the grain section of Curry County reported larger numbers of cattle normally kept on their farms than did those in the row-crop section.

Following the 1934 drought large numbers of livestock were sold by the farmers in the Southern Great Plains. From a normal average of 30 head of cattle per farm in the row-crop section of Dallam County the average number per farm had been reduced to 17 by the spring of 1935. In the grain section the number of cattle had been reduced from 21 to 13. Numbers of milk cows had been reduced by about one-half in both sections. Numbers of beef cows were reduced from an average of 16 to 6 per farm in the row-crop section and from 5 to 4 in the grain section (appendix table 63).

Reduction of cattle was marked in the grain section of Curry County, possibly as a result of overstocking, but approximately normal numbers were retained in the row-crop section. In Hale County the number of all cattle was reduced from an average of 16 to 11 per farm, milk cows from 9 to 6 per farm, and other cattle from 7 to 5 per farm.

Most of the cattle sold in 1934 were purchased by the Government during the Emergency Livestock Purchase Program. The farmers' reports show that approximately 2 out of 3 of the cattle sold in Dallam and Curry Counties and 7 out of 10 of those sold in Hale County

Works Progress Administration.

Drying Water Holes Force Cattle Sales.

were sold to the Government (fig. 9, p. 27). Approximately 12,000 head of cattle were purchased in Dallam County by the Government and about the same number in Hale County. Nearly 15,000 head were purchased in Curry County.

The number of work stock was reduced by about one-third in Dallam County and one-fourth in Curry County. It was generally maintained at normal levels in Hale County. Poultry flocks were reduced to about one-half to two-thirds of normal in the three counties.

The farmers' reports of livestock numbers and their estimates of the carrying capacity of their pastures indicate that on the average most farmers had retained as many livestock as their depleted pastures would support in the spring of 1935. Feed loans had enabled most farmers to maintain the young animals in their cow herds, and sufficient stock remained in the areas to rebuild cattle numbers as the carrying capacity of pastures increased. Some farmers, however, had sold nearly all of their livestock and were in need of replacements.

The majority of the selected farmers still had some cattle in April 1935, including one or more milk cows, but few farmers had any beef cows and about one-half of them had no hogs (appendix table 64). Most of the farmers had chickens although more than one-half of those in Dallam and Hale Counties had not more than 50. The proportion of the farmers who had no work stock ranged from about one-sixth in Hale County to more than one-half in the grain section of Dallam County.

The farmers on general relief reported much smaller numbers of the various classes of livestock in all of the counties studied than did the selected farmers (appendix tables 59 and 63). Numbers on even the largest farms operated by relief clients were less than those reported on the smallest selected farms. A large proportion of the relief clients owned no livestock. Since the relief clients' reports were taken from their relief applications, many of which were filed before the general drastic reduction of livestock in 1934, their dependence on livestock for income as compared with that of the selected farmers must have been even smaller than these reports indicate.

In Dallam County one-fourth of the relief clients who had been approved for rehabilitation had no milk cows, one-half had no work stock, three-fifths had no hogs, and 1 out of 14 had no poultry. The proportions of the relief clients who had not been approved for rehabilitation and who had none of the various classes of livestock were much larger than those just cited. In Hale County nearly three-fifths of the relief clients who had been approved for rehabilitation loans had no cattle, three-fourths had no work stock, nine-tenths had no hogs, and three-fifths had no poultry. In Curry County about one-seventh of the relief clients had no milk cows, over one-third had no work stock, one-half had no hogs, and one-seventh had no poultry.

Use of Machinery and Labor

Power machinery is used extensively throughout the grain-producing sections of the Southern Great Plains. In the small grain sections of the cash-grain area tractors and combines were part of the usual equipment and trucks were used on about one-half of the selected farms. Tractors were part of the usual equipment throughout the row-crop sections of the cash-grain area and in the area where both grain and cotton are produced. The average investment in machinery was smaller and power machinery was used less extensively on the smaller farms of the cotton area.

Nine-tenths of the selected farmers in the grain section of Dallam County and seven-tenths of those in the grain section of Curry County were using tractors (appendix table 65). In the row-crop section of Dallam County and in Hale County three-fifths of the farmers were using tractors. In the row-crop section of Curry County two-thirds of the farmers were using tractors.

The average estimated value per farm of all farm machinery and equipment was $1,067 in the row-crop section and $1,749 in the grain section of Dallam County, $911 in the row-crop section and $1,103 in the grain section of Curry County, and $1,183 in Hale County (appendix table 72).

Machinery on many of the farms was badly in need of repair, particularly in the small grain section. In many instances at least a portion of the machinery needed replacement. The average estimated cost of machinery repairs needed per farm was $55 in the row-crop section and $131 in the grain section of Dallam County, $41 in the row-crop section and $113 in the grain section of Curry County, and $44 in Hale County.

The average estimated cost of machinery repairs needed was proportionally highest in the grain sections of Dallam and Curry Counties and lowest in Hale County. It ranged from less than 4 percent of the value of the machinery in Hale County to 10 percent in the grain section of Curry County, and in most instances it was higher on tenant-operated than on owner-operated farms.

The use of power machinery was an important factor in determining the labor requirements of farms. Few of the farms were operated by more than two men.

In all of the selected areas, as would be expected, the crop acreage operated was generally larger on farms with two or more workers than on those with one worker, and it was larger on farms operated with tractors than on farms operated without tractors. In Dallam and Curry Counties crop acreage on farms operated by one man without a tractor averaged about two-fifths of the crop acreage on farms operated by one man with a tractor. In Hale County it was only a little over one-third of that operated by a man with a tractor (appendix table 65).

Under the systems of farming commonly practiced in the area, the crop acreage which one man operated without a tractor and without additional help averaged about 200 to 220 acres in the row-crop sections, about 250 to 260 acres in the grain sections, and about 130 acres in Hale County. Some additional labor was no doubt needed during the harvest season. Those who operated larger acreages satisfactorily reported either a tractor or additional help regularly employed on the farm.

Farm Buildings

Buildings on many farms in the cash-grain area of the Southern Great Plains were small, poorly constructed, and in need of paint and repairs. They were particularly poor on the small farms.

On the whole, farm buildings in the row-crop sections were more nearly adequate and in a better state of repair than those in the grain sections. In the cotton area, where crop yields in recent years have been relatively reliable, where livestock production is not an extensive enterprise, and where the climate is less severe than in the northern areas, farm buildings were in a better state of repair than those in the cash-grain area.

In all of the selected areas the average value of dwellings constituted about two-fifths of the value of all farm buildings (table 23 and appendix table 66).

Table 23.—Average Value of Farm Buildings and Estimated Cost of Needed Repairs per Farm on Selected Farms in Representative Counties in the Southern Great Plains, 1935

County	Number of farms reporting	Value of buildings			Cost of needed repairs		
		Total	Dwelling	Other	Total	Dwelling	Other
Dallam:							
Row-crop section	43	$2, 331	$909	$1, 422	$105	$63	$42
Grain section	37	1, 956	776	1, 180	143	76	67
Hale	156	1, 953	838	1, 115	78	47	31
Curry:							
Row-crop section	63	1, 615	660	955	93	53	40
Grain section	46	1, 334	557	777	159	93	66

The value of all farm buildings tended to be proportional to the size of farm. Within each area the estimated cost of needed repairs was relatively high on the small farms. The average estimated value of all farm buildings per farm ranged from $1,334 in the grain section of Curry County to $2,331 in the row-crop section of Dallam County. The average estimated cost of needed repairs ranged from $78 per farm in Hale County, or 4 percent of the total value of all buildings, to $159 per farm in the grain section of Curry County, or 12 percent of the value of all buildings.

Failure to maintain farm buildings must have been due, for the most part, to depleted finances rather than to a lack of incentive or responsibility on the part of the farm operators. This is indicated by the fact that in the areas where the estimated cost of building repairs was highest in relation to the total value of buildings, the proportion of the selected farms which were owner-operated tended to be higher than in the other areas.

INDEBTEDNESS

Throughout the Southern Great Plains farmers are burdened by taxes and carrying charges on indebtedness which are relatively high when compared with the productivity of their farms. In their efforts to meet these charges they tend to follow soil-depleting practices.

Real-estate mortgages were the primary source of indebtedness on the owner-operated farms surveyed, ranging from an average of one-third of the estimated value of all owner-operated real estate in the grain section of Curry County to approximately two-thirds of the value of all owner-operated real estate in both the row-crop and grain sections of Dallam County (appendix table 72). Real-estate mortgages and chattel mortgages, which included Government feed and seed loans, represented more than nine-tenths of the owner-operators' indebtedness in the Southern Great Plains.

Chattel mortgages were the primary source of the tenant-operators' indebtedness. They were reported by most tenants and represented from seven-tenths to more than nine-tenths of their indebtedness.

In portions of the Southern Great Plains affected most adversely by drought the burden to farmers of taxes and carrying charges on indebtedness can be seen in the reports of 10 owner-operators in the grain section of Dallam County who were operating farms approximating 320 acres. Their average indebtedness, by sources, consisted of real-estate mortgages, $2,691; chattel mortgages (including crop and feed loans), $1,040; delinquent taxes, $115; and other debts, $182. If assessed for taxes at the usual rates and if charged the usual interest rates on these various sources of indebtedness, these farmers would have an annual fixed cost of at least $240. The average yield of wheat per acre is only 9 bushels, and at 75 cents a bushel about 36 acres, or more than one-fourth of the wheat usually produced, would be utilized in meeting these fixed charges. In adverse years all of the crops produced on these farms would not pay the taxes and interest, and it is in such years that the farmers' indebtedness accumulates. In 1934 these same farmers reported an average gross cash income of only $510, or little more than twice the amount of these fixed charges. Their average cash income in 1934 from other than governmental expenditures would pay about one-half of their annual taxes and interest charges.

Real-Estate Indebtedness

Mortgages of record taken from the registration books in the selected counties indicate that 44 percent of the land in Dallam County, 39 percent in Hale County, and 36 percent in Curry County were mortgaged in 1935 (table 24). More than one mortgage was outstanding on 15 percent of the land in Dallam County, 14 percent in Hale County, and 10 percent in Curry County.

Table 24.—Acreage Mortgaged and Average Indebtedness per Acre, Mortgages of Record in Representative Counties in the Southern Great Plains, 1935

County	Number of acres mortgaged		Percent of all land mortgaged		Average indebtedness per acre
	First mortgage	Other mortgage	First mortgage	Other mortgage	
Dallam	432,350	146,931	44	15	$8.42
Hale	259,351	90,169	39	14	15.85
Curry	319,774	86,941	36	10	6.67

In Dallam County the amount of the mortgage was usually between $2.50 and $15 per acre, averaging $8.42 per acre for all mortgages, or 74 percent of the average value placed by the census [14] on all farm land and buildings in the county. A number of the farmers were evidently carrying mortgage indebtedness greater than the current value of their farms.

In Curry County, also, a number of the farmers must have been carrying a debt approximately equal to, or greater than, the current value of their farms. Seventeen percent of the encumbered acreage was mortgaged for more than $10 an acre and the land and buildings were valued at $12.45 an acre.[15] The usual mortgage indebtedness was less than $10 per acre and the average indebtedness was $6.67 per acre.

In Hale County, on the other hand, few of the farms were mortgaged for more than their current value. Only 2 percent of the encumbered acreage was mortgaged for more than $30 an acre, the approximate average value per acre of all farm land and buildings in the county.[16] The usual amount of mortgage indebtedness was between $7.50 and $22.50 an acre and the average was $15.85.

Most of the mortgages in the Southern Great Plains were held by the Federal Land Bank, Federal Land Bank Commissioner, private individuals, and lending corporations. Mortgages held by the Fed-

[14] Bureau of the Census, *United States Census of Agriculture: 1935*, U. S. Department of Commerce, Washington, D. C.

[15] *Ibid.*

[16] *Ibid.*

eral Land Bank were first mortgages, whereas most of those held by the Federal Land Bank Commissioner were second mortgages. Together, these two agencies held 55 percent of the first mortgages and 62 percent of all mortgages in Dallam County (appendix table 67). They held 80 percent of the first mortgages and 84 percent of all mortgages in Hale County and 76 percent of the first mortgages and 75 percent of all mortgages in Curry County. Between 1933 and 1935 a number of farmers throughout the entire area refinanced through the Federal Land Bank and the Federal Land Bank Commissioner mortgages which had previously been held by other lending agencies.

Crop and Feed Loans

Federal crop and feed loans of 1934 outstanding in Dallam County on December 31, 1934, totaled $253,571, while feed loans of 1934–1935 outstanding on February 28, 1935, totaled $30,834. Together they averaged $401 for every farm in the county (appendix table 68). In Curry County these loans averaged $151 per farm, but in Hale County they averaged only $57 per farm.

Taxation and Tax Delinquencies

Tax delinquency has been chronic in the Southern Great Plains. That the farmers' ability to pay taxes declined between 1928 and 1932 is shown by reports on tax delinquency of rural real estate in 10 New Mexico counties, 55 Texas counties, and 15 Oklahoma counties.[17] From 1928 to 1932 the accumulated unpaid delinquency per acre in the 10 New Mexico counties increased from 10 cents to 31 cents, or 210 percent. In the 55 Texas counties it increased from 21 cents per acre to 40 cents, or 90 percent, and in the 15 Oklahoma counties it increased from 37 cents to 76 cents, or 105 percent. In each State the accumulated unpaid delinquency of each year exceeded that of the preceding year, indicating that new delinquencies in each year of the period exceeded all previous delinquencies which had been redeemed during that year.

Records on file in the county indicate that tax certificates on 236,156 acres in Dallam County had been redeemed between 1932 and 1935, but that in 1935, 252,011 acres, or 26 percent of all land, were still delinquent on 1931, 1932, or 1933 taxes (appendix table 69). About 80 percent of this land was delinquent for 1933 only. A large number of the redemptions were made in 1934 and 1935, partly as a result of the refinancing of mortgages previously mentioned and partly as

[17] Bureau of Agricultural Economics, Division of Finance, *Tax Delinquency of Rural Real Estate in 10 New Mexico Counties, 1928–33*, June 18, 1935; *Tax Delinquency of Rural Real Estate in 55 Texas Counties, 1928–33*, September 27, 1935; and *Tax Delinquency of Rural Real Estate in 15 Oklahoma Counties, 1928–33*, mimeographed reports, U. S. Department of Agriculture, Washington, D. C., July 9, 1935.

a result of a State law passed in January 1935 rescinding all penalties and interest on general property taxes delinquent before August 1, 1934, if paid before March 15, 1935.

In Hale County tax certificates on 133,465 acres of tax-delinquent land had been redeemed, but taxes on 262,239 acres, or 40 percent of all land, were still delinquent for 1931, 1932, 1933, or 1934. Approximately one-third of the delinquent land was delinquent for 3 or 4 years while two-thirds was delinquent for only 1 or 2 years.

In Curry County 105,639 acres, or only 12 percent of all land, remained delinquent in 1935 for 1931, 1932, or 1933 taxes. About one-half of this delinquent acreage was delinquent for taxes due in all 3 of the years and more than one-third was for 1933 only. Tax certificates on 9,510 acres had been redeemed during the first 5 months of 1935.

The total tax levied against real estate in 1934 averaged about $2.45 per $100 valuation in Dallam County, $2.50 in Curry County, and $2.67 in Hale County. In 1934 assessed valuations in Dallam County averaged about $5 per acre and the usual tax on a 320-acre farm was about $40. In Hale County assessed valuations in 1934 ranged from $7 to $12 with $8 as the modal valuation. The usual tax was about $68 on a 320-acre farm.

Relief Clients' Indebtedness

Statements of the relief clients' liabilities (appendix table 70) indicate an average indebtedness smaller than that reported by the selected farmers. In Curry County, however, the relief clients who were owner-operators of farms of 559 acres or less reported more indebtedness than did the selected farmers who were owner-operators of farms of similar size (appendix table 71). Tenant-operators on relief rolls in this county who were operating farms of less than 280 acres reported larger indebtedness than the selected tenants on farms of the same size. The indebtedness reported by relief clients who were tenant-operators of farms larger than 280 acres was somewhat smaller than that reported by selected tenant-operators of farms similar in size. However, in view of the fact that the relief clients had less livestock and probably less other mortgageable property, it is probable that their net worth was considerably smaller than that of the selected farmers.

OWNERSHIP OF LAND AND TENURE OF OPERATORS

Corporate-owned land does not present a pressing problem in connection with the rehabilitation of farmers in the Southern Great Plains. Ownership data taken from the county records indicate that most of the land in the selected counties in the Southern Great Plains was owned by private individuals. Of the land with recorded ownership, corporations owned only 5 percent in Dallam County, 4 percent in Hale County, and 3 percent in Curry County (table 25).

Table 25.—Type and Residence of Owners of Land in Representative Counties in the Southern Great Plains, 1935

County	Total area (acres)	Ownership of land (percent)				
		Private individuals		Corporations		Others
		Resident	Nonresident	Resident	Nonresident	
Dallam	[1] 958, 167	44	41	2	3	10
Hale	[2] 604, 647	68	27	*	4	1
Curry	[3] 881, 451	73	22	1	2	2

*Less than 0.5 percent.

[1] Data represent 97 percent of all land in the county.
[2] Data represent 92 percent of all land in the county.
[3] Data represent 98 percent of all land in the county.

Sources: Agricultural Adjustment Administration contracts and records in offices of county tax assessors.

On the other hand, nonresident ownership is a major problem. Nearly one-half of the privately-owned land and three-fifths of the corporate-owned land in Dallam County were owned by nonresidents. Nonresidents owned nearly three-tenths of the privately-owned land and nearly all of the corporate-owned land in Hale County and more than one-fifth of the privately-owned land and two-thirds of the corporate-owned land in Curry County.

Nonresident owners who rent out their land may not be in a position to counteract soil-depleting practices which are encouraged by the usual rental agreement. Those in the wheat sections of Dallam and Curry Counties who operate their own farms may not be able to check wind erosion when it occurs since they live on or near their holdings only during the seeding and harvesting seasons. Not only their own farms but also those adjacent to them may be damaged.

Tenancy is another major problem in the rehabilitation of farmers in the area. In 1934 tenants operated 44 percent of the farm land represented by corn-hog contracts in Dallam County, 52 percent of the land represented by cotton contracts in Hale County, and 28 percent of the land represented by corn-hog contracts in Curry County (table 26).

The proportion of the farmers who were classed as tenants and the proportion of all land in farms that was operated by tenants had increased considerably in all of the selected counties from 1920 to 1935.[18] In Dallam County the proportion of farmers who were tenants

[18] Bureau of the Census, *Fifteenth Census of the United States: 1930*, Agriculture Vol. II, and *United States Census of Agriculture: 1935*, Vol. I, U. S. Department of Commerce, Washington, D. C.

had increased from 32 to 47 percent and the proportion of farm land operated by tenants had increased from 12 to 29 percent (table 27). In Hale County the proportion of tenants had increased from 40 to 55 percent and the land operated by tenants had increased from 29 to 48 percent. In Curry County the proportion of all farmers classed as tenants had increased from 18 to 39 percent and the proportion of all farm land which they were operating had increased from 14 to 29 percent.

Table 26.—Tenure of Operators of Farm Land in Representative Counties in the Southern Great Plains, 1934

County	Total acres reported	Operators of farm land (percent)			
		Owner	Tenant		Not specified
			Resident owner	Nonresident owner	
Dallam	[1] 295, 038	55	21	23	1
Hale	[2] 413, 944	48	29	23	—
Curry	[1] 273, 272	72	17	11	—

[1] Under corn-hog production control contracts.
[2] Under cotton production control contracts.

Tenants were heavily overrepresented among farmers in need of public assistance in the spring of 1935. They comprised about three-fourths of the relief clients in Dallam and Curry Counties, whereas they made up only one-fourth of the interviewed farmers. In Hale County 45 of the 46 relief clients who had been approved for rehabilitation were tenants as compared with only 60 out of 154 selected farmers (appendix tables 59 and 72).

Table 27.—Farm Tenancy in Representative Counties in the Southern Great Plains, 1920, 1930, and 1935

County	Percent of farm operators who were tenants			Percent of farm land operated by tenants		
	1920	1930	1935	1920	1930	1935
Dallam	32	34	47	12	27	29
Hale	40	52	55	29	47	48
Curry	18	34	39	14	31	29

Sources: Bureau of the Census, *Fourteenth Census of the United States: 1920* and *United States Census of Agriculture: 1935*, U. S. Department of Commerce, Washington, D. C.

In all of the selected areas owner-operators were stronger financially than tenant-operators as measured by total assets and liabilities. The average net worth of both owners and tenants was higher in Hale County than in Dallam and Curry Counties. In Dallam County both owners and tenants in the row-crop section were considerably stronger financially than were those in the grain section (fig. 19 and appendix table 72).

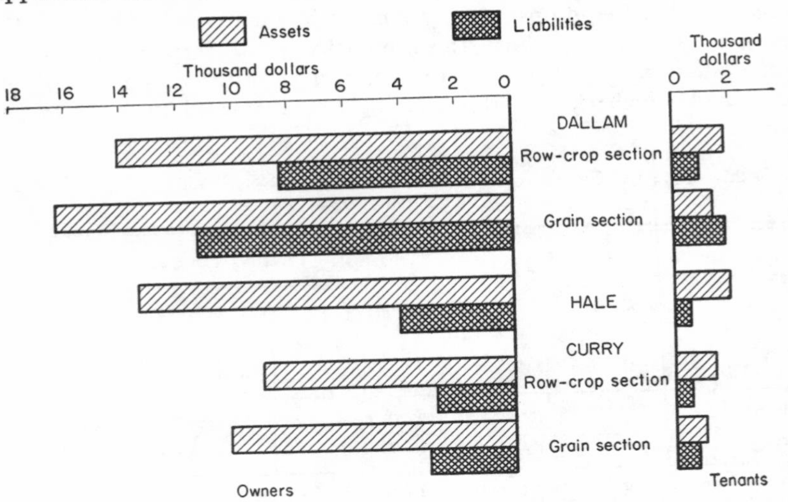

FIG. 19-AVERAGE VALUE OF FARM ASSETS AND AMOUNT OF LIABILITIES OF SELECTED FARMERS IN REPRESENTATIVE COUNTIES IN THE SOUTHERN GREAT PLAINS BY TENURE 1935

AF-2707, WPA

Chapter IV

PROSPECTS FOR REHABILITATION OF FARMERS

CONTINUED DROUGHT and low crop yields in 1935 and 1936 intensified the economic and agricultural distress of farmers in the Great Plains drought area of 1934, and additional loans to finance their crops ran the farmers further into debt. Because the future of the Great Plains depends upon the economic recovery of the thousands of financially crippled or destitute farmers, agricultural agencies have concerned themselves with the possibilities for their permanent rehabilitation.

In most of the areas studied such rehabilitation involves an increase in size of some of the farms, the movement of some farmers out of the area, retirement of some land from crops, an increase in pasture acreage, replacement of depleted livestock herds, repairs to buildings, and repairs or replacement of machinery. Adjustment of the farmers' debts and advances of working capital will often be necessary to accomplish these changes in farm economy and organization. Only by such reorganization, however, can many of the farmers hope to build up adequate reserves against future drought periods. Accomplishment of this result will have some repercussions on the community structure.

In the Northern Great Plains four of the six areas studied presented most of these rehabilitation problems to a greater or less degree. The areas represented by Divide and Hettinger Counties, N. Dak., and Hyde County, S. Dak., were seriously in need of rehabilitation measures, while in the area represented by Sheridan County, N. Dak., the problems were somewhat less urgent. Two areas—those represented by Traill County, N. Dak., and Moody County, S. Dak.—presented no rehabilitation problems at all or no pressing ones.

Throughout the Northern Great Plains, but particularly in the central and western sections, the livestock enterprise on many farms should be increased beyond the point considered normal in 1934 in order that the farmers may have more diversified and more stable sources of income. A rehabilitation program should assist the farmers with least reserves in acquiring replacements. An increase in the livestock enterprise, however, should go hand in hand with an increase in the size of operating units and should be accompanied by a shifting of some cropland to permanent pasture and some replacement of cash crops by feed crops. An increase in livestock with no increase in feed will only intensify the present overgrazing and feed shortages. Under such circumstances future drought periods might necessitate a reduction of livestock even greater than that which occurred in 1934. To encourage farmers to seed large acreages to permanent grasses, provisions of grass seed, soil-conserving payments, and tax exemptions while the sod is being established will probably be necessary.

Increased size of operating units would also make possible more extensive use of summer fallow farming.

A rehabilitation program would need to make provision for the repair and replacement of machinery on many farms in the central and western counties. In some cases new buildings are needed, particularly if livestock numbers should be markedly expanded.

Many farmers in the Northern Great Plains are so overburdened with debt that a fundamental rehabilitation need is either downward adjustment of their indebtedness or assistance in paying carrying charges. Some means of caring for or deferring payments on mortgages, interest, and taxes appears necessary.

In the Central Great Plains the sections represented by Cheyenne County, Colo., and Goshen County, Wyo., were seriously in need of rehabilitation, but problems were less urgent in Sherman County, Nebr., and there were no pressing problems in Perkins County, Nebr. The variations among the counties studied illustrate the range in the severity of land-use problems throughout the Central Great Plains.

In many sections farmers needed assistance in restoring livestock numbers, while in others practically normal numbers had been retained. Since the farmers who needed livestock replacements or increases in the size of their normal herds were the financially weakest, and since in the event of a good year competition would place livestock in the hands of the financially strongest, it is probable that some assistance would be required to obtain a desirable distribution of stock among the farmers. Return of eroded acreages to natural grass is needed in many sections, together with the adoption of sound soil conservation practices to prevent further erosion.

As in other sections of the Great Plains, many farms in the central counties were too small to provide for carrying charges and operating costs and yet insure adequate support of the operator's family. While crop and feed loans are not so extensive as in many areas, they represent an increased financial burden which also should be considered in any attempt to rehabilitate the families of the area.

In order to effect redistribution of land so as to enlarge the smaller holdings, some counties could care for the present farm population through greater concentration in the more fertile sections. In other cases, such as in Cheyenne County, emigration was already under way. Emigration from this area following extensive periods of drought in the past serves to emphasize the importance of anticipating future periods of drought through rehabilitation measures.

In the Southern Great Plains also it is apparent that the recurrence of drought periods must be anticipated in the organization of any successful rural rehabilitation program. The three areas studied, however, illustrate marked contrasts in farm conditions. That represented by Dallam County, Tex., was the only one where rehabilitation problems were urgent at the time of the survey. Some adjustment to the natural requirements of the area had already been made in Curry County, N. Mex. The region represented by Hale County, Tex., was favorably situated as to soil and precipitation and presented few immediate problems.

Wind erosion is a special problem to be met in portions of the southern area. A vegetative cover has proved the most effective means of controlling wind erosion, but, since periods of drought have destroyed and then prevented the reestablishment of a vegetative cover on cropland, cultivated land which is most susceptible to wind erosion should be diverted from crop production. To accomplish the comprehensive program of soil conservation which is needed requires governmental assistance and concerted action on the part of farmers.

Any farmer who is entirely dependent on grain production for his livelihood is in a precarious position because of the frequent low yields and crop failures. Such farmers need drastic adjustments in land use to provide for a livestock enterprise and the requisite pasturage. Moreover, only the growing of feed crops in all years and the carrying over of supplies from years of good production to years of poor production will insure ample feed for livestock.[1] Where pasture is available, range livestock should often form the primary basis of the farm enterprise.

Rehabilitation of farmers in the cash-grain section of the Southern Great Plains will require extensive repairs to farm buildings. On the other hand, rehabilitation of farmers in the cotton section, represented by Hale County, for the most part will require only minor repairs to farm buildings.

Throughout the Southern Great Plains many farmers are in need of advances of working capital as a result of exhausted credit. In such relatively favorable areas as that represented by Hale County,

[1] Mathews, O. R. and Brown, L. A., *Winter Wheat and Sorghum Production Under Limited Rainfall*, Circular 477, U. S. Department of Agriculture, Washington, D. C., July 1938.

temporary financial assistance will be sufficient to rehabilitate most operators.

Although rehabilitation problems are generally similar in all drought-stricken areas of the Great Plains, the measures needed to restore financial independence or to prevent future dependency differ somewhat from one county to another. More detailed suggestions for the rehabilitation of farmers and the improvement of the farm economy in the Great Plains are therefore presented below for the counties surveyed, each county being considered typical of conditions in its geographic and type-of-farming area.

NORTHWESTERN NORTH DAKOTA AND NORTHEASTERN MONTANA

As Typified by Divide County, N. Dak.

Permanent removal of northwestern North Dakota and northeastern Montana from the frequently distressed class implies a drastic change in producing units. The weather hazard cannot be eliminated, and, according to their own statements of financial progress, farmers in Divide County, which is typical of the area, have not been generally successful. Operators of the smaller farms reported least success.

Summer fallow can to some extent reduce the drought hazard, but on a small farm a summer fallow practice leaves an unprofitably small acreage of crops. Permanent pasture lends stability to livestock production, but the size of many farms does not provide for a sufficient acreage of both pasture and cropland.

Before the drastic reduction in livestock in this county in 1934 many farms in the North Dakota Black Prairies Section and some of the smaller farms in the Scobey-Plentywood Section were overstocked. Hence, an increase in pasture acreage and a more equitable distribution of pasture land constitute desirable steps in a rehabilitation program for this area. While farms of 800 acres or more in the Scobey-Plentywood Section of Divide County had one-half of their acreage in pasture, smaller farms in that section and practically all farms in the North Dakota Black Prairies Section had a much smaller proportion in pasture.

The majority of interviewed farmers considered 320 to 480 acres to be the minimum-sized farm for profitable operation, but statements of the financial progress of these farmers indicate that a larger acreage is desirable. Wheat contracts indicated that almost two-thirds of the farms are smaller than even this minimum size.

A readjustment of land holdings to bring the average of small farms to 480 acres would probably displace about 7 percent of the farmers reported by the census in 1935. A trend in this direction would make feasible the reseeding of some of the less desirable cropland to permanent grasses. Farmers might be encouraged to shift crop acre-

Resettlement Administration (Lange).

Drought Refugees.

age to pasture by advances to provide grass seed and tax exemptions on land during the process of establishing a permanent sod. Organization of grazing districts is desirable as a means of adjusting the control of pasturage as well as a means of preventing overgrazing.

The crop yields usually obtained, the frequency of failures in the area, and the low earning capacity per acre cast doubt on the proposition that much of the land, even with a revised organization, would be able to support a valuation or debt burden heavier than that carried in 1935. Partial losses of past investment, with no marked rise of the price level, may be unavoidable, but adjustments of size of farm and farm organization to the productive capacity of the area may avoid a future return of the condition found in 1935.

In a number of cases machinery repairs and even replacement of worn-out machinery and repairs of buildings are needed for continuation of farm operations. If ownership by the operator is to be retained, some means of caring for or deferring payments on mortgages, interest, and taxes is necessary. When normal crop production is resumed and feed is available, intermediate term loans to finance purchase of breeding stock will be in order.

SOUTHWESTERN NORTH DAKOTA

As Typified by Hettinger County

Some adjustment is needed in the present organization of southwestern North Dakota farms. Farm tenancy has increased, indicating that farm operators are now less able than formerly to acquire land. Real-estate mortgage indebtedness has mounted, and, since land values have declined, the burden of mortgage indebtedness has been accelerated even more rapidly than the value of mortgages. The vast amount of indebtedness incurred through Federal emergency loans and the inability of many farmers to pay either the principal or interest when due, the increase in tax deliquencies, and the resultant financial difficulties of school districts and other taxing units are all indicative of inadequate incomes under the present system of farming.

Many farms are not large enough to yield sufficient income to meet the carrying charges on the land and other operating expenses and to provide the operator and his family with a living. Until reduced, outstanding indebtedness, which has increased so rapidly in recent years, will tend to keep fixed costs at a relatively high level.

On the basis of the size of farm recommended and the income and financial progress statements made by farmers operating farms of different sizes in Hettinger County, representative of the area, farms of less than 480 acres appear not to be economical units, on the whole. The census report in 1930 showed 541 farms in the county between 50 and 500 acres in size. To combine those smaller farms so that all operators would have a unit of 480 acres would involve the displacement of about 15 percent of the total number of farmers reported in Hettinger County by the 1935 Census.

Pasture acreage on the small farms must be expanded if the operators are to be encouraged to increase their livestock. These small farms were apparently overgrazed before reductions took place in 1934 and the remaining numbers are all that their present pasturage can support.

A rehabilitation program should provide for minor repairs on most farm buildings and machinery in the area. The average cost of needed building repairs on all farms was estimated at $348, or 15 percent of the estimated value of all buildings.

A portion of the lighter soils in the area should be returned to permanent grass cover in the interest of soil conservation and sound farm management. Farm operators should be induced to seed to permanent grass at least part of the cropland which has been unprofitable in recent years. Possible inducements could be in the form of advances to provide grass seed and tax exemptions on the acreage during the process of establishing the sod. Although the percentage of farm land in crops dropped between 1929 and 1934 and 11 percent of the farm land became idle, this cannot be regarded as a permanent tendency in the area. Unless restrictions are placed on the planting of crops, the land that was left idle will probably be put back into crops as soon as moisture supplies become favorable.

CENTRAL NORTH DAKOTA

As Typified by Sheridan County

Frequent crop failures need not be expected in central North Dakota, and with the return to normal crop production most of the farmers should no longer need assistance. However, a rehabilitation program in the area should, as far as possible, assist the farmers in reorganizing their operating units so that they will be able to build up reserves against future drought periods.

From a short-time standpoint those farmers who were forced to sell nearly all of their livestock need assistance in reestablishing breeding herds. Other farmers need help in reconditioning farm buildings to prevent rapid depreciation and high replacement expense. Many need assistance in the repair or replacement of farm machinery.

From a long-time standpoint some adjustment in the size of operating units is desirable. Many of the farms are too small to provide the operator with an income sufficient to pay his high fixed costs, support himself and his family, and accumulate reserves for years of low income. If a more nearly equal distribution of acreage can be effected among the farmers operating in the area by assisting farmers on the smaller farms to acquire portions of the larger farms, few, if any, farmers need be displaced.

Because of the rolling topography and the prevalence of glacial boulders on the surface, much of the present crop acreage is suited to range production of livestock rather than to crop production. From the standpoint of soil conservation and the maintenance of soil productivity such acreage should be shifted to permanent grasses and the farmers' livestock enterprises increased proportionately. Such a shift in land use might be encouraged by making advances for the purchase of grass seed, by soil-conserving payments, and by tax exemptions on the land during the process of establishing permanent sod. The change to permanent grasses will not only help to retard soil erosion but it will also tend to reduce the farmers' dependence on crops and increase the reliability of their incomes. Without some shift in land use it is probable that soil erosion in the area will become more acute and that another drought period will bring more distress to central North Dakota farmers than that experienced in 1934.

CENTRAL SOUTH DAKOTA

As Typified by Hyde County

The decided increase in planted crop acreage in the Missouri Plateau Area of central South Dakota during the relatively productive period of 1918–1930, followed by the decrease during the calamitous 1931–1934 period, would indicate that under the present system of operation crop acreage will be restored when climatic and economic factors are favorable and that another adverse period will again cause the majority of the farmers to need public assistance.

The tendency to overcapitalize land during the post World War period, with the drastic reduction in land values since 1930, has retarded the accumulation of capital in recent years. The high rate of foreclosures indicates the need for adjustment of land values.

It appears that the lower limits in size for economical farming units in the area, as typified by Hyde County, are from 480 to 640 acres, depending on the ability of the operators, with an average unit of approximately 640 acres.

Some increase in the present pasture acreage seems advisable. However, the present custom of renting pasture acreage for cash should be considered, and care should be taken not to overburden the operators with fixed costs. The increase in pasture acreage could be accomplished by shifting present cropland, which has proved unprofitable for crop production, to permanent grass.

Under the present organization many farmers need assistance in the replacement of livestock. If the farm and pasture acreages are increased, the need will be even more pronounced. Farmers on the larger farms need assistance in restoring beef cattle but, until pasture acreages are increased, the small farmers' needs for replacements will be largely confined to restoring poultry and swine and in some instances work stock and milk cows.

Under the present setup the smaller farms with a larger percentage of crop acres are concentrated in the central portion of the county where the terrain is less undulating and the soils are productive. Consequently, farm dwellings and other improvements are more or less concentrated in this section. In order to increase the size of operating units and at the same time utilize the present improvements most economically, it is suggested that additions to the present units be made by adding pasture acreage in the rougher sections to the present units in the better sections. This could be accomplished by additions to individual units or by the organization of grazing districts in the rougher sections to be utilized by the operators located in the better sections. The latter method would permit restricted grazing and conserve the native sod.

RED RIVER VALLEY OF EASTERN NORTH DAKOTA

As Typified by Traill County

Traill County was the only county in North Dakota that had no relief agency in the early months of 1935. There were some relief cases in the other four counties of the Red River Valley, but the actual relief burden in this area was light. Traill County was included in the survey because, due to its favorable agricultural situation, it was considered an area for possible closer settlement.

Highly productive soils and a climate suitable for the production of spring grains and potatoes have resulted in consistently high crop yields in the Red River Valley over a long period of years. In the period between 1931 and 1934, when crops in most midwestern farming areas were either seriously or totally damaged by the continued drought, precipitation was very little below normal in Traill County, and crop yields did not depart greatly from normal.

From the financial records of the 52 farmers interviewed, it is evident that 160-, 240-, and 320-acre units have offered farmers in this area something more than a bare living, and units of this size can be suggested for new farms in a resettlement program. A farm of 200 acres or less can be operated by one man without help and without a tractor. However, efficient operation of larger farms requires extra help or tractors. A somewhat higher net income may be expected from farms of 240 and 320 acres or even larger units, but the capital investment necessary to establish a family on the larger farms may be prohibitive.

By acquiring portions of the larger farms it is believed that resettlement of new farmers in the area would be possible without displacing the present farm operators and with no disturbance of the present farm organization except a reduction in size of some of the larger units. Tenant-operated land could probably be acquired more readily than owner-operated land. It is estimated that in 1935 there were approximately 300 farms in Traill County of over 400 acres in size which were either tenant or part-owner operated. Portions of such farms, if available, could be used in establishing new farmers in the area.

There are very few unused farm buildings in Traill County, and establishment of new farms in the area would, in most instances, necessitate the construction of new buildings. Since the average estimated value in 1935 of all farm buildings on 160-acre farms was $2,684, and of those on 320-acre farms, $3,793, new buildings of the same proportions and quality might involve prohibitive capital expenditures. Many farm buildings in the county, however, are more than adequate to meet the farmers' needs, and less expensive buildings can be erected.

The acquiring of new land in Traill County would be facilitated by the fact that a relatively small proportion is tax delinquent. But the unusually high value of farms in Traill County, the second highest in value in the State, might prove to be a deterrent in the purchase of land.

The desirability of making actual cash advancements to new farmers would depend on whether the land was purchased or leased, the type of buildings, and the grade of livestock provided, whether the machinery was new or used, and the amount of capital which each individual had to invest. The cost of moving from his present location to the Red River Valley, and the provision of operating and living expenses until the new unit could provide such expenses, should be carefully considered on an individual basis.

SOUTHEASTERN SOUTH DAKOTA

As Typified by Moody County

Although the drought of 1934 limited crop production and curtailed incomes in southeastern South Dakota, both agricultural and economic conditions were much better in this area than in any other section of the State in the summer of 1935. Only about one-fourth of the acreage intended for harvest in 1934 was a failure as compared with almost total failure in some counties of South Dakota.

To the high productivity of the soils in this region, combined with stable crop yields and precipitation, was attributed the relatively strong financial condition of farmers in Moody County, representative of the area, throughout the drought years. Like Traill County it was selected for study for purposes of comparison with areas seriously affected by drought.

Moody County, however, offers few opportunities for resettlement of farmers from other areas. If all Moody County farm land was divided equally into units of 160 acres, more than 2,000 farm families, or 665 new families, might be established in the county. Such an equal distribution, however, is not practicable. Since there is an unsatisfied demand for farm land within the county, it is doubtful if much acreage could be acquired without displacing farmers already operating there.

Rural distress in Moody County was not marked until 1934. The immediate cause was low crop yields; and the farmers affected were primarily tenant-operators with small farms, who were not well established in the area or who had unusually high indebtedness. Farm owners' fixed costs, such as taxes and carrying charges on real-estate indebtedness, were high, but owner-operators had accumulated more financial reserves than tenant-operators.

The few requirements for rehabilitation in Moody County are little more than needs for working capital loans. There is apparently little need for livestock and equipment replacements.

The selected farmers reported that with livestock production as their major enterprise both owner- and tenant-operators could maintain a desirable standard of living for themselves and their families on a farm of 160 acres. The financial record of selected farmers who were operating 160-acre farms appeared to substantiate these estimates.

In general, farmers who derived a high percentage of their income from livestock sales experienced more years in which they were able to accumulate capital than did those who depended on crop sales for a large proportion of their income. Normally, operators of less than 121 acres derived approximately half of their income from crop sales. Operators of farms of this size were able to accumulate capital or reduce debts on an average of only two-fifths of the years. Increased dependence on livestock and livestock products probably would improve the financial status of such operators.

Farm buildings in the county were in good condition and only minor repairs were needed. There were few buildings not in use, however, and any program looking toward closer settlement would require some new construction.

LOESS HILLS OF CENTRAL NEBRASKA

As Typified by Sherman County

Severe droughts and total loss of crops have been so infrequent in the Loess Hills area of central Nebraska that rapid recovery of the farmers from the recent drought period can be expected. Amounts advanced for crop and feed loans have been high, however, reflecting the dependence of the farmers on governmental assistance.

A large number of farms in Sherman County, which represents conditions throughout the area, were found to be too small to provide more than a living for a family. The product from 160 acres, with average use of land and no more than average yields, will not meet carrying charges on the land and operating costs on the farm and provide sufficient surplus for the support of a family.

The small operating unit common in the area has tended to force land that should be in grass into cultivated crops. Tillage on the slopes and lack of cover have subjected the land to damage from water erosion, and the more erosive areas should be maintained permanently in grass.

A program to conserve productivity or even to bring about a shift in the use of land should be instituted on a number of farms. This might take the form of advances to provide grass seed for seeding the steeper slopes and advances to obtain cattle to use the additional pastures. Some farmers need assistance in restoring hogs and poultry to their normal numbers. Changes in production or the continuation of certain classes of livestock depend to some extent on the replacement or reconditioning of buildings although the rehabilitation of most farmers in the areas would not involve a heavy outlay for farm improvements.

SOUTHWESTERN WHEAT AREA OF NEBRASKA

As Typified by Perkins County, Nebr.

In the spring of 1935 rural relief and rehabilitation problems were not pressing in the southwestern wheat-producing area of Nebraska, of which Perkins County is representative. Farmers in several different sections of the county had had fair crop yields in 1934 and had received good prices for their products. Most farmers had signed both wheat and corn-hog adjustment contracts and had received substantial payments in 1934. Few farmers were on the relief rolls.

Although cattle numbers had been reduced somewhat by the drought, breeding herds had been maintained and few, if any, replacements were necessary. Hog numbers had been more drastically reduced, but sufficient breeding stock had been retained to restore numbers quickly when grain became available from farm production.

The consensus among farmers in Perkins County was that a 400-acre farm, including 80 acres of native grass pasture, is necessary to provide an adequate income for the average family even in the best farming sections of the county. It is doubtful, however, whether the income even from this size unit will permit the accumulation of the surplus necessary to carry most farm families through the frequent abnormally dry years.

Many farms in April 1935 had less than 400 acres. Readjustments to increase the size of small farms will displace some farmers, especially in the sandy loam areas where there are many farms of 160 and 320 acres. It seems probable that all of these farmers could be resettled on newly improved farms in the more fertile parts of the area.

In the interest of conservation some of the land in the sandy sections that is too light to withstand soil blowing should be retired from cultivation and returned to grass.

No urgent need for readjustment or reorganization of farms is apparent in the loam soil area. Moreover, if suitable buildings are provided on farms now unimproved, this area possibly can absorb the displaced farmers from other parts of the county.

SOUTHEASTERN WYOMING

As Typified by Goshen County

Some adjustment is needed in the present organization of dry-land farms in southeastern Wyoming, many of which were found to be too small to provide reserves necessary to maintain the operators' financial independence in adverse periods. Resumption of a normal flow of irrigation water will remove the need for assistance of most farmers operating irrigated farms in this area.

The consensus among selected farmers in Goshen County was that in the dry-land farming section a diversified farm of 640 acres or more was necessary to provide an adequate income for the average family. Financial records of farmers operating nonirrigated farms appeared to verify this opinion; yet two-fifths of all farmers in the dry-land farming section with corn-hog contracts were operating farms of 460 acres or less.

An increase in the acreage of Goshen County farms would lead to a reduction in the number of farmers, but many of them could probably be established in the irrigated sections if a more dependable supply of irrigation water were provided. Farmers in the irrigated section estimated that 80 to 90 acres were sufficient to provide an adequate income for the average family.

The small operating unit has tended to force nonirrigated land that should be in grass into cultivated crops. The return of most of the eroded acreage to grass should be part of any rehabilitation program. The practice of strip farming on cropland should be encouraged.

To utilize acreage returned to grass and to provide diversification of sources of farm income, livestock numbers should be increased. As a result of livestock reductions in 1934, many farmers did not retain sufficient numbers of cows to rebuild their cattle herds. Two-thirds of the selected farmers in both the dry-land and the irrigated sections had retained no brood sows.

Since most farm buildings in the irrigated section are occupied, a rehabilitation program involving moving many farmers from the nonirrigated to the irrigated section would require the construction of new buildings. If farmers are to be rehabilitated on their present units in the nonirrigated section, minor repairs should be provided for buildings on most of the farms.

Resettlement Administration (Rothstein).

Once an Excellent Farming Section.

HIGH PLAINS OF EASTERN COLORADO

As Typified by Cheyenne County

Need of rural rehabilitation is general in the High Plains of eastern Colorado, the area represented by Cheyenne County, as a result of 11 years of generally deficient moisture. The records of annual precipitation in the area show that recurrent dry periods with resultant low crops are to be expected. If the area continues under cultivation, some provision to meet conditions during these adverse periods must be made. The low average yields of all crops since 1931 indicate the high risk of wheat production and the necessity of feed reserves to carry the livestock through unfavorable periods. Crops in this area normally provide about 50 percent of the farmers' cash receipts; in 1934 they provided only 11 percent of the cash receipts. Low productivity of much of the land, frequent subnormal precipitation, and the tendency of the soil to blow when cultivated intensely limit the extent of profitable crop production.

The opinion of selected farmers in this area was that a system of farming based on livestock production with only minor emphasis on cash crops would offer the best chances for future success. Only 1 of the 56 farmers interviewed recommended cash crop production and only 3 recommended strictly range production. The others suggested some combination of feed crops and cattle production.

In spite of the small proportion of land in pasture on the farms of less than 440 acres, livestock numbers, even after reductions made in 1934, were still near normal in 1935. Available range land with no restrictions on grazing undoubtedly made possible the maintenance of breeding herds up to 1935 in spite of the succession of crop failures.

Only 6 of the farmers interviewed considered a farm smaller than 640 acres large enough for profitable operation; 32 considered 640 to 1,280 acres and 18 considered more than 1,280 acres as the minimum size of farm that would provide the average family an adequate income. For farm operations based on a herd of about 50 head of breeding cattle, a farmer should have about 300 acres of cropland and a minimum of 900 acres of pasture land. Recent experience indicates that a larger acreage would be desirable to maintain a herd of that size during a series of unfavorable years.

To provide even 960 acres for farmers in the county would require the consolidation of some of the smaller farms or a reduction in the acreage of a number of the larger farms in the more thickly populated parts of the county. Rehabilitation on this basis would mean that a large number of farmers would need to be established elsewhere.

Soil conservation is a pressing need in Cheyenne County. Successive dry seasons and lack of crop cover had resulted in some damage by wind erosion to an area equivalent to more than four-fifths of the cropland on the farms studied. More than one-fourth of this land was so badly damaged that its productivity had been greatly reduced. Precautions to prevent further erosion on the less severely damaged fields, therefore, and reversion of the land most severely damaged by wind erosion to natural grass are major needs in this area.

Immediate requirements of most farmers who could be rehabilitated in place include replacement of their worn-out machinery, building repairs and improvements, and a supply of working capital for living and operating expenses while their farms are being reestablished on a productive basis.

NORTH PLAINS OF TEXAS

As Typified by Dallam County

The recent drought served to aggravate an agricultural condition that had been developing in some portions of the Panhandle. Because of the frequency of years of subnormal rainfall and the tendency of the sandy soils to blow when moisture is insufficient, a comprehensive program of soil conservation is urgent.

Although less than three-tenths of the farmers in Dallam County, which is representative of the area, were on relief rolls in May 1935, those receiving such assistance were concentrated in the sections most severely affected by wind erosion. A scattered few were in the heavier loam soil areas.

Successive years with low crop yields amounting to almost complete crop failures from 1932 to 1934 had exhausted reserves and depleted livestock on farms throughout the area, but the farmers with eroded land or soil subject to erosion had a much more difficult problem than those on undamaged or slightly damaged land. On farms in the grain section nearly one-half and on farms in the row-crop section one-third of the income in 1934 came from crop reduction or relief payments. A large share of income came from livestock sales, which represented reductions in inventory rather than produced income. Few farmers reported capital gains since beginning farming in the area and these were primarily on the larger farms.

As crop production has been unsatisfactory, there is an apparent need for drastic adjustments in farm organization and land use if farmers are to avoid a repetition of the situation existing in 1932–1936.

The difficulty of rehabilitation on the light soils is intensified by the fact that so many of the farmers are on farms containing less than 320 acres, on which the percent of land in crops is relatively high. If the size of the farm unit can be increased, a larger proportion of the land may be left for grass or cover crops without interfering greatly with crop practice or income.

In estimating the size of the most economical farm units 16 farmers in the row-crop section thought that the farm should have about

540 acres with 172 acres in pasture and the remainder about evenly divided between wheat and row crops. Similarly the average estimate of 70 farmers in the grain section placed the most economical unit at 866 acres with 163 acres in pasturage, 560 acres in wheat, and 143 acres in row crops. The summaries of financial gains and losses over a number of years substantiate the proposition that farmers to be rehabilitated should be established on farm units of between 480 and 800 acres.

In the area of the Amarillo sandy loam soils many farms had an insufficient amount of native sod to arrest the shifting of the soils. On these light soils prevention of soil blowing in cultivated fields is extremely difficult. Much of the cropland in this area already has been abandoned, and rehabilitation of farmers on the abandoned sandy soils should not be attempted. Instead, efforts should be made to restore some permanent vegetative cover. A unified community or county-wide program of soil conservation, through the planting of cover crops or the leaving of stubble on the land until late spring, should be adopted. An alternative is a system of crop production aimed to control soil erosion.

Since the process of restoring permanent cover to the land is likely to be an expensive operation with little or no immediate returns, it could hardly be carried out by the farmers without governmental assistance. Some provision for sufficient grass land seems essential to farmers to be rehabilitated since this pasture acreage would lend an element of stability by helping to carry livestock through the usual drought period.

In addition to more pasturage per farm unit rehabilitation in the area represented by Dallam County should include financial assistance which would give adequate working capital, especially for building up small herds of cattle. Most farmers had to dispose of a large percentage of their livestock prior to 1935 and may need additional breeding stock to reestablish a cattle or hog enterprise. It has been suggested that where pasture is available, range cattle should form the basis of the farm enterprise with cash crops second in importance.

Working capital is needed in both grain and row-crop areas for repairs to and replacement of worn-out farm machinery and for repairs to buildings.

SOUTH PLAINS OF THE TEXAS PANHANDLE

As Typified by Hale County

The drought-resistant and moisture-absorbing qualities of the productive Amarillo clay loam soil favor the cultivation of wheat and small grains on this type of soil in the South Plains of the Texas Panhandle. Cotton production is favored on the lighter soils. A system of farming based on the production of these crops plus some livestock production has proved fairly profitable for both owners and tenants in Hale County, which is typical of the area.

The fact that only a small proportion of farmers had applied for relief or rehabilitation loans would indicate little need for a rehabilitation program providing more than temporary financial assistance. Some farmers lacked working capital, but most of them had equipment and livestock. The situation in Hale County was probably better than in many counties of the South Plains. Agricultural distress in the county was occasioned primarily by the short feed and cotton crops of 1934 and would be relieved by a return to normal conditions.

Few farms in the area can be divided and still leave an acreage large enough for a satisfactory unit. Experience in the area indicates that farmers on farms smaller than 160 acres have less chance to succeed than farmers on the larger acreages. Wheat farmers can handle a larger acreage than cotton farmers, and larger acreages probably are required.

Livestock production should form a part of the organization of most farms, which means that sorghums for feed are necessary and that pasture acreage is desirable. The experience in 1934 should warn against too heavy stocking of cattle without adequate provision for feed reserves.

UPPER SOUTH PLAINS OF THE TEXAS PANHANDLE AND HIGH PLAINS OF EASTERN NEW MEXICO

As Typified by Curry County, N. Mex.

Apparently the area represented by Curry County had been affected less by drought than some other areas of the Great Plains in 1934, and farmers had previously adjusted their farming systems to the quantity and variability of precipitation.

Mortgage indebtedness and tax delinquencies were not high in 1935, but farmers had allowed feed and seed loan indebtedness to accumulate. The proportion of nonresident operators was unduly high, frequently resulting in inadequate attention to soil conservation.

The chief contribution of a rehabilitation program in this and similar areas would be to advance working capital to those farmers with exhausted credit who did have land, equipment, or livestock. In extreme instances replacement of machinery or livestock might be necessary. Farmers on land subject to severe wind erosion could be aided either in restoring their land to permanent grass cover or in adopting a system of crop production and practices which would minimize erosion.

The interviewed farmers considered the average farm in the wheat section to be large enough to maintain a family although more land should be used for pasture and feed crops. They estimated that the average farm in the row-crop section should have an extra 80 acres of pasture.

A long-time program should consider the possibility of reducing the number of small farms. The trend has been for farms to increase in size, but not all farmers have had sufficient acreage to make the best use of their labor and equipment. With a larger acreage, and particularly with more pasture land, the normal number of livestock per farm could be maintained with less danger of depleted feed reserves or overgrazing pastures.

Part of the cropland in the extreme northeastern section of the county should be retired from crop production as a preventive against further damage from wind erosion. A definite soil conservation program is needed for the land that has already been damaged by wind erosion.

It seems probable that all farmers on relief can be reestablished within the county as only 9 percent of all farmers were actually receiving relief in May 1935 and only 6 percent had applied for rehabilitation.

Appendixes

Appendix A

SUPPLEMENTARY TABLES

Table 1.—Normal Gross Cash Receipts, Source of Receipts, and Adequacy of Income on Selected Farms in Representative Counties in the Northern Great Plains, by Size of Farm

County and size of farm	Number of farms reporting	Normal gross cash receipts	Source of receipts (percent)			Average length of record (years)	Adequacy of income	
			Crops	Livestock and livestock products	Work off farm		Percent of years income was sufficient to meet expenses	Percent of years income was sufficient to increase capital
DIVIDE								
North Dakota Black Prairies Section								
Total farms	44	$1,934	74	25	1	19	58	26
Less than 281 acres	5	880	81	19	—	13	77	31
281–400 acres	12	1,733	69	31	—	20	60	30
401–600 acres	17	1,612	72	27	1	20	50	30
601–800 acres	7	2,929	82	18	—	21	62	29
801 acres or more	3	4,000	80	20	—	18	72	17
Scobey-Plentywood Section								
Total farms	22	1,352	67	30	3	20	75	30
Less than 281 acres	5	540	63	25	12	15	80	13
281–400 acres	5	1,440	85	15	—	21	71	33
401–600 acres	3	1,333	67	30	3	24	67	38
601–800 acres	4	1,213	61	39	—	20	80	25
801 acres or more	5	2,200	58	42	—	21	71	43
HETTINGER								
Total farms	[1] 61	1,583	69	30	1	—	[2] 77	[2] 39
Less than 280 acres	9	828	67	29	4	—	56	11
280–439 acres	14	1,207	71	28	1	—	64	36
440–559 acres	7	2,229	58	39	3	—	100	57
560–719 acres	11	1,482	72	26	2	—	73	45
720–879 acres	7	1,857	70	30	—	—	100	57
880 acres or more	13	2,100	69	31	—	—	85	38
SHERIDAN								
Total farms	57	1,489	60	40	—	17	75	52
Less than 240 acres	8	771	51	49	—	12	75	63
240–399 acres	12	892	54	46	—	13	79	46
400–559 acres	13	1,146	66	34	—	18	60	42
560–719 acres	9	1,922	67	33	—	17	53	41
720–879 acres	9	2,367	60	40	—	23	84	53
880 acres or more	6	2,417	53	47	—	27	97	64

See footnotes at end of table.

Table 1.—**Normal Gross Cash Receipts, Source of Receipts, and Adequacy of Income on Selected Farms in Representative Counties in the Northern Great Plains, by Size of Farm—Continued**

County and size of farm	Number of farms reporting	Normal gross cash receipts	Source of receipts (percent)			Average length of record (years)	Adequacy of income	
			Crops	Livestock and livestock products	Work off farm		Percent of years income was sufficient to meet expenses	Percent of years income was sufficient to increase capital
HYDE								
Total farms	[3] 47	$1,686	34	65	1	—	[2] 77	[2] 58
Less than 280 acres	9	1,411	16	83	1	—	80	40
280–439 acres	11	1,782	35	62	3	—	73	73
440–559 acres	10	1,715	35	65	—	—	90	60
560–719 acres	7	1,243	43	57	—	—	43	29
720 acres or more	10	2,108	43	56	1	—	90	80
TRAILL								
Total farms	52	2,010	77	22	1	13	77	38
Less than 200 acres	8	1,013	65	35	—	14	79	36
200–399 acres	19	2,100	75	24	1	15	80	40
400–599 acres	12	1,917	83	17	—	11	64	27
600–799 acres	8	2,663	78	22	—	8	87	37
800 acres or more	5	2,440	89	11	—	15	80	53
MOODY								
Total farms	[4] 85	1,729	31	68	1	14	86	50
Less than 121 acres	4	1,100	49	45	6	18	83	39
121–200 acres	32	1,384	30	70	—	13	85	46
201–280 acres	16	1,762	20	80	—	17	82	47
281–360 acres	23	2,252	34	66	—	14	79	43
361–440 acres	4	1,800	45	55	—	7	86	14
441–520 acres	2	1,750	25	75	—	32	91	47
521 acres or more	4	1,900	31	69	—	14	93	71

[1] Data not available for 2 farms.
[2] Reports on adequacy of income for Hettinger and Hyde Counties are for percent of farmers reporting incomes sufficient to meet expenses and percent of farmers reporting incomes sufficient to increase capital.
[3] Data not available for 1 farm.
[4] Data not available for 2 farms.

Table 2.—**Age of Farm Operators Receiving Relief in Representative Counties in the Northern Great Plains and Number Unable to Work,[1] April–May 1935**

Age	Divide		Hettinger		Sheridan		Hyde		Moody	
	Number of farm operators	Number unable to work	Number of farm operators	Number unable to work	Number of farm operators	Number unable to work	Number of farm operators	Number unable to work	Number of farm operators	Number unable to work
Total	175	7	198	6	150	5	[2] 239	5	100	4
Under 21 years	—	—	—	—	—	—	—	—	—	—
21–30 years	14	—	65	—	51	—	42	—	29	—
31–40 years	40	—	52	—	44	—	62	1	31	1
41–50 years	55	1	45	1	31	2	57	—	26	1
51–60 years	40	—	22	1	15	2	42	2	9	1
61 years and over	26	6	12	4	7	—	36	2	5	1
Unknown	—	—	2	—	2	1	—	—	—	—

[1] Based on disabilities reported.
[2] Reports available for only 239 of the 247 farm operators receiving relief in April 1935.

Table 3.—Number of Children of Different Ages and Adult Members Other Than Parents in Farm Families Receiving Relief in Representative Counties in the Northern Great Plains, April–May 1935

County and item	Total families	Number of families with specified number of persons												
		None	1	2	3	4	5	6	7	8	9	10	11	12
DIVIDE														
Total children	175	26	19	37	30	30	12	10	6	3	1	1	—	—
Children under 16 years	175	55	30	31	30	15	6	4	2	2	—	—	—	—
Boys 16 years and over	175	106	38	22	9	—	—	—	—	—	—	—	—	—
Girls 16 years and over	175	122	36	14	3	—	—	—	—	—	—	—	—	—
Others	175	153	18	3	1	—	—	—	—	—	—	—	—	—
HETTINGER														
Total children	198	31	26	32	27	25	16	10	13	6	7	2	3	—
Children under 16 years	198	47	29	42	13	22	19	11	5	5	4	1	—	—
Boys 16 years and over	198	150	31	11	2	3	—	1	—	—	—	—	—	—
Girls 16 years and over	198	152	33	7	5	—	1	—	—	—	—	—	—	—
Others	198	184	10	4	—	—	—	—	—	—	—	—	—	—
SHERIDAN														
Total children	150	14	21	32	20	23	12	9	7	5	4	1	—	2
Children under 16 years	150	18	27	32	24	18	11	9	5	6	—	—	—	—
Boys 16 yeers and over	150	113	22	12	2	—	1	—	—	—	—	—	—	—
Girls 16 years and over	150	130	14	6	—	—	—	—	—	—	—	—	—	—
Others	150	135	11	2	1	1	—	—	—	—	—	—	—	—
HYDE														
Total children	247	80	53	24	37	20	12	10	8	1	1	1	—	—
Children under 16 years	247	107	43	31	25	22	11	6	1	1	—	—	—	—
Boys 16 years and over	247	195	36	15	1	—	—	—	—	—	—	—	—	—
Girls 16 years and over	247	207	30	8	2	—	—	—	—	—	—	—	—	—
Others	247	199	25	15	6	1	1	—	—	—	—	—	—	—
MOODY														
Total children	100	21	19	25	11	10	6	5	1	1	1	—	—	—
Children under 16 years	100	27	18	28	8	12	5	2	—	—	—	—	—	—
Boys 16 years and over	100	85	6	7	1	1	—	—	—	—	—	—	—	—
Girls 16 years and over	100	87	10	3	—	—	—	—	—	—	—	—	—	—
Others	100	72	14	7	3	1	1	1	1	—	—	—	—	—

***Table 4.*—Relative Importance of Different Causes of Crop Damage on Selected Farms in Representative Counties in the Northern Great Plains, by Degree of Loss**

County and cause of damage	Total number of records	Length of record			Percent of years			
		Less than 10 years	10–19 years	20 years or more	Damage was reported	Degree of loss was		
						Total	Serious	Slight
Divide:	66	12	20	34				
Drought					40	12	15	13
Insects					10	2	3	5
Hail					17	4	4	9
Soil blowing					2	1	1	*
Rust					9	1	2	6
Frost					1	*	*	1
Hettinger:	63	12	21	30				
Drought					43	9	16	18
Insects					14	4	5	5
Hail					15	4	5	6
Soil blowing					3	1	1	1
Rust					4	1	1	2
Frost					1	*	1	*
Sheridan:	[1] 56	22	11	23				
Drought					41	10	16	15
Insects					13	3	2	8
Hail					12	3	3	6
Soil blowing					3	1	1	1
Rust					5	1	2	2
Frost					*	—	—	*
Hyde:	48	6	21	21				
Drought					55	18	20	17
Insects					15	7	6	2
Hail					13	3	6	4
Soil blowing					3	1	1	1
Rust					5	1	2	2
Frost					4	1	2	1
Traill:	52	28	11	13				
Drought					26	1	6	19
Insects					12	1	2	9
Hail					10	3	2	5
Soil blowing					3	1	1	1
Rust					11	*	2	9
Frost					1	1	—	—
Moody:	87	38	25	24				
Drought					19	3	7	9
Insects					3	*	*	3
Hail					10	3	2	5
Soil blowing					1	—	*	1
Rust					1	—	*	1
Frost					5	*	1	4

*Less than 0.5 percent.

[1] Records not available for 1 farm.

Table 5.—Average Annual Yield per Harvested Acre of Important Crops in Representative Counties in the Northern Great Plains, 1911–1931

Crop and county	Average yield per harvested acre (bushels)																					Average yield for years reported (bushels)
	1911	1912	1913	1914	1915	1916	1917	1918	1919	1920	1921	1922	1923	1924	1925	1926	1927	1928	1929	1930	1931	
WHEAT																						
Divide	11.4	20.5	11.9	18.2	21.0	7.0	7.0	8.5	5.5	3.9	12.1	17.0	10.9	15.1	11.6	15.9	12.3	14.1	11.2	7.8	2.5	11.7
Hettinger	2.0	15.5	6.6	12.3	16.0	4.0	5.0	8.0	2.5	6.8	1.9	14.7	6.6	13.6	11.6	5.9	13.3	17.4	9.6	7.9	4.2	8.8
Sheridan	10.8	16.9	6.3	9.3	18.0	6.0	2.5	6.5	4.4	7.8	9.6	13.2	5.5	12.7	12.7	5.9	14.0	16.3	8.0	10.5	4.9	9.6
Hyde	(1)	(1)	(1)	(1)	(1)	(1)	(1)	(1)	8.0	7.0	8.0	16.9	8.9	13.9	9.0	5.1	15.0	5.9	7.0	13.9	2.3	9.3
Traill	11.3	16.0	19.2	9.5	18.0	3.5	15.0	23.0	8.7	8.8	8.7	13.2	8.9	19.5	10.6	12.9	10.1	11.6	10.2	14.6	9.2	12.5
Moody	(1)	(1)	(1)	(1)	(1)	(1)	(1)	(1)	9.0	7.0	10.0	12.0	13.8	16.0	14.0	9.3	16.8	13.0	9.5	12.7	13.8	12.1
BARLEY																						
Divide	28.3	26.2	23.5	36.7	32.7	16.0	8.0	12.0	8.0	6.0	19.0	21.5	20.0	23.5	17.0	17.0	24.5	22.5	10.5	7.0	2.5	18.2
Hettinger	0.5	33.5	16.8	19.8	34.0	25.0	5.0	15.0	3.0	15.5	2.0	26.0	20.0	24.5	12.5	12.5	27.5	28.0	15.0	9.5	8.0	16.8
Sheridan	12.0	33.8	17.4	18.3	36.7	20.0	5.0	9.0	8.0	14.5	15.0	24.0	14.5	23.5	13.5	8.5	22.0	27.0	11.4	18.5	8.0	17.2
Hyde	(1)	(1)	(1)	(1)	(1)	(1)	(1)	26.0	25.0	21.0	20.0	33.0	24.0	24.0	26.0	3.0	31.0	11.0	11.0	25.0	3.2	20.2
Traill	25.7	24.2	21.8	16.8	30.7	12.0	20.0	30.0	16.0	18.5	15.0	21.5	17.5	24.0	24.5	21.0	24.0	21.5	13.8	19.0	15.0	20.6
Moody	(1)	(1)	(1)	(1)	(1)	(1)	(1)	30.0	30.0	19.0	19.0	21.0	21.0	33.0	31.0	15.0	33.0	29.0	30.0	33.0	17.9	25.9
OATS																						
Divide	31.9	44.5	23.4	37.0	41.9	30.0	12.0	17.0	13.5	8.0	28.5	34.5	28.0	29.0	19.0	29.0	24.0	30.5	13.5	8.5	3.2	24.1
Hettinger	2.9	38.0	15.6	33.4	49.6	20.0	6.0	14.0	5.0	19.0	4.0	34.5	27.0	30.5	13.0	13.0	25.0	34.0	17.0	15.0	8.0	20.2
Sheridan	14.5	44.7	20.0	25.0	39.5	25.0	6.0	12.0	11.5	18.0	18.0	29.0	17.0	30.5	18.0	10.0	24.0	30.0	12.5	19.0	9.0	20.6
Hyde	(1)	(1)	(1)	(1)	(1)	(1)	(1)	30.0	30.0	34.0	20.0	41.5	34.0	39.0	34.0	5.0	30.0	14.0	12.5	26.0	1.9	25.1
Traill	33.0	33.9	29.5	16.4	42.0	15.0	25.0	30.0	20.0	28.0	20.0	29.0	26.0	32.5	30.5	27.0	16.5	29.0	21.0	25.5	17.0	26.0
Moody	(1)	(1)	(1)	(1)	(1)	(1)	(1)	40.0	31.5	36.0	27.5	31.0	33.0	37.0	41.0	13.0	33.0	28.0	38.0	38.0	17.9	31.8
CORN																						
Divide	(1)	(1)	(1)	(1)	(1)	(1)	(1)	(1)	20.7	14.0	25.6	29.3	23.5	17.2	20.6	21.7	19.6	20.2	11.5	18.0	10.0	19.4
Hettinger	(1)	(1)	(1)	(1)	(1)	(1)	6.0	20.0	16.4	21.6	12.3	26.5	31.0	19.0	21.5	20.8	26.5	24.0	17.0	14.0	20.5	19.8
Sheridan	19.3	(1)	25.0	23.3	40.0	(1)	(1)	(1)	20.7	19.0	22.7	25.5	35.7	20.0	18.7	23.6	17.6	25.9	11.5	12.5	22.0	22.5
Hyde	(1)	(1)	(1)	(1)	(1)	(1)	(1)	32.0	28.0	33.5	21.0	30.0	34.0	17.0	13.0	5.0	26.0	8.0	8.0	13.0	0.4	19.2
Traill	35.3	26.0	32.5	26.0	30.0	15.0	(1)	20.0	32.8	68.0	31.2	34.0	33.8	20.0	25.3	21.0	23.5	24.9	18.0	17.5	16.0	25.5
Moody	(1)	(1)	(1)	(1)	(1)	(1)	(1)	32.0	35.0	23.5	35.5	33.0	36.0	23.0	23.0	27.0	28.0	28.0	38.0	25.0	16.3	29.7
FLAX																						
Divide	7.7	12.7	6.5	7.8	7.8	10.0	4.0	7.0	4.7	2.5	6.8	8.0	9.7	8.2	6.0	6.5	7.8	6.9	4.5	3.4	2.0	6.7
Hettinger	2.1	9.1	4.5	6.8	14.5	10.0	2.0	4.0	2.0	2.5	0.5	8.3	8.8	8.7	6.1	3.4	9.9	9.8	4.0	2.4	2.2	5.8
Sheridan	8.1	7.9	7.4	9.0	11.6	14.0	2.5	8.0	2.0	4.1	4.8	9.0	7.9	5.8	4.0	5.8	10.7	8.2	3.7	5.0	3.8	6.8
Hyde	(1)	(1)	(1)	(1)	(1)	(1)	(1)	8.5	9.0	11.5	5.5	10.0	11.0	8.5	4.5	4.0	9.5	7.0	4.5	4.4	0.5	7.0
Traill	8.0	8.5	8.8	10.0	9.7	5.0	7.5	10.0	7.0	8.2	8.5	11.2	7.8	9.2	6.2	7.9	7.2	7.8	6.0	6.2	5.0	7.9
Moody	(1)	(1)	(1)	(1)	(1)	(1)	(1)	10.6	6.5	8.5	8.0	11.0	10.0	12.0	9.5	8.0	11.0	8.5	9.5	10.0	5.3	9.2

[1] Yield not available.

Sources: Willard, Rex E. and Fuller, O. M., *Type-of-Farming Areas in North Dakota*, Bulletin 212, North Dakota Agricultural Experiment Station, Fargo, N. Dak., July 1927, pp. 254–259; reports of the North Dakota agricultural statistician, Fargo, N. Dak., 1919–1931; and reports of the South Dakota agricultural statistician, Brookings, S. Dak., 1922–1931.

***Table 6.*—Percent of Years Specified Crop Yield per Harvested Acre Was Obtained in Selected Areas in the Northern Great Plains, 1911–1931**

Crop and area	Period included	Total reports		Yield per harvested acre								
		Number	Percent	Less than 2.5 bushels	2.5–7.4 bushels	7.5–12.4 bushels	12.5–17.4 bushels	17.5–22.4 bushels	22.5–27.4 bushels	27.5–32.4 bushels	32.5–37.4 bushels	37.5 bushels or more
WHEAT												
North Dakota Black Prairies Section [1]	1911–1931	105	100.0	3	29	35	23	10	—	—	—	—
Scobey-Plentywood Section [2]	1922–1931	60	100.0	5	14	33	23	13	2	—	—	—
Southwestern North Dakota [3]	1911–1931	101	100.0	9	33	27	39	2	—	—	—	—
Central North Dakota [4]	1911–1931	126	100.0	—	34	30	26	10	—	—	—	—
Central South Dakota [5]	1919–1931	91	100.0	3	24	46	22	5	—	—	—	—
Red River Valley [6]	1911–1931	105	100.0	—	7	47	30	13	3	—	—	—
Southeastern South Dakota [7]	[8]1919–1932	126	100.0	—	12	29	38	19	1	1	—	—
BARLEY												
North Dakota Black Prairies Section [1]	1911–1931	104	100.0	—	13	17	25	11	20	7	5	2
Scobey-Plentywood Section [2]	1922–1931	58	100.0	—	14	15	17	14	33	7	—	—
Southwestern North Dakota [3]	1911–1931	101	100.0	5	16	17	18	13	16	12	3	—
Central North Dakota [4]	1911–1931	126	100.0	—	6	22	21	25	16	5	4	1
Central South Dakota [5]	1919–1931	91	100.0	—	12	12	12	25	22	12	5	—
Red River Valley [6]	1911–1931	105	100.0	—	—	5	30	30	25	9	1	—
Southeastern South Dakota [7]	1918–1931	126	100.0	—	—	9	5	12	21	35	18	—
OATS												
North Dakota Black Prairies Section [1]	1911–1931	105	100.0	—	9	10	16	20	9	17	8	11
Scobey-Plentywood Section [2]	1922–1931	60	100.0	—	8	13	17	10	12	18	20	2
Southwestern North Dakota [3]	1911–1931	101	100.0	1	19	10	15	13	11	11	12	8
Central North Dakota [4]	1911–1931	126	100.0	—	4	10	21	19	20	13	5	8
Central South Dakota [5]	1919–1931	91	100.0	3	9	4	15	11	7	19	18	14
Red River Valley [6]	1911–1931	105	100.0	—	—	—	12	20	24	26	9	9
Southeastern South Dakota [7]	1918–1931	126	100.0	—	—	7	6	2	6	25	28	26
CORN												
North Dakota Black Prairies Section [1]	1919–1931	65	100.0	—	—	9	20	35	28	8	—	—
Scobey-Plentywood Section [2]	1922–1931	60	100.0	1	—	27	15	30	20	7	—	—
Southwestern North Dakota [3]	1917–1931	75	100.0	—	4	9	27	36	15	5	4	—
Central North Dakota [4]	1919–1931	78	100.0	—	1	5	17	33	32	9	3	—
Central South Dakota [5]	1919–1931	91	100.0	7	5	17	19	14	19	12	7	—
Red River Valley [6]	1911–1931	95	100.0	—	—	2	11	22	28	20	15	2
Southeastern South Dakota [7]	1918–1931	126	100.0	—	4	2	2	8	17	11	29	27
FLAX												
North Dakota Black Prairies Section [1]	1911–1931	105	100.0	8	49	42	1	—	—	—	—	—
Scobey-Plentywood Section [2]	1922–1931	60	100.0	10	38	52	—	—	—	—	—	—
Southwestern North Dakota [3]	1911–1931	100	100.0	19	48	32	1	—	—	—	—	—
Central North Dakota [4]	1911–1931	126	100.0	3	51	44	2	—	—	—	—	—
Central South Dakota [5]	1919–1931	89	100.0	6	49	43	2	—	—	—	—	—
Red River Valley [6]	1911–1931	104	100.0	—	37	60	3	—	—	—	—	—
Southeastern South Dakota [7]	1918–1931	112	100.0	2	20	75	3	—	—	—	—	—

[1] North Dakota Black Prairies Section includes Bottineau, Burke, Divide, Renville, and Ward Counties, N. Dak.

[2] Scobey-Plentywood Section includes McLean, Mountrail, and Williams Counties, N. Dak., and Daniels, Roosevelt, and Sheridan Counties, Mont.

[3] Southwestern North Dakota Area includes Adams, Bowman, Hettinger, Slope, and Stark Counties, N. Dak.

[4] Central North Dakota Area includes Benson, Burleigh, Kidder, Pierce, Sheridan, and Wells Counties, N. Dak.

[5] Central South Dakota Area includes Buffalo, Faulk, Hand, Hughes, Hyde, Potter, and Sully Counties, S. Dak.

[6] Red River Valley Area includes Cass, Grand Forks, Pembina, Traill, and Walsh Counties, N. Dak.

[7] Southeastern South Dakota Area includes Bon Homme, Clay, Lake, Lincoln, Minnehaha, Moody, Turner, Union, and Yankton Counties, S. Dak.

[8] Data available for 1919–1932 rather than for 1918–1931.

Sources: Willard, Rex E. and Fuller, O. M., *Type-of-Farming Areas in North Dakota*, Bulletin 212, North Dakota Agricultural Experiment Station, Fargo, N. Dak., July 1927, pp. 254–259; reports of the North Dakota agricultural statistician, Fargo, N. Dak., 1919–1931; and reports of the South Dakota agricultural statistician, Brookings, S. Dak., 1922–1931.

***Table 7.*—Average Yield per Seeded Acre of Important Crops on Selected Farms in Representative Counties in the Northern Great Plains and Frequency of Occurrence of Yields Which Were Good, Medium, Poor, or Failures**

Crop and county	Number of crops reported	Yield per seeded acre (bushels)				Percent of years yield was obtained				Average yield per acre (bushels)
		Good	Medium	Poor	Failure	Good	Medium	Poor	Failure	
WHEAT										
Divide:										
North Dakota Black Prairies Section	691	21	11	5	—	17	42	26	15	10
Scobey-Plentywood Section	414	18	10	7	3	20	31	26	23	9
Hettinger	936	21	10	4	1	17	44	25	14	9
Sheridan	881	18	11	5	1	19	41	25	15	9
Hyde	778	18	11	4	—	15	37	24	24	8
Traill	630	24	16	8	2	27	48	20	5	16
Moody	183	21	17	10	3	29	50	15	6	16
BARLEY										
Divide:										
North Dakota Black Prairies Section	400	32	17	8	1	21	39	21	19	15
Scobey-Plentywood Section	241	32	20	11	5	19	19	28	34	15
Hettinger	784	35	18	8	2	16	37	27	20	15
Sheridan	624	32	19	9	2	21	40	24	15	17
Hyde	929	35	21	10	1	19	35	24	22	16
Traill	609	41	26	14	5	29	46	20	5	27
Moody	1,025	40	26	14	10	24	56	11	9	26
OATS										
Divide:										
North Dakota Black Prairies Section	623	41	21	10	1	17	42	25	16	18
Scobey-Plentywood Section	347	37	23	12	6	26	20	24	30	19
Hettinger	639	45	21	10	3	16	39	27	18	18
Sheridan	713	38	23	10	2	18	41	23	18	19
Hyde	919	44	25	10	1	21	31	26	22	20
Traill	610	45	30	16	6	29	46	18	7	30
Moody	1,201	49	33	17	4	26	55	11	8	33
CORN										
Divide:										
North Dakota Black Prairies Section	—	—	—	—	—	—	—	—	—	—
Scobey-Plentywood Section	26	20	—	—	2	12	—	—	88	5
Hettinger	586	30	15	7	2	19	28	31	22	12
Sheridan	44	26	16	8	1	34	11	23	32	13
Hyde	877	30	15	7	1	14	21	33	32	10
Traill	—	—	—	—	—	—	—	—	—	—
Moody	1,200	45	30	16	5	25	53	14	8	30

Table 8.—Average Yield per Seeded Acre of Important Crops on Selected Farms in Representative Counties in the Northern Great Plains, 1930–1934

County and year	Number of farms reporting	Average yield per seeded acre					
		Bushels					Tons
		Wheat	Barley	Oats	Flax	Corn for grain	Corn for fodder
DIVIDE							
North Dakota Black Prairies Section							
1930	16	5.6	13.1	8.2	6.8	—	1.1
1931	19	0.2	—	0.1	—	—	0.6
1932	33	7.6	9.4	14.7	1.5	—	1.5
1933	42	4.2	2.6	3.5	0.9	—	0.8
1934	44	—	—	—	—	—	0.1
Scobey-Plentywood Section							
1930	2	5.5	10.0	10.0	6.0	—	—
1931	4	0.1	—	—	—	—	—
1932	20	8.1	9.0	15.1	3.0	—	1.0
1933	22	4.3	3.7	5.1	1.4	—	1.0
1934	22	—	0.1	—	—	—	0.2
HETTINGER							
1930	6	5.9	7.4	5.0	—	25.0	—
1931	13	4.8	3.5	0.4	10.0	14.7	1.3
1932	50	10.9	18.7	22.6	0.7	11.2	0.8
1933	57	4.3	5.8	6.3	0.7	6.1	0.8
1934	63	0.4	0.2	0.5	0.6	0.1	0.3
SHERIDAN							
1930	2	7.3	10.0	26.7	—	13.3	—
1931	8	5.6	10.3	16.3	—	3.8	0.1
1932	36	10.2	16.1	20.5	—	20.9	1.7
1933	52	5.8	9.2	10.6	—	13.4	1.2
1934	57	0.6	1.0	0.3	—	0.3	0.5
HYDE							
1930	3	12.2	10.0	21.4	—	2.1	—
1931	16	0.4	6.6	0.1	—	*	—
1932	43	11.0	13.8	18.6	—	3.1	0.1
1933	45	—	0.5	1.1	—	—	0.2
1934	48	—	—	—	—	—	0.3
TRAILL							
1930	—	—	—	—	—	—	—
1931	2	10.5	10.0	10.3	—	—	2.6
1932	12	11.1	27.2	22.9	8.5	—	2.0
1933	32	13.5	20.3	26.8	3.8	—	1.7
1934	52	15.0	20.0	26.0	5.0	—	1.6
MOODY							
1930	—	—	—	—	—	—	—
1931	3	—	15.1	28.5	5.0	22.7	—
1932	36	17.2	35.7	42.9	12.2	34.7	—
1933	72	7.2	16.3	18.3	4.9	21.2	1.3
1934	87	0.4	5.0	4.4	0.8	6.1	0.8

*Less than 0.05 bushel.

Table 9.—Financial Progress of Selected Farmers in Representative Counties in the Northern Great Plains Since Beginning Farming in the Area, by Size of Farm, 1935

County and size of farm	Number of farms reporting	Financial status at beginning			Capital additions to business			Net put into business	Financial status in 1935			Average increase per farm	
		Assets	Liabilities	Net worth	Additions	Deductions	Net additions		Assets	Liabilities	Net worth	Total	Per year
DIVIDE													
Total farms	66	$1, 829	$315	$1, 514	$876	$287	$589	$2, 103	$6, 548	$3, 528	$3, 020	$917	$47
Less than 281 acres	10	1, 627	76	1, 551	494	88	406	1, 957	2, 337	1, 238	1, 099	−858	−55
281–400 acres	17	1, 933	400	1, 533	348	288	60	1, 593	6, 169	3, 123	3, 046	1, 453	71
401–600 acres	20	1, 691	141	1, 550	649	438	211	1, 761	6, 507	4, 005	2, 502	741	37
601–800 acres	11	1, 659	727	932	591	321	270	1, 202	7, 427	3, 582	3, 845	2, 643	128
801 acres or more	8	2, 438	300	2, 138	3, 434	113	3, 321	5, 459	11, 512	5, 985	5, 527	68	3
HETTINGER													
Total farms	63	1, 064	297	767	301	271	30	797	6, 700	3, 121	3, 579	2, 782	152
Less than 280 acres	11	525	90	435	536	7	529	964	2, 635	1, 254	1, 381	417	23
280–439 acres	14	950	186	764	500	246	254	1, 018	3, 960	2, 342	1, 618	600	33
440–559 acres	7	971	235	736	—	1, 143	−1, 143	−407	7, 372	6, 430	942	1, 349	71
560–719 acres	11	998	405	593	232	89	143	736	5, 420	2, 528	2, 892	2, 156	113
720–879 acres	7	657	571	86	500	143	357	443	10, 610	3, 302	7, 308	6, 865	327
880 acres or more	13	1, 970	385	1, 585	—	277	−277	1, 308	11, 705	4, 162	7, 543	6, 235	363
SHERIDAN													
Total farms	57	2, 265	844	1, 421	535	538	−3	1, 418	7, 279	2, 874	4, 405	2, 987	171
Less than 240 acres	8	1, 438	425	1, 013	—	48	−48	965	2, 294	1, 540	754	−211	−18
240–399 acres	12	1, 612	300	1, 312	317	329	−12	1, 300	3, 512	2, 149	1, 363	63	5
400–559 acres	13	1, 266	1, 245	21	111	69	42	63	6, 536	2, 325	4, 211	4, 148	235
560–719 acres	9	4, 844	1, 544	3, 300	1, 000	430	570	3, 870	10, 476	5, 533	4, 943	1, 073	64
720–879 acres	9	2, 385	914	1, 471	—	1, 982	−1, 982	−511	8, 616	3, 712	4, 904	5, 415	427
880 acres or more	6	2, 794	467	2, 327	2, 717	631	2, 086	4, 413	16, 269	2, 045	14, 224	9, 811	366

Table 9.—Financial Progress of Selected Farmers in Representative Counties in the Northern Great Plains Since Beginning Farming in the Area, by Size of Farm, 1935—Continued

County and size of farm	Number of farms reporting	Financial status at beginning			Capital additions to business			Net put into business	Financial status in 1935			Average increase per farm	
		Assets	Liabilities	Net worth	Additions	Deductions	Net additions		Assets	Liabilities	Net worth	Total	Per year
HYDE													
Total farms	48	$2,345	$733	$1,612	$1,278	$566	$712	$2,324	$7,010	$3,210	$3,800	$1,476	$78
Less than 280 acres	10	2,430	990	1,440	284	420	−136	1,304	5,397	2,853	2,544	1,240	76
280–439 acres	11	1,502	255	1,247	3,494	237	3,257	4,504	6,121	2,436	3,685	−819	−36
440–559 acres	10	5,940	1,560	4,380	713	630	83	4,463	3,606	2,283	1,323	−3,140	−160
560–719 acres	7	550	64	486	478	500	−22	464	6,898	3,010	3,888	3,424	250
720 acres or more	10	849	645	204	965	1,057	−92	112	13,087	5,487	7,600	7,488	374
TRAILL													
Total farms	52	4,666	1,355	3,311	291	1,051	−760	2,551	9,140	3,228	5,912	3,361	260
Less than 200 acres	8	5,613	838	4,775	1,375	1,152	223	4,998	8,289	2,609	5,680	682	47
200–399 acres	19	6,143	2,260	3,883	13	1,445	−1,432	2,451	8,537	2,804	5,733	3,282	221
400–599 acres	12	1,442	850	592	250	929	−679	−87	8,144	2,300	5,844	5,931	535
600–799 acres	8	6,213	1,013	5,200	106	103	3	5,203	10,992	5,024	5,968	765	90
800 acres or more	5	2,800	500	2,300	—	1,200	−1,200	1,100	12,220	5,183	7,037	5,937	401
MOODY													
Total farms	87	5,045	1,588	3,457	488	1,573	−1,085	2,372	7,998	3,291	4,707	2,335	150
Less than 121 acres	4	1,875	475	1,400	2,500	—	2,500	3,900	4,656	1,994	2,662	−1,238	−67
121–200 acres	32	5,234	1,617	3,617	38	525	−487	3,130	6,059	2,765	3,294	164	12
201–280 acres	16	6,233	1,317	4,916	533	6,646	−6,113	−1,197	8,156	3,440	4,716	5,913	328
281–360 acres	24	4,941	2,122	2,819	970	607	363	3,182	9,801	4,055	5,746	2,564	167
361–440 acres	5	8,700	1,720	6,980	—	40	−40	6,940	2,684	384	2,300	−4,640	−380
441–520 acres	2	250	500	−250	—	125	−125	−375	13,142	9,500	3,642	4,017	127
521 acres or more	4	675	800	−125	—	690	−690	−815	19,982	4,381	15,601	16,416	1,094

***Table 10.*—Size of Farm, Number of Livestock per Farm, and Tenure of Farm Operators Receiving Relief in Representative Counties in the Northern Great Plains, April–May 1935**

County and size of farm	Number of farms reporting	Average size of farm [1] (acres)	Average number of livestock				Tenure of operator		
			Cattle	Hogs	Chickens	Horses	Owner	Tenant	Unknown
DIVIDE									
Total farms	175	373	6	2	42	3	118	55	2
Less than 281 acres	53	169	4	1	36	2	24	29	—
281–400 acres	51	324	6	2	40	3	36	15	—
401–600 acres	27	484	6	2	52	4	26	1	—
601–800 acres	19	653	8	2	53	5	17	2	—
801 acres or more	5	1,384	10	5	65	12	5	—	—
Not specified	20	—	6	1	32	7	10	8	2
HETTINGER									
Total farms	198	413	8	3	26	5	78	57	63
Less than 280 acres	50	153	6	2	31	4	22	28	—
280–439 acres	44	331	10	5	36	6	26	18	—
440–559 acres	18	482	14	4	28	7	13	5	—
560–719 acres	9	622	16	4	28	8	5	4	—
720–879 acres	4	810	8	5	22	8	3	1	—
880 acres or more	5	2,784	17	1	35	12	4	1	—
Not specified	68	—	4	2	14	2	5	—	63
SHERIDAN									
Total farms	150	289	11	2	31	6	55	87	8
Less than 240 acres	54	154	10	2	26	5	26	28	—
240–399 acres	47	298	13	2	38	6	17	30	—
400–559 acres	12	450	15	2	38	7	6	6	—
560–719 acres	7	644	13	2	43	6	2	5	—
720–879 acres	4	751	21	3	31	8	1	3	—
880 acres or more	1	960	12	—	—	6	—	1	—
Not specified	25	—	8	2	22	4	3	14	8
HYDE									
Total farms	[2] 214	464	27	5	58	6	86	128	—
Less than 280 acres	53	164	15	3	47	5	23	30	—
280–439 acres	68	330	22	3	54	5	26	42	—
440–559 acres	26	486	44	6	63	7	12	14	—
560–719 acres	23	630	28	7	73	6	11	12	—
720 acres or more	31	1,126	51	10	78	8	13	18	—
Not specified	13	—	8	2	32	3	1	12	—
MOODY									
Total farms	100	199	17	23	105	4	16	74	10
Less than 121 acres	12	57	3	9	72	2	5	7	—
121–200 acres	38	160	17	27	114	5	5	33	—
201–280 acres	16	231	23	24	112	6	1	15	—
281–360 acres	15	321	25	38	129	7	2	13	—
361–440 acres	3	390	54	37	125	7	1	2	—
441–520 acres	1	480	13	8	—	4	—	1	—
Not specified	15	—	9	6	83	2	2	3	10

[1] Reporting acreage.
[2] Reports available for only 214 of the 247 farm operators receiving relief in April 1935.

Table 11.—Utilization of Land on Selected Farms in Representative Counties in the Northern Great Plains, by Size of Farm, 1934

County and size of farm	Number of farms reporting	Average number of acres per farm					
		Total	Crop-land	Native grass		Former crop-land	Farm-stead and waste
				Hay	Pasture		
DIVIDE							
North Dakota Black Prairies Section							
Total farms	44	499	368	23	82	4	22
Less than 281 acres	5	160	120	—	32	—	8
281–400 acres	12	329	244	10	57	7	11
401–600 acres	17	495	376	20	69	3	27
601–800 acres	7	742	565	29	114	9	25
801 acres or more	3	1,200	754	88	295	—	63
Scobey-Plentywood Section							
Total farms	22	549	287	7	208	4	43
Less than 281 acres	5	184	135	5	39	2	3
281–400 acres	5	320	206	6	92	8	8
401–600 acres	3	493	299	—	126	—	68
601–800 acres	4	699	422	17	216	12	32
801 acres or more	5	1,060	407	8	534	—	111
HETTINGER							
Total farms	63	606	371	7	213	2	13
Less than 280 acres	11	175	114	—	52	4	5
280–439 acres	14	339	240	6	88	—	5
440–559 acres	7	474	279	—	173	14	8
560–719 acres	11	627	413	7	202	—	5
720–879 acres	7	796	438	19	318	5	16
880 acres or more	13	1,210	707	6	462	—	35
SHERIDAN							
Total farms	57	547	324	21	184	1	17
Less than 240 acres	8	176	101	6	60	—	9
240–399 acres	12	306	197	—	90	3	16
400–559 acres	13	455	303	18	118	2	14
560–719 acres	9	632	390	32	184	—	26
720–879 acres	9	805	486	34	273	—	12
880 acres or more	6	1,205	578	53	546	—	28
HYDE							
Total farms	48	523	217	48	224	22	12
Less than 280 acres	10	192	115	1	71	—	5
280–439 acres	11	323	194	—	109	11	9
440–559 acres	10	485	211	66	201	2	5
560–719 acres	7	629	206	122	216	69	16
720 acres or more	10	1,036	359	75	532	45	25
TRAILL							
Total farms	52	433	393	7	19	1	13
Less than 200 acres	8	161	136	—	13	—	12
200–399 acres	19	305	277	—	16	1	11
400–599 acres	12	473	430	13	18	—	12
600–799 acres	8	648	589	11	32	—	16
800 acres or more	5	915	846	24	30	—	15
MOODY							
Total farms	87	260	211	9	31	—	9
Less than 121 acres	4	60	51	—	5	—	4
121–200 acres	32	161	138	3	14	—	6
201–280 acres	16	238	192	4	32	—	10
281–360 acres	24	323	266	13	33	—	11
361–440 acres	5	400	338	—	46	—	16
441–520 acres	2	480	376	12	80	—	12
521 acres or more	4	640	432	64	130	—	14

***Table 12.*—Use of Farm Land on Selected Farms in Representative Counties in the Northern Great Plains, 1934**

Use of farm land	Average number of acres per farm						
	Divide						
	North Dakota Black Prairies Section (44 farms)	Scobey-Plentywood Section (22 farms)	Hettinger (63 farms)	Sheridan (57 farms)	Hyde (48 farms)	Traill (52 farms)	Moody (87 farms)
Total land operated	499	549	606	547	523	433	260
Total cropland	368	287	371	324	217	393	211
Wheat	98	103	155	135	34	100	2
Wheat on fallow	36	5	14	8	—	22	—
Barley	11	19	35	23	32	68	35
Oats	35	23	15	23	12	41	51
Rye	1	—	20	16	4	7	2
Corn for grain	1	—	8	3	18	—	52
Corn for fodder	14	8	20	27	6	28	23
Flax	1	10	3	2	—	12	3
Tame hay	1	3	7	12	3	20	13
Feed crops	4	2	3	—	22	2	7
Other crops	7	4	6	3	4	7	1
Annual pasture	3	2	—	4	—	17	13
Fallow	27	26	19	22	1	47	—
Idle cropland	129	82	66	46	81	22	9
Former cropland	4	4	2	1	22	1	—
Native hay	23	7	7	21	48	7	9
Native pasture	82	208	213	184	224	19	31
Farmstead and waste	22	43	13	17	12	13	9

***Table 13.*—Average Acreage of Important Crops on Selected Farms [1] in Representative Counties in the Northern Great Plains, 1930–1934**

County and year	Number of farms reporting	Average number of acres per farm					
		Wheat	Barley	Oats	Flax	Corn for grain	Corn for fodder
DIVIDE							
North Dakota Black Prairies Section							
1930	16	190	23	34	12	—	5
1931	19	183	16	28	—	—	6
1932	33	180	20	28	12	—	6
1933	42	170	16	30	14	—	8
1934	44	134	11	35	1	—	14
Scobey-Plentywood Section							
1930	2	257	15	8	5	—	—
1931	4	220	6	21	—	—	—
1932	20	120	18	17	35	—	1
1933	22	138	23	14	29	—	2
1934	22	108	19	23	10	—	8
HETTINGER							
1930	6	227	25	13	—	7	—
1931	13	156	24	10	8	18	4
1932	50	179	26	12	12	15	9
1933	57	195	32	13	7	16	12
1934	63	169	35	15	3	8	20
SHERIDAN							
1930	2	150	13	38	(2)	15	—
1931	8	113	20	17	(2)	5	4
1932	36	177	18	19	(2)	3	13
1933	52	158	27	23	(2)	3	20
1934	57	143	23	23	(2)	3	27
HYDE							
1930	3	51	52	27	(2)	35	—
1931	16	47	45	12	(2)	63	—
1932	43	66	54	24	(2)	39	11
1933	45	63	51	19	(2)	36	6
1934	48	34	32	12	—	18	6
TRAILL							
1930	—	—	—	—	—	—	—
1931	2	50	13	15	—	—	8
1932	12	105	30	30	7	—	12
1933	32	127	41	36	12	—	22
1934	52	122	68	41	12	—	28
MOODY							
1930	—	—	—	—	—	—	—
1931	3	—	14	35	7	62	—
1932	36	1	34	51	2	86	—
1933	72	2	34	44	4	82	1
1934	87	2	35	51	3	52	23

[1] Reporting acreage.
[2] Not calculated.

Table 14.—**Percent of Owned and Rented Land in Crops and Grass on Selected Farms in Representative Counties in the Northern Great Plains, 1934**

Item	Divide		Hettinger (63 farms)	Sheridan (57 farms)	Hyde (48 farms)	Traill (52 farms)	Moody (87 farms)
	North Dakota Black Prairies Section (44 farms)	Scobey-Plentywood Section (22 farms)					
Total operated land [1]	100.0	100.0	100.0	100.0	100.0	100.0	100.0
Cropland	73.5	52.3	61.2	59.3	41.5	90.9	81.2
Hay and pasture	21.1	39.1	36.2	37.4	52.0	6.1	15.2
Other	5.4	8.6	2.6	3.3	6.5	3.0	3.6
Total owned land	54.2	51.2	43.7	44.8	36.3	34.7	37.1
Cropland	40.2	27.4	28.5	32.1	18.0	30.4	29.6
Hay and pasture	11.2	20.3	13.8	11.5	17.1	2.8	6.2
Other	2.8	3.5	1.4	1.2	1.2	1.5	1.3
Total share-rented land	43.6	41.2	44.5	44.7	38.1	65.3	60.6
Cropland	32.6	20.8	31.9	26.3	20.1	60.5	50.0
Hay and pasture	8.3	15.3	11.3	16.4	14.2	3.3	8.4
Other	2.7	5.1	1.3	2.0	3.8	1.5	2.2
Total cash-rented land	2.9	7.6	13.1	10.8	25.6	—	4.2
Cropland	1.3	4.1	2.0	1.0	3.4	—	3.5
Hay and pasture	1.6	3.5	11.1	9.7	20.7	—	0.6
Other	—	—	—	0.1	1.5	—	0.1
Land rented out	0.7	—	1.3	0.3	—	—	1.9
Cropland	0.6	—	1.2	0.1	—	—	1.9
Hay and pasture	—	—	—	0.2	—	—	—
Other	0.1	—	0.1	—	—	—	—

[1] Total operated land is the sum of owned and rented land less land rented out.

Table 15.—Number of Livestock on Hand April 1, 1935, and Normal Number on Selected Farms in Representative Counties in the Northern Great Plains, by Size of Farm

County and size of farm	Average number of livestock																			
	All cattle		Milk cows		Beef cows		Other cattle		All hogs		Brood sows		Other hogs		Sheep		Poultry		Work stock	
	April 1, 1935	Normal	April 1, 1935	Normal	April 1, 1935	Normal	April 1, 1935	Normal	April 1, 1935	Normal	April 1, 1935	Normal	April 1, 1935	Normal	April 1, 1935	Normal	April 1, 1935	Normal	April 1, 1935	Normal
DIVIDE																				
North Dakota Black Prairies Section																				
Total farms	9	20	5	7	—	1	4	12	3	3	1	1	2	2	4	6	47	62	6	6
Less than 281 acres	5	9	3	4	—	—	2	5	—	2	—	—	—	2	—	—	48	63	5	5
281–400 acres	7	16	5	7	—	—	2	9	1	2	—	1	1	1	3	4	52	70	5	5
401–600 acres	11	24	6	8	—	—	5	16	3	7	1	2	2	5	—	—	53	65	6	8
601–800 acres	10	16	4	4	2	2	4	10	1	4	—	1	1	3	5	3	29	40	5	5
801 acres or more	18	39	6	8	2	10	10	21	6	—	—	—	6	—	27	67	31	63	7	9
Scobey-Plentywood Section																				
Total farms	12	20	2	4	3	5	7	11	2	7	1	3	1	4	14	11	49	65	7	7
Less than 281 acres	9	11	2	3	2	2	5	6	1	7	1	2	—	5	—	—	45	49	3	3
281–400 acres	11	17	—	—	5	6	6	11	2	11	—	6	2	5	18	10	65	91	7	10
401–600 acres	17	22	4	6	3	3	10	13	1	3	1	3	—	—	—	—	42	74	3	6
601–800 acres	15	26	7	9	1	5	7	12	3	3	1	2	2	1	—	—	45	48	7	5
801 acres or more	15	27	1	5	4	6	10	16	3	12	1	3	2	9	45	44	47	64	8	8
HETTINGER																				
Total farms	17	21	7	8	2	3	8	10	3	13	1	2	2	11	5	3	52	90	6	6
Less than 280 acres	6	11	3	5	—	—	3	6	2	6	1	1	1	5	—	—	30	49	3	4
280–439 acres	8	18	3	5	1	3	4	10	1	12	1	2	—	10	9	12	50	73	4	5
440–559 acres	15	30	7	8	3	8	5	14	5	25	1	3	4	22	—	—	46	132	5	7
560–719 acres	20	26	8	11	2	2	10	13	2	8	2	2	—	6	6	—	50	104	7	7
720–879 acres	28	26	11	13	3	3	14	10	2	14	2	4	—	10	—	—	64	130	7	5
880 acres or more	26	23	12	10	2	2	12	11	8	17	2	4	6	13	6	—	70	95	8	8

SHERIDAN																				
Total farms	21	28	8	10	2	3	11	15	3	7	1	2	2	5	13	21	43	105	6	7
Less than 240 acres	16	22	5	7	2	2	9	13	2	4	1	1	1	3	9	8	22	129	4	5
240–399 acres	16	21	7	8	1	1	8	12	2	6	1	1	1	5	—	—	36	74	4	5
400–559 acres	18	22	8	9	1	1	9	12	4	7	1	2	3	5	10	—	45	106	6	6
560–719 acres	25	28	8	11	4	2	13	15	3	7	2	3	1	4	12	13	46	113	8	10
720–879 acres	25	46	9	15	3	7	13	24	4	8	1	4	3	4	7	4	51	120	7	7
880 acres or more	26	36	11	14	2	4	13	18	5	8	1	2	4	6	68	168	58	93	8	8
HYDE																				
Total farms	28	50	7	10	8	14	13	26	2	45	1	7	1	38	9	9	47	144	7	8
Less than 280 acres	13	29	6	10	3	10	4	9	3	67	1	9	2	58	2	6	24	79	4	6
280–439 acres	27	48	8	12	7	11	12	25	2	38	1	6	1	32	7	5	59	137	6	8
440–559 acres	22	41	6	9	5	10	11	22	4	32	2	5	2	27	21	23	46	239	6	8
560–719 acres	28	52	8	11	11	13	9	28	2	32	1	5	1	27	16	15	5	65	7	7
720 acres or more	53	80	8	10	15	27	30	43	6	50	2	7	4	43	3	—	73	177	10	10
TRAILL																				
Total farms	19	19	7	7	2	2	10	10	4	6	1	2	3	4	11	8	69	72	6	6
Less than 200 acres	12	12	4	4	2	2	6	6	*	—	*	*	*	—	3	—	52	53	5	3
200–399 acres	20	21	7	7	2	2	11	12	6	12	1	3	5	9	3	4	70	80	6	6
400–599 acres	16	18	6	7	2	2	8	9	4	4	1	1	3	3	22	19	51	71	5	4
600–799 acres	29	29	7	9	6	6	16	14	4	7	3	4	1	3	22	13	57	52	5	5
800 acres or more	25	20	11	10	2	—	12	10	2	2	2	2	—	—	6	1	152	105	12	12
MOODY																				
Total farms	28	29	7	7	4	4	17	18	18	48	5	9	13	39	24	29	84	130	4	5
Less than 121 acres	5	4	3	2	—	—	2	2	3	4	1	2	2	2	9	18	44	115	2	2
121–200 acres	18	20	5	5	2	3	11	12	10	38	3	6	7	32	21	15	77	116	4	4
201–280 acres	34	32	8	7	6	6	20	19	17	37	5	7	12	30	11	15	91	123	4	5
281–360 acres	35	39	9	9	4	5	22	25	16	45	6	12	10	33	37	64	78	148	6	6
361–440 acres	26	28	8	8	—	—	18	20	6	70	3	10	3	60	4	4	136	174	3	5
441–520 acres	58	55	10	10	11	11	37	34	140	172	22	22	118	150	86	100	88	88	6	7
521 acres or more	46	41	8	6	6	6	32	29	70	127	13	16	57	111	12	2	108	138	6	6

* Less than 0.5.

***Table 16.*—Number of Selected Farms With Livestock in Representative Counties in the Northern Great Plains, April 1, 1935**

Number of livestock	Number of farms reporting						
	Divide						
	North Dakota Black Prairies Section (44 farms)	Scobey-Plentywood Section (22 farms)	Hettinger (63 farms)	Sheridan (57 farms)	Hyde (48 farms)	Traill (52 farms)	Moody (87 farms)
MILK COWS							
None	2	13	15	13	11	6	22
1–5	26	3	16	4	9	13	18
6 or more	16	6	32	40	28	33	47
BEEF COWS							
None	42	9	50	45	28	42	50
1–5	—	7	7	2	6	2	11
6–15	2	6	5	8	8	6	23
16 or more	—	—	1	2	6	2	3
OTHER CATTLE							
None	2	2	3	2	2	—	3
1–10	26	4	23	8	12	14	11
11–25	15	16	29	30	20	23	35
26–50	1	—	5	16	7	13	28
51 or more	—	—	3	1	7	2	10
BROOD SOWS							
None	22	13	21	21	19	25	21
1–3	22	9	38	36	27	22	21
4 or more	—	—	4	—	2	5	45
OTHER HOGS							
None	30	16	45	37	33	35	18
1–5	8	3	12	10	10	7	27
6 or more	6	3	6	10	5	10	42
SHEEP							
None	39	15	59	49	35	38	48
1–10	2	2	1	1	6	2	6
11–50	2	2	—	2	4	9	21
51 or more	1	3	3	5	3	3	12
CHICKENS							
None	2	—	2	4	4	—	2
1–50	31	16	36	41	33	29	32
51–100	7	5	18	12	7	16	37
101 or more	4	1	7	—	4	7	16
WORK STOCK							
None	3	3	5	3	5	3	4
1–6	26	11	37	31	22	32	69
7 or more	15	8	21	23	21	17	14

Table 17.—Utilization of Labor and Tractors on Selected Farms in Representative Counties in the Northern Great Plains, by Size of Farm, 1935

County and size of farm	Number of farms reporting			Farms operated by specified number of men											
				1			2			3			4		
	Total	With tractor	Without tractor	Total	With tractor	Without tractor	Total	With tractor	Without tractor	Total	With tractor	Without tractor	Total	With tractor	Without tractor
DIVIDE															
Total farms	66	38	28	41	21	20	13	10	3	10	6	4	2	1	1
Less than 401 acres	27	11	16	21	8	13	3	2	1	2	1	1	1	—	1
401–600 acres	20	12	8	13	8	5	2	1	1	5	3	2	—	—	—
601 acres or more	19	15	4	7	5	2	8	7	1	3	2	1	1	1	—
HETTINGER															
Total farms	63	43	20	35	20	15	22	17	5	5	5	—	1	1	—
Less than 440 acres	25	11	14	19	7	12	6	4	2	—	—	—	—	—	—
440–719 acres	18	15	3	12	11	1	5	3	2	1	1	—	—	—	—
720 acres or more	20	17	3	4	2	2	11	10	1	4	4	—	1	1	—
SHERIDAN															
Total farms	57	28	29	26	9	17	14	9	5	13	7	6	4	3	1
Less than 400 acres	20	7	13	13	4	9	3	1	2	4	2	2	—	—	—
400–719 acres	22	11	11	10	3	7	8	6	2	3	1	2	1	1	—
720 acres or more	15	10	5	3	2	1	3	2	1	6	4	2	3	2	1
HYDE															
Total farms	48	27	21	23	11	12	23	14	9	2	2	—	—	—	—
Less than 440 acres	21	8	13	11	3	8	9	4	5	1	1	—	—	—	—
440–719 acres	17	11	6	8	5	3	8	5	3	1	1	—	—	—	—
720 acres or more	10	8	2	4	3	1	6	5	1	—	—	—	—	—	—
TRAILL															
Total farms	52	38	14	28	18	10	16	12	4	6	6	—	2	2	—
Less than 200 acres	8	2	6	5	—	5	3	2	1	—	—	—	—	—	—
200–399 acres	19	13	6	13	9	4	4	2	2	2	2	—	—	—	—
400 acres or more	25	23	2	10	9	1	9	8	1	4	4	—	2	2	—
MOODY															
Total farms	87	41	46	55	23	32	26	14	12	6	4	2	—	—	—
Less than 281 acres	52	17	35	39	12	27	10	4	6	3	1	2	—	—	—
281 acres or more	35	24	11	16	11	5	16	10	6	3	3	—	—	—	—

Table 18.—Acreage Operated by Specified Number of Men, With or Without Tractors, on Selected Farms in Sheridan and Traill Counties, N. Dak., by Size of Farm, 1935

County and size of farm	Number of farms reporting			Average acreage in farms operated by specified number of men											
				1			2			3			4		
	Total	With tractor	Without tractor	Total	With tractor	Without tractor	Total	With tractor	Without tractor	Total	With tractor	Without tractor	Total	With tractor	Without tractor
SHERIDAN															
All farms:															
Total farms	57	28	29	26	9	17	14	9	5	13	7	6	4	3	1
Total acres operated	547	611	484	429	483	401	559	569	540	636	656	613	971	1,014	840
Crop acres operated	324	431	221	215	312	164	359	389	305	366	438	281	773	896	405
Less than 400 acres:															
Total farms	20	7	13	13	4	9	3	1	2	4	2	2	—	—	—
Total acres operated	254	274	242	241	290	219	313	240	350	250	260	240	—	—	—
Crop acres operated	159	219	126	150	242	109	200	235	182	155	165	145	—	—	—
400–719 acres:															
Total farms	22	11	11	10	3	7	8	6	2	3	1	2	1	1	—
Total acres operated	527	537	517	484	515	470	566	541	640	533	480	560	640	640	—
Crop acres operated	338	390	287	289	378	251	370	384	330	376	388	370	465	465	—
720 acres or more:															
Total farms	15	10	5	3	2	1	3	2	1	6	4	2	3	2	1
Total acres operated	965	927	1,040	1,067	820	1,560	787	820	720	945	898	1,040	1,081	1,202	840
Crop acres operated	522	623	320	247	350	40	487	480	500	501	587	328	876	1,112	405
TRAILL															
All farms:															
Total farms	52	38	14	28	18	10	16	12	4	6	6	—	2	2	—
Total acres operated	433	497	259	376	455	234	441	481	320	584	584	—	720	720	—
Crop acres operated	393	455	227	345	425	201	392	425	294	526	526	—	685	685	—
Less than 200 acres:															
Total farms	8	2	6	5	—	5	3	2	1	—	—	—	—	—	—
Total acres operated	161	160	162	163	—	163	160	160	160	—	—	—	—	—	—
Crop acres operated	136	152	131	131	—	131	145	152	130	—	—	—	—	—	—
200–399 acres:															
Total farms	19	13	6	13	9	4	4	2	2	2	2	—	—	—	—
Total acres operated	305	316	282	298	314	262	320	320	320	320	320	—	—	—	—
Crop acres operated	277	292	245	273	295	223	296	302	290	270	270	—	—	—	—
400 acres or more:															
Total farms	25	23	2	10	9	1	9	8	1	4	4	—	2	2	—
Total acres operated	617	629	480	583	595	480	588	602	480	716	716	—	720	720	—
Crop acres operated	564	573	464	547	556	462	517	523	465	653	653	—	685	685	—

Table 19.—Average Value of Farm Buildings and Estimated Cost of Needed Repairs per Farm on Selected Farms in Representative Counties in the Northern Great Plains, by Size of Farm, 1935

County and size of farm	Number of farms reporting		Value of buildings			Cost of needed repairs		
	Total	Owned	Total	Dwelling	Other	Total	Dwelling	Other
DIVIDE								
North Dakota Black Prairies Section								
Total farms	44	31	$3, 084	$1, 195	$1, 889	$374	$143	$231
Less than 281 acres	5	3	1, 693	900	793	168	29	139
281–400 acres	12	9	2, 846	1, 167	1, 679	331	105	226
401–600 acres	17	11	3, 499	1, 247	2, 252	472	221	251
601–800 acres	7	5	2, 949	1, 243	1, 706	364	139	225
801 acres or more	3	3	4, 317	1, 400	2, 917	363	50	313
Scobey-Plentywood Section								
Total farms	22	17	1, 204	652	552	232	140	92
Less than 281 acres	5	2	831	470	361	51	25	26
281–400 acres	5	5	1, 605	960	645	508	395	113
401–600 acres	3	2	1, 076	533	543	185	38	147
601–800 acres	4	3	1, 231	650	581	110	58	52
801 acres or more	5	5	1, 232	600	632	263	127	136
HETTINGER								
Total farms	63	46	2, 321	990	1, 331	348	118	230
Less than 280 acres	11	8	1, 022	400	622	272	92	180
280–439 acres	14	10	1, 941	782	1, 159	287	94	193
440–559 acres	7	6	1, 875	1, 021	854	298	139	159
560–719 acres	11	7	2, 237	1, 045	1, 192	413	171	242
720–879 acres	7	5	2, 694	1, 343	1, 351	444	74	370
880 acres or more	13	10	3, 940	1, 462	2, 478	399	133	266
SHERIDAN								
Total farms	57	37	2, 299	902	1, 397	241	82	159
Less than 240 acres	8	4	826	480	346	168	77	91
240–399 acres	12	8	1, 392	658	734	230	80	150
400–559 acres	13	6	1, 894	677	1, 217	154	50	104
560–719 acres	9	8	2, 770	1, 211	1, 559	362	105	257
720–879 acres	9	5	3, 644	1, 350	2, 294	356	114	242
880 acres or more	6	6	4, 228	1, 300	2, 928	194	78	116
HYDE								
Total farms	48	23	2, 699	1, 153	1, 546	336	100	236
Less than 280 acres	10	4	2, 378	1, 195	1, 183	311	105	206
280–439 acres	11	5	3, 133	1, 173	1, 960	346	99	247
440–559 acres	10	4	2, 516	1, 185	1, 331	311	88	223
560–719 acres	7	3	2, 340	1, 071	1, 269	318	137	181
720 acres or more	10	7	2, 975	1, 113	1, 862	386	82	304
TRAILL								
Total farms	52	27	3, 977	1, 665	2, 312	301	94	207
Less than 200 acres	8	7	2, 684	1, 038	1, 646	325	138	187
200–399 acres	19	8	3, 793	1, 595	2, 198	196	70	126
400–599 acres	12	5	4, 728	1, 875	2, 853	242	55	187
600–799 acres	8	4	4, 426	2, 075	2, 351	585	168	417
800 acres or more	5	3	4, 228	1, 780	2, 448	344	90	254
MOODY								
Total farms	87	44	3, 880	1, 395	2, 485	380	90	290
Less than 121 acres	4	4	1, 587	675	912	104	30	74
121–200 acres	32	15	3, 362	1, 241	2, 121	306	86	220
201–280 acres	16	9	3, 406	1, 428	1, 978	362	90	272
281–360 acres	24	13	4, 753	1, 575	3, 178	452	102	350
361–440 acres	5	—	4, 376	1, 140	3, 236	338	56	282
441–520 acres	2	1	7, 385	3, 500	3, 885	990	150	840
521 acres or more	4	2	4, 612	1, 400	3, 212	640	125	515

Table 20.—Percent of Acreage With Mortgages of Record Held by Different Types of Lending Agencies in Representative Counties in the Northern Great Plains, 1935

Type of lending agency	Percent of mortgaged acres					
	Divide	Hettinger	Sheridan	Hyde	Traill	Moody
ALL MORTGAGES						
Total	100	100	100	100	100	100
Private	14	13	14	33	15	24
Corporate	1	1	5	4	6	27
Commercial banks	11	3	6	12	9	9
Federal Land Bank	35	35	28	9	41	21
Federal Land Bank Commissioner	29	38	31	15	27	14
State lending agencies	10	10	16	11	2	5
Other	—	—	—	16	—	—
FIRST MORTGAGES						
Total	100	100	100	100	100	100
Private	12	17	16	34	19	27
Corporate	3	2	6	4	8	31
Commercial banks	8	3	6	12	11	8
Federal Land Bank	48	49	38	9	55	25
Federal Land Bank Commissioner	18	17	12	12	4	3
State lending agencies	11	12	22	12	3	6
Other	—	—	—	17	—	—

Source: County records.

Table 21.—Federal Emergency Loans to Farmers in Representative Counties in the Northern Great Plains and Loans Outstanding, December 31, 1934

County	Number of loans per 100 farms						Average amount per loan					
	Total	Crop and feed loans				Drought loans 1934	Total	Crop and feed loans				Drought loans 1934
		1931 or before	1932	1933	1934			1931 or before	1932	1933	1934	
TOTAL LOANS MADE												
Divide	544	270	90	35	84	65	$186	$163	$294	$116	$146	$218
Hettinger	199	64	55	18	27	35	153	160	213	137	128	75
Sheridan	153	20	48	11	11	63	112	126	152	81	113	82
Hyde	168	—	62	7	25	74	165	—	251	108	151	103
Traill	58	—	16	20	14	8	141	—	153	142	130	135
Moody	56	—	14	1	1	40	95	—	189	78	110	61
LOANS OUTSTANDING DECEMBER 31, 1934												
Divide	456	189	85	33	84	65	177	148	264	117	146	218
Hettinger	141	17	47	15	27	35	137	178	178	128	128	75
Sheridan	132	11	38	9	11	63	99	119	120	78	113	83
Hyde	166	—	60	7	25	74	149	—	[1] 212	[1] 106	[1] 150	101
Traill	34	—	9	7	10	8	116	—	117	108	104	135
Moody	52	—	11	1	1	39	78	—	[1] 139	[1] 75	[1] 110	60

[1] Outstanding January 15, 1935.

Source: Compiled from data supplied by the Farm Credit Administration.

***Table 22.*—Average Indebtedness of Farm Operators Receiving Relief [1] in Representative Counties in the Northern Great Plains, by Tenure, April–May 1935**

County and size of farm	Owners						Tenants				
	Number of farms reporting	Average size of farm [2] (acres)	Average indebtedness	Kind of indebtedness (percent)			Number of farms reporting	Average size of farm [2] (acres)	Average indebtedness	Kind of indebtedness (percent)	
				Real-estate mortgages	Chattel mortgages	Other debts				Chattel mortgages	Other debts
DIVIDE											
Total farms	118	422	$2, 997	72	6	22	55	245	$988	47	53
Less than 281 acres	24	167	1, 754	64	6	30	29	171	759	37	63
281–400 acres	36	326	3, 141	75	6	19	15	320	1, 237	56	44
401–600 acres	26	485	3, 151	70	7	23	1	480	750	—	—
601–800 acres	17	654	3, 453	77	7	16	2	640	622	—	—
801 acres or more	5	1, 384	7, 217	85	1	14	—	—	—	—	—
Not specified	10	—	2, 366	70	9	21	8	—	1, 470	63	37
HETTINGER											
Total farms	78	502	3, 940	80	11	9	57	299	1, 064	74	26
Less than 280 acres	22	144	2, 084	83	3	14	28	161	536	61	39
280–439 acres	26	335	3, 634	77	13	10	18	324	1, 098	70	30
440–559 acres	13	480	5, 776	84	9	7	5	488	1, 454	91	9
560–719 acres	5	624	6, 314	98	—	2	4	620	1, 254	88	12
720–879 acres	3	813	5, 525	59	22	19	1	800	11, 553	82	18
880 acres or more	4	3, 240	6, 531	58	33	9	1	960	2, 050	64	36
Not specified	5	—	3, 530	93	—	7	—	—	—	—	—
SHERIDAN											
Total farms	55	261	2, 700	71	23	6	87	310	863	87	13
Less than 240 acres	26	152	1, 789	65	28	7	28	155	589	83	17
240–399 acres	17	293	2, 606	66	27	7	30	301	884	84	16
400–559 acres	6	443	6, 099	78	17	5	6	457	1, 336	92	8
560–719 acres	2	600	8, 360	90	10	—	5	661	1, 983	88	12
720–879 acres	1	764	650	—	100	—	3	747	1, 061	95	5
880 acres or more	—	—	—	—	—	—	1	960	20	—	100
Not specified	3	—	1, 241	75	24	1	14	—	779	92	8

See footnotes at end of table.

Table **22.**—Average Indebtedness of Farm Operators Receiving Relief [1] in Representative Counties in the Northern Great Plains, by Tenure, April–May 1935—Continued

County and size of farm	Owners						Tenants				
	Number of farms reporting	Average size of farm [2] (acres)	Average indebtedness	Kind of indebtedness (percent)			Number of farms reporting	Average size of farm [2] (acres)	Average indebtedness	Kind of indebtedness (percent)	
				Real-estate mortgages	Chattel mortgages	Other debts				Chattel mortgages	Other debts
HYDE											
Total farms	92	485	$4, 313	73	20	7	147	448	$917	76	24
Less than 280 acres	23	174	3, 008	66	29	5	30	157	566	81	19
280–439 acres	26	331	4, 064	76	15	9	42	329	1, 039	79	21
440–559 acres	12	486	5, 867	69	21	10	14	486	1, 233	76	24
560–719 acres	11	586	4, 415	79	13	8	12	636	661	70	30
720 acres or more	13	1, 227	7, 562	73	22	5	18	1, 053	2, 217	73	27
Not specified	7	—	678	86	—	14	31	—	292	70	30
MOODY											
Total farms	16	143	7, 225	90	4	6	74	197	1, 323	62	38
Less than 121 acres	5	53	1, 872	91	2	7	7	60	621	84	16
121–200 acres	5	157	6, 674	87	6	7	33	160	1, 264	52	48
201–280 acres	1	240	10, 015	85	3	12	15	230	940	76	24
281–360 acres	2	316	18, 548	95	1	4	13	322	1, 557	77	23
361–440 acres	1	370	19, 300	93	5	2	2	400	2, 528	60	40
441–520 acres	—	—	—	—	—	—	1	480	450	78	22
Not specified	2	—	3, 228	77	14	9	3	—	4, 005	—	100

[1] For whom reports were available.
[2] Reporting acreage.

Table 23.—Average Value of Farm Assets, Amount of Liabilities, and Net Worth of Selected Farmers in Representative Counties in the Northern Great Plains, by Tenure, 1935

Item	Owners						Tenants					
	Divide (48 farms)	Hettinger (46 farms)	Sheridan (37 farms)	Hyde (23 farms)	Traill (27 farms)	Moody (44 farms)	Divide (18 farms)	Hettinger (17 farms)	Sheridan (20 farms)	Hyde (25 farms)	Traill (25 farms)	Moody (43 farms)
Total assets	$8, 339	$8, 604	$10, 629	$12, 967	$14, 477	$13, 624	$1, 775	$1, 550	$1, 537	$1, 531	$3, 376	$2, 757
Real estate	6, 174	6, 290	7, 682	7, 831	9, 862	10, 369	—	—	—	—	—	—
Machinery	973	1, 024	967	753	1, 365	812	718	805	554	534	1, 547	892
Livestock	776	956	1, 257	2, 166	1, 658	1, 649	716	698	880	940	1, 132	1, 356
Farm products	40	73	71	52	127	29	5	3	10	16	102	13
Other	376	261	652	2, 165	1, 465	765	336	44	93	41	595	496
Total liabilities	4, 395	3, 861	3, 976	5, 476	5, 658	5, 731	1, 218	1, 121	985	1, 126	604	1, 018
Mortgages:												
Real estate	2, 859	2, 511	2, 839	3, 888	4, 747	4, 899	—	—	—	—	—	—
Chattel	1, 198	894	813	1, 138	576	284	1, 116	954	849	858	526	800
Delinquent taxes	175	97	124	198	30	20	31	39	19	27	1	13
Other debts	163	359	200	252	305	528	71	128	117	241	77	205
Net worth	3, 944	4, 743	6, 653	7, 491	8, 819	7, 893	557	429	552	405	2, 772	1, 739

Table 24.—Normal Gross Cash Receipts, Source of Receipts, and Adequacy of Income on Selected Farms in Representative Counties in the Central Great Plains, by Size of Farm

County and size of farm	Number of farms reporting	Normal gross cash receipts	Source of receipts (percent)			Adequacy of income		
			Crops	Livestock and livestock products	Work off farm	Number of farms reporting	Number of farms with income sufficient to meet expenses	Number of farms with income sufficient to increase capital
SHERMAN								
Total farms	[1] 55	$1,534	31	69	—	52	48	32
Less than 200 acres	30	1,148	25	75	—	27	26	20
200–279 acres	10	1,415	43	56	1	10	9	6
280–359 acres	9	1,833	29	71	—	9	8	3
360 acres or more	6	3,217	38	62	—	6	5	3
PERKINS								
Loam section								
Total farms	36	4,536	77	22	1	36	35	29
Less than 281 acres	—	—	—	—	—	—	—	—
281–400 acres	7	2,356	80	20	—	7	7	6
401–880 acres	20	3,865	76	23	1	20	19	15
881 acres or more	9	7,722	78	20	2	9	9	8
Sandy loam section								
Total farms	37	3,647	72	25	3	36	36	25
Less than 281 acres	6	1,375	75	19	6	6	6	2
281–400 acres	10	2,010	76	19	5	10	10	6
401–880 acres	12	4,541	71	25	4	11	11	10
881 acres or more	9	5,789	65	35	—	9	9	7
GOSHEN								
Irrigated section								
Total farms	29	4,972	77	22	1	29	29	23
Less than 101 acres	6	3,433	78	22	—	6	6	5
101–280 acres	14	4,914	79	19	2	14	14	9
281–460 acres	6	6,167	62	38	—	6	6	6
461–640 acres	2	5,900	90	10	—	2	2	2
641 acres or more	1	6,000	100	—	—	1	1	1
Nonirrigated section								
Total farms	43	2,534	70	26	4	43	41	36
Less than 101 acres	—	—	—	—	—	—	—	—
101–280 acres	2	900	58	42	—	2	2	1
281–460 acres	11	1,164	68	26	6	11	10	8
461–640 acres	7	1,771	76	21	3	7	6	5
641–960 acres	9	3,200	72	21	7	9	9	8
961 acres or more	14	3,796	68	31	1	14	14	14
CHEYENNE								
Total farms	[2] 55	1,798	49	51	—	55	53	48
Less than 400 acres	12	1,383	46	54	—	12	11	9
400–559 acres	11	1,362	68	32	—	11	10	9
560–719 acres	14	1,829	35	65	—	14	14	14
720 acres or more	18	2,317	51	49	—	18	18	16

[1] Data not available for 2 farms.
[2] Data not available for 1 farm.

***Table 25.*—Age of Farm Operators Receiving Relief [1] in Representative Counties in the Central Great Plains and Number Unable to Work,[2] April–May 1935**

Age	Sherman		Perkins		Goshen		Cheyenne	
	Number of farm operators	Number unable to work	Number of farm operators	Number unable to work	Number of farm operators	Number unable to work	Number of farm operators	Number unable to work
Total	272	9	52	1	193	20	193	4
Under 21 years	—	—	—	—	3	—	3	—
21–25 years	15	—	3	—	23	2	23	—
26–30 years	38	—	9	—	25	—	25	—
31–35 years	49	—	11	—	30	1	29	—
36–40 years	45	1	7	—	33	4	32	2
41–45 years	41	—	7	—	21	—	21	—
46–50 years	28	1	5	—	28	9	31	2
51–55 years	16	2	5	—	15	3	15	—
56–60 years	20	—	4	1	6	—	6	—
61 years and over	16	4	1	—	7	1	7	—
Unknown	4	1	—	—	2	—	1	—

[1] For whom reports were available.
[2] Based on disabilities reported.

***Table 26.*—Number of Children of Different Ages and Adult Members Other Than Parents in Farm Families Receiving Relief in Representative Counties in the Central Great Plains, April–May 1935**

County and item	Total families	Number of families with specified number of persons											
		None	1	2	3	4	5	6	7	8	9	10	11
SHERMAN													
Total children	272	35	49	50	39	36	22	22	9	4	2	3	1
Children under 16 years	272	58	50	60	39	27	15	15	5	3	—	—	—
Boys 16 years and over	272	208	42	14	4	3	1	—	—	—	—	—	—
Girls 16 years and over	272	213	34	21	4	—	—	—	—	—	—	—	—
Others	272	262	8	1	1	—	—	—	—	—	—	—	—
PERKINS													
Total children	[1] 44	3	10	9	11	8	1	—	1	1	—	—	—
Children under 16 years	44	9	10	10	7	5	1	—	1	1	—	—	—
Boys 16 years and over	44	33	9	2	—	—	—	—	—	—	—	—	—
Girls 16 years and over	44	36	7	1	—	—	—	—	—	—	—	—	—
Others	44	41	2	1	—	—	—	—	—	—	—	—	—
GOSHEN													
Total children	193	41	31	24	28	15	21	18	3	3	7	2	—
Children under 16 years	193	54	30	26	30	15	15	15	4	2	2	—	—
Children 16 years and over	193	145	17	16	8	3	4	—	—	—	—	—	—
Others	193	177	11	3	—	2	—	—	—	—	—	—	—
CHEYENNE													
Total children	218	36	40	48	29	25	14	11	5	5	2	3	—
Children under 16 years	218	72	39	40	25	23	12	3	3	—	1	—	—
Boys 16 years and over	218	145	45	17	5	3	2	1	—	—	—	—	—
Girls 16 years and over	218	173	29	12	3	1	—	—	—	—	—	—	—
Others	218	187	25	4	2	—	—	—	—	—	—	—	—

[1] Reports were available for only 44 of the 52 farm families receiving relief in April 1935.

86869°—38——12

Table 27.—Relative Importance of Different Causes of Crop Damage on Selected Farms in Representative Counties in the Central Great Plains, by Degree of Loss

County and cause of damage	Total number of records	Length of record			Percent of years			
		Less than 10 years	10–19 years	20 years or more	Damage was reported	Degree of loss was		
						Total	Serious	Slight
SHERMAN								
Drought					45	8	16	21
Hail					9	3	3	3
Soil blowing					6	2	2	2
Rust	57	13	21	23	5	—	1	4
Insects					2	*	—	2
Frost					2	1	1	*
Excessive precipitation					2	1	1	*
PERKINS								
Loam section								
Drought					47	14	15	18
Hail					21	3	6	12
Soil blowing					12	4	5	3
Rust	36	10	24	2	6	3	1	2
Insects					17	*	3	14
Frost					6	3	1	2
Excessive precipitation					3	1	1	1
Sandy loam section								
Drought					38	12	11	15
Hail					15	5	4	6
Soil blowing					10	4	3	3
Rust	37	13	19	5	4	3	1	*
Insects					9	2	4	3
Frost					8	3	2	3
Excessive precipitation					—	—	—	—
GOSHEN								
Irrigated section								
Drought					14	1	8	5
Hail					15	4	6	5
Soil blowing					8	—	3	5
Rust	29	7	14	8	2	—	—	2
Insects					20	—	7	13
Frost					9	1	2	6
Excessive precipitation					2	—	1	1
Nonirrigated section								
Drought					27	8	12	7
Hail					11	4	4	3
Soil blowing					15	4	6	5
Rust	43	6	21	16	6	1	2	3
Insects					5	1	2	2
Frost					4	1	2	1
Excessive precipitation					1	—	1	—
CHEYENNE								
Drought					52	20	18	14
Hail					21	4	5	12
Soil blowing					7	2	3	2
Rust	56	14	24	18	7	1	1	5
Insects					9	2	3	4
Frost					3	*	1	2
Excessive precipitation					6	*	2	4

*Less than 0.5 percent.

Table 28.—Average Annual Yield per Harvested Acre of Important Crops in Representative Counties in the Central Great Plains, 1910–1932

Year	Average yield per harvested acre (bushels)															
	Wheat				Barley				Oats				Corn			
	Sherman	Perkins	Goshen	Cheyenne	Sherman	Perkins	Goshen	Cheyenne	Sherman	Perkins	Goshen	Cheyenne	Sherman	Perkins	Goshen	Cheyenne
1910	13	8	—	—	—	10	—	—	26	8	—	—	26	10	—	—
1911	10	4	—	—	10	5	—	—	18	13	—	—	21	8	—	—
1912	16	9	—	—	18	12	—	—	19	18	—	—	20	30	—	—
1913	15	8	—	—	22	7	—	—	20	8	—	—	17	11	—	—
1914	18	13	—	—	24	25	—	—	34	25	—	—	26	24	—	—
1915	16	15	—	—	22	35	—	—	34	31	—	—	25	27	—	—
1916	18	19	—	—	25	20	—	—	31	27	—	—	23	21	—	—
1917	15	13	—	14	34	24	—	11	36	25	—	20	20	20	—	11
1918	11	12	—	—	21	22	—	—	24	21	—	—	20	28	—	—
1919	10	16	—	8	24	28	—	13	33	30	—	35	29	24	—	16
1920	9	16	—	12	21	29	—	20	30	32	—	18	33	24	—	20
1921	10	10	—	13	23	23	—	16	28	20	—	20	25	14	—	17
1922	12	11	10	13	15	15	25	8	20	15	25	14	18	20	24	18
1923	10	5	16	6	24	33	32	22	30	33	32	23	29	32	28	27
1924	20	18	13	13	23	27	32	21	31	26	30	14	24	17	13	6
1925	15	16	17	6	18	26	34	11	26	28	38	16	28	21	25	15
1926	10	11	16	5	11	11	32	6	15	15	31	4	10	7	22	3
1927	21	21	15	4	28	31	33	6	29	29	31	13	32	23	20	10
1928	16	19	14	9	26	33	28	19	29	33	28	18	13	20	18	10
1929	11	18	14	7	21	26	21	10	21	27	24	11	21	22	13	11
1930	20	19	13	10	28	27	20	13	28	35	15	17	28	27	21	19
1931	20	10	10	11	14	17	16	8	14	12	13	9	14	17	10	10
1932	12	8	—	7	14	21	—	7	14	20	—	4	14	21	—	3
Average yield for years reported	14.3	13.0	13.8	9.2	21.2	22.0	27.3	12.7	25.7	23.0	26.7	15.7	22.4	20.3	19.4	13.1

Sources: *Annual Reports*, Nebraska State Board of Agriculture, Lincoln, Nebr., 1913–1922; *Nebraska Agricultural Statistics*, Department of Agriculture, Lincoln, Nebr., 1923–1932; *Wyoming Agricultural Statistics*, State Department of Agriculture, Cheyenne, Wyo., 1923–1932; and *Yearbooks of the State of Colorado*, State Board of Immigration, Denver, Colo., 1918–1933.

***Table 29.*—Percent of Years Specified Crop Yield per Harvested Acre Was Obtained in Selected Areas in the Central Great Plains, 1905–1934**

Crop and area	Period included	Total reports		Yield per harvested acre								
		Number	Percent	Less than 2.5 bushels	2.5–7.4 bushels	7.5–12.4 bushels	12.5–17.4 bushels	17.5–22.4 bushels	22.5–27.4 bushels	27.5–32.4 bushels	32.5–37.4 bushels	37.5 bushels or more
WHEAT												
Central Nebraska [1]	1910–1932	184	100.0	—	2	38	43	17	—	—	—	—
Southwestern Nebraska [2]	1910–1932	115	100.0	—	8	32	24	25	11	—	—	—
Southeastern Wyoming [3]	1922–1931	50	100.0	—	6	36	58	—	—	—	—	—
Western Kansas [4]	1911–1932	176	100.0	6	33	31	21	8	1	—	—	—
BARLEY												
Central Nebraska [1]	1911–1932	169	100.0	—	1	8	12	30	30	15	4	—
Southwestern Nebraska [2]	1910–1932	115	100.0	—	3	6	14	18	26	19	10	4
Southeastern Wyoming [3]	1922–1931	50	100.0	—	—	8	12	22	24	26	8	—
Western Kansas [4]	1905–1932	224	100.0	4	10	21	24	21	12	6	1	1
OATS												
Central Nebraska [1]	1910–1932	183	100.0	—	1	2	12	14	24	29	15	3
Southwestern Nebraska [2]	1910–1932	115	100.0	—	—	6	12	20	15	21	11	15
Southeastern Wyoming [3]	1922–1931	50	100.0	—	—	4	20	12	24	34	4	2
Western Kansas [4]	1905–1932	222	100.0	15	6	16	18	18	17	8	1	1
CORN												
Central Nebraska [1]	1910–1932	184	100.0	—	1	4	13	27	35	13	6	1
Southwestern Nebraska [2]	1910–1932	115	100.0	—	3	13	14	24	29	11	5	1
Southeastern Wyoming [3]	1922–1931	50	100.0	—	2	16	24	34	18	6	—	—
Western Kansas [4]	1905–1934	224	100.0	10	16	25	23	16	4	4	2	—

[1] Central Nebraska Area includes Custer, Dawson, Garfield, Greeley, Loup, Sherman, Valley, and Wheeler Counties.
[2] Southwestern Nebraska Area includes Chase, Cheyenne, Deuel, Keith, and Perkins Counties.
[3] Southeastern Wyoming Area includes Converse, Goshen, Laramie, Niobrara, and Platte Counties.
[4] Western Kansas Area includes Finney, Greeley, Hamilton, Kearny, Logan, Scott, Wallace, and Wichita Counties. This area is adjacent to Cheyenne County, Colo., 1 of the sample counties.

Sources: *Annual Reports*, Nebraska State Board of Agriculture, Lincoln, Nebr., 1913–1922; *Nebraska Agricultural Statistics*, Department of Agriculture, Lincoln, Nebr., 1923–1932; *Wyoming Agricultural Statistics*, State Department of Agriculture, Cheyenne, Wyo., 1923–1932; and *Biennial Reports*, Kansas State Board of Agriculture, Topeka, Kans., 1905–1906 and 1933–1934.

Table 30.—**Average Yield per Seeded Acre of Important Crops on Selected Farms in Representative Counties in the Central Great Plains and Frequency of Occurrence of Yields Which Were Good, Medium, Poor, or Failures**

Crop and county	Number of crops reported	Yield per seeded acre (bushels)				Percent of years yield was obtained				Average yield per acre (bushels)
		Good	Medium	Poor	Failure	Good	Medium	Poor	Failure	
WHEAT										
Sherman	559	26	17	8	2	15	53	20	12	15
Perkins:										
Loam section	420	26	15	9	4	23	36	21	20	14
Sandy loam section	320	24	14	8	3	20	40	19	21	13
Goshen:										
Irrigated section	34	34	23	13	6	15	53	17	15	20
Nonirrigated section	429	24	14	8	4	18	42	20	20	13
Cheyenne	138	19	9	5	2	14	25	15	46	7
BARLEY										
Sherman	560	36	26	11	2	18	53	14	15	22
Perkins:										
Loam section	292	35	19	11	6	24	32	19	25	18
Sandy loam section	163	33	21	14	4	15	40	19	26	17
Goshen:										
Irrigated section	207	68	45	25	—	24	52	24	—	46
Nonirrigated section	223	31	17	9	4	16	45	24	15	15
Cheyenne	406	25	14	9	6	16	34	18	32	12
OATS										
Sherman	767	42	27	13	3	18	51	19	12	24
Perkins:										
Loam section	273	42	24	12	5	23	37	19	21	22
Sandy loam section	186	38	23	12	5	28	35	18	19	22
Goshen:										
Irrigated section	126	72	58	35	—	32	40	28	—	56
Nonirrigated section	295	33	20	14	4	20	44	21	15	19
Cheyenne	16	25	13	5	3	13	25	6	56	8
CORN										
Sherman	808	38	24	11	2	22	48	19	11	22
Perkins:										
Loam section	417	31	21	11	4	24	39	21	16	18
Sandy loam section	384	34	21	12	5	24	45	15	16	20
Goshen:										
Irrigated section	57	48	40	10	—	25	44	31	—	33
Nonirrigated section	489	26	17	9	4	17	52	18	13	15
Cheyenne	798	24	13	8	5	22	28	19	31	12

Table 31.—Average Yield per Seeded Acre of Important Crops on Selected Farms in Representative Counties in the Central Great Plains, 1930–1934

County and year	Number of farms reporting	Average yield per seeded acre							
		Bushels					Tons		
		Wheat	Barley	Oats	Corn	Potatoes	Alfalfa	Sugar beets	Cane
SHERMAN									
1930	10	18.6	—	20.9	21.2	[1]	1.9	[1]	[1]
1931	25	13.2	14.8	19.2	17.4	[1]	2.1	[1]	[1]
1932	49	15.2	19.9	25.4	18.1	[1]	1.5	[1]	[1]
1933	55	9.7	8.2	10.7	18.4	[1]	1.2	[1]	[1]
1934	57	*	—	*	0.2	[1]	0.2	[1]	[1]
PERKINS									
Loam section									
1930	24	22.9	30.3	24.7	25.5	[1]	0.9	[1]	[1]
1931	27	9.4	13.2	24.5	18.3	[1]	0.9	[1]	[1]
1932	31	9.1	9.2	8.7	15.8	[1]	0.8	[1]	[1]
1933	35	5.6	3.9	5.1	13.4	[1]	0.7	[1]	[1]
1934	36	3.9	2.0	3.0	0.4	[1]	0.1	[1]	[1]
Sandy loam section									
1930	26	16.5	19.3	29.3	29.5	[1]	1.2	[1]	[1]
1931	29	7.4	19.1	14.9	21.3	[1]	0.8	[1]	[1]
1932	32	6.6	11.7	18.5	18.7	[1]	0.5	[1]	[1]
1933	35	4.8	3.8	5.5	14.4	[1]	0.3	[1]	[1]
1934	37	4.2	2.1	3.7	0.8	[1]	*	[1]	[1]
GOSHEN									
Irrigated section									
1930	23	1.8	48.8	39.7	33.8	311	2.6	13.1	[1]
1931	24	5.4	50.6	66.3	14.8	345	2.4	13.4	[1]
1932	28	7.3	44.8	54.3	30.3	320	2.1	12.1	[1]
1933	29	25.0	36.7	51.0	24.3	213	2.0	12.2	[1]
1934	29	6.9	26.6	21.5	6.4	89	1.7	9.5	[1]
Nonirrigated section									
1930	30	19.8	23.0	19.0	19.0	259	2.1	[1]	[1]
1931	39	6.3	16.6	15.9	13.4	134	1.9	[1]	[1]
1932	42	8.7	10.6	15.5	8.8	183	1.5	[1]	[1]
1933	43	5.7	7.9	7.1	9.5	111	1.4	[1]	[1]
1934	43	2.1	0.2	0.7	0.6	63	1.3	[1]	[1]
CHEYENNE									
1930	39	3.9	16.1	—	15.5	[1]	[1]	[1]	0.8
1931	51	6.7	11.7	—	11.1	[1]	[1]	[1]	0.6
1932	54	6.8	8.5	—	5.0	[1]	[1]	[1]	0.5
1933	56	4.6	4.9	—	11.6	[1]	[1]	[1]	1.4
1934	56	2.7	0.5	—	0.2	[1]	[1]	[1]	0.4

*Less than 0.05 bushel or ton.

[1] Not calculated.

Table 32.—Financial Progress of Selected Farmers in Representative Counties in the Central Great Plains Since Beginning Farming in the Area, by Size of Farm, 1935

County and size of farm	Number of farms reporting	Financial status at beginning			Capital additions to business			Net put into business	Financial status in 1935			Average increase per farm	
		Assets	Liabilities	Net worth	Additions	Deductions	Net additions		Assets	Liabilities	Net worth	Total	Per year
SHERMAN													
Total farms	57	$1,824	$831	$993	$1,461	$764	$697	$1,690	$4,316	$2,735	$1,581	−$109	−$7
Less than 200 acres	31	2,024	927	1,097	1,181	361	820	1,917	3,123	1,867	1,256	−661	−41
200–279 acres	11	836	379	457	1,445	291	1,154	1,611	2,164	2,062	102	−1,509	−92
280–359 acres	9	2,192	364	1,828	2,316	132	2,184	4,012	6,269	3,383	2,886	−1,126	−80
360 acres or more	6	2,050	1,862	188	1,650	4,653	−3,003	−2,815	11,499	7,484	4,015	6,830	293
PERKINS													
Loam section													
Total farms	36	8,613	1,647	6,966	1,011	2,516	−1,505	5,461	14,783	5,367	9,416	3,955	288
Less than 281 acres	—	—	—	—	—	—	—	—	—	—	—	—	—
281–400 acres	7	10,714	1,286	9,428	—	4,250	−4,250	5,178	5,723	2,357	3,366	−1,812	−136
401–880 acres	20	6,180	840	5,340	1,647	1,699	−52	5,288	12,943	4,750	8,193	2,905	238
881 acres or more	9	12,389	3,722	8,667	383	2,984	−2,601	6,066	25,920	9,078	16,842	10,776	614
Sandy loam section													
Total farms	37	4,467	696	3,771	850	1,122	−272	3,499	10,618	5,001	5,617	2,118	156
Less than 281 acres	6	2,013	333	1,680	183	623	−440	1,240	3,524	1,958	1,566	326	19
281–400 acres	10	1,860	188	1,672	755	687	68	1,740	5,114	2,778	2,336	596	50
401–880 acres	12	3,250	508	2,742	1,016	899	117	2,859	8,901	2,724	6,177	3,318	265
881 acres or more	9	10,622	1,755	8,867	1,178	2,233	−1,055	7,812	23,752	12,535	11,217	3,405	236
GOSHEN													
Irrigated section													
Total farms	29	2,324	73	2,251	1,005	1,385	−380	1,871	8,816	3,091	5,725	3,854	244
Less than 101 acres	6	2,537	—	2,537	417	517	−100	2,437	5,865	1,557	4,308	1,871	105
101–280 acres	14	2,361	2	2,359	1,321	1,485	−164	2,195	9,054	2,777	6,277	4,082	290
281–460 acres	6	2,269	350	1,919	858	2,362	−1,504	415	9,084	4,849	4,235	3,820	189
461–640 acres	2	2,250	—	2,250	1,250	1,050	200	2,450	17,109	5,395	11,714	9,264	713
641 acres or more	1	1,000	—	1,000	500	—	500	1,500	5,010	1,530	3,480	1,980	248

Table 32.—Financial Progress of Selected Farmers in Representative Counties in the Central Great Plains Since Beginning Farming in the Area, by Size of Farm, 1935—Continued

County and size of farm	Number of farms reporting	Financial status at beginning			Capital additions to business			Net put into business	Financial status in 1935			Average increase per farm	
		Assets	Liabilities	Net worth	Additions	Deductions	Net additions		Assets	Liabilities	Net worth	Total	Per year
GOSHEN—continued													
Nonirrigated section													
Total farms	43	$1, 546	$52	$1, 494	$827	$1, 109	−$282	$1, 212	$7, 057	$2, 417	$4, 640	$3, 428	$198
Less than 101 acres	—	—	—	—	—	—	—	—	—	—	—	—	—
101–280 acres	2	425	—	425	5, 500	50	5, 450	5, 875	3, 249	525	2, 724	−3, 151	−197
281–460 acres	11	1, 309	93	1, 216	355	1, 141	−786	430	3, 368	1, 423	1, 945	1, 515	86
461–640 acres	7	1, 086	47	1, 039	1, 200	1, 420	−220	819	5, 605	1, 964	3, 641	2, 822	165
641–960 acres	9	2, 839	—	2, 839	305	646	−341	2, 498	6, 086	1, 773	4, 313	1, 815	126
961 acres or more	14	1, 292	64	1, 228	679	1, 379	−700	528	11, 851	4, 110	7, 741	7, 213	378
CHEYENNE													
Second-grade land													
Total farms	46	5, 949	453	5, 496	428	835	−407	5, 089	5, 096	1, 649	3, 447	−1, 642	−103
Less than 400 acres	11	4, 016	501	3, 515	446	330	116	3, 631	3, 100	1, 500	1, 600	−2, 031	−168
400–559 acres	10	9, 640	50	9, 590	20	515	−495	9, 095	5, 224	1, 232	3, 992	−5, 103	−325
560–719 acres	12	8, 396	813	7, 583	800	1, 458	−658	6, 925	5, 710	1, 639	4, 071	−2, 854	−141
720 acres or more	13	2, 487	392	2, 095	384	933	−549	1, 546	6, 118	2, 105	4, 013	2, 467	162
Third-grade land													
Total farms	10	1, 105	85	1, 020	600	421	179	1, 199	5, 181	1, 639	3, 542	2, 343	117
Less than 400 acres	2	1, 150	200	950	2, 000	—	2, 000	2, 950	4, 912	3, 820	1, 092	−1, 858	−162
400–559 acres	1	200	—	200	—	—	—	200	2, 260	1, 200	1, 060	860	43
560–719 acres	2	3, 075	75	3, 000	—	—	—	3, 000	9, 710	2, 554	7, 156	4, 156	189
720 acres or more	5	480	60	420	400	842	−442	−22	4, 061	489	3, 572	3, 594	158

Table 33.—Size of Farm, Number of Livestock per Farm, and Tenure of Farm Operators Receiving Relief [1] in Representative Counties in the Central Great Plains, April–May 1935

County and size of farm	Number of farms reporting	Average size of farm (acres)	Average number of livestock				Tenure of operator		
			Cattle	Hogs	Chickens	Horses	Owner	Tenant	Unknown
SHERMAN									
Total farms	220	200	9	10	97	5	48	172	—
Less than 61 acres	9	18	4	4	57	2	3	6	—
61–100 acres	7	79	9	4	49	4	3	4	—
101–140 acres	5	122	5	3	69	3	2	3	—
141–180 acres	125	160	9	9	101	5	30	95	—
181 acres or more	74	305	12	12	101	6	10	64	—
PERKINS									
Total farms	51	212	4	1	33	1	9	41	1
Less than 61 acres	10	12	3	1	30	1	3	6	1
61–100 acres	—	—	—	—	—	—	—	—	—
101–140 acres	2	115	4	1	7	1	2	—	—
141–180 acres	16	161	3	1	30	2	3	13	—
181 acres or more	23	349	5	2	39	2	1	22	—
GOSHEN									
Total farms	119	411	6	1	30	3	45	70	4
Less than 81 acres	15	62	2	1	16	1	3	10	2
81–260 acres	28	157	4	2	22	2	9	18	1
261–400 acres	43	328	5	1	37	2	16	27	—
401–580 acres	7	486	10	1	27	6	3	3	1
581–800 acres	14	657	15	1	41	5	8	6	—
801 acres or more	12	1,410	8	1	33	4	6	6	—
CHEYENNE									
Total farms	202	403	26	2	58	5	72	129	1
Less than 400 acres	133	275	23	2	55	5	50	83	—
400–559 acres	16	458	27	3	46	5	3	13	—
560–719 acres	34	639	33	3	67	6	10	23	1
720 acres or more	18	857	41	4	77	7	8	10	—
Unknown	1	—	28	—	36	1	1	—	—

[1] For whom reports were available.

Table 34.—Utilization of Land on Farms Having Corn-Hog Contracts in Representative Counties in the Central Great Plains, by Size of Farm, 1934

County and size of farm	Number of farms	Number owned	Average number of acres per farm				
			Total	Cropland	Native grass		Other
					Hay	Pasture	
SHERMAN							
Total farms	1,097	433	248	144	16	75	13
Less than 200 acres	540	212	147	95	6	38	8
200–279 acres	167	60	231	141	13	65	12
280–359 acres	233	89	317	183	23	95	16
360 acres or more	157	72	512	260	44	183	25
PERKINS							
Total farms	798	305	577	428	9	107	33
Less than 281 acres	174	53	158	126	*	19	13
281–440 acres	190	54	337	268	3	50	16
441–880 acres	293	112	618	480	11	94	33
881 acres or more	141	86	1,330	908	23	320	79
GOSHEN							
Irrigated section							
Total farms	175	103	201	120	1	64	16
Less than 101 acres	40	21	70	51	—	11	8
101–280 acres	102	61	176	114	1	43	18
281–460 acres	22	15	351	190	*	144	17
461–640 acres	9	4	583	307	2	243	31
641 acres or more	2	2	740	221	—	514	5
Nonirrigated section							
Total farms	395	288	724	269	8	430	17
Less than 101 acres	2	1	3	—	—	2	1
101–280 acres	27	16	190	121	*	58	11
281–460 acres	131	88	343	190	*	138	15
461–640 acres	95	73	581	253	5	309	14
641–960 acres	65	52	846	270	9	548	19
961 acres or more	75	58	1,680	489	27	1,138	26
CHEYENNE							
Total farms	397	258	548	291	—	249	8
Less than 281 acres	47	23	179	125	—	48	6
281–440 acres	169	115	323	179	—	138	6
441–880 acres	121	71	634	340	—	282	12
881 acres or more	60	49	1,303	635	—	656	12

*Less than 0.5 acre.

Source: Corn-hog production control contracts of the Agricultural Adjustment Administration.

Table 35.—Utilization of Land on Selected Farms in Representative Counties in the Central Great Plains, by Size of Farm, 1934

County and size of farm	Number of farms reporting	Average number of acres per farm					
		Total	Crop-land	Native grass		Former crop-land	Farm-stead and waste
				Hay	Pasture		
SHERMAN							
Total farms	57	241	144	15	74	—	8
Less than 200 acres	31	161	108	6	41	—	6
200–279 acres	11	243	151	10	74	—	8
280–359 acres	9	321	191	21	93	—	16
360 acres or more	6	532	239	71	212	—	10
PERKINS							
Loam section							
Total farms	36	714	588	1	94	—	31
Less than 281 acres	—	—	—	—	—	—	—
281–400 acres	7	320	260	1	47	—	12
401–880 acres	20	626	556	1	45	—	24
881 acres or more	9	1, 215	913	1	239	—	62
Sandy loam section							
Total farms	37	619	465	3	126	10	15
Less than 281 acres	6	219	149	3	58	—	9
281–400 acres	10	323	255	4	48	—	16
401–880 acres	12	630	491	2	111	9	17
881 acres or more	9	1, 199	873	4	276	29	17
GOSHEN							
Irrigated section							
Total farms	29	276	122	3	120	7	24
Less than 101 acres	6	83	58	1	9	—	15
101–280 acres	14	173	115	—	28	8	22
281–460 acres	6	360	163	11	157	9	20
461–640 acres	2	560	178	—	294	25	63
641 acres or more	1	1, 820	250	—	1, 518	—	52
Nonirrigated section							
Total farms	43	959	410	1	505	17	26
Less than 101 acres	—	—	—	—	—	—	—
101–280 acres	2	174	115	—	56	—	3
281–460 acres	11	340	200	—	121	—	19
461–640 acres	7	634	295	—	313	1	25
641–960 acres	9	865	414	3	420	10	18
961 acres or more	14	1, 780	671	—	1, 023	46	40
CHEYENNE							
Total farms	56	666	327	—	310	7	22
Less than 400 acres	13	307	184	—	109	—	14
400–559 acres	11	454	256	—	174	6	18
560–719 acres	14	641	296	—	299	18	28
720 acres or more	18	1, 071	495	—	544	6	26

***Table 36.*—Percent of Owned and Rented Land in Crops and Grass on Selected Farms in Representative Counties in the Central Great Plains, 1934**

Item	Sherman (57 farms)	Perkins		Goshen		Cheyenne	
		Loam section (36 farms)	Sandy loam section (37 farms)	Irrigated section (29 farms)	Non-irrigated section (43 farms)	Second-grade land (46 farms)	Third-grade land (10 farms)
Total operated land [1]	100	100	100	100	100	100	100
Cropland	59	82	79	45	43	50	49
Hay and pasture	37	13	17	44	53	46	46
Other	4	5	4	11	4	4	5
Total owned land	24	42	43	54	59	42	41
Cropland	16	35	34	29	27	22	20
Hay and pasture	7	5	7	17	28	18	19
Other	1	2	2	8	4	2	2
Total share-rented land	54	51	49	28	21	52	52
Cropland	38	47	45	17	14	27	27
Hay and pasture	14	2	2	8	7	23	22
Other	2	2	2	3	*	2	3
Total cash-rented land	24	11	10	20	21	7	8
Cropland	7	5	3	1	3	1	2
Hay and pasture	16	5	7	19	18	6	6
Other	1	1	*	—	*	*	*
Free land	—	1	1	—	—	—	—
Hay and pasture	—	1	1	—	—	—	—
Land rented out	2	5	3	2	1	1	1
Cropland	2	5	3	2	1	*	*
Hay and pasture	—	—	—	—	*	1	1
Other	—	*	*	—	—	*	—

*Less than 0.5 percent.

[1] Total operated land is the sum of owned, rented, and free land less land rented out.

***Table 37.*—Use of Farm Land on Selected Farms in Representative Counties in the Central Great Plains, 1934**

Use of farm land	Average number of acres per farm					
	Sherman (57 farms)	Perkins		Goshen		Cheyenne (56 farms)
		Loam section (36 farms)	Sandy loam section (37 farms)	Irrigated section (29 farms)	Nonirrigated section (43 farms)	
Total land operated	241	714	619	276	959	666
Total cropland	144	588	465	122	[1] 410	327
Wheat	12	228	148	3	74	13
Wheat on fallow	—	26	5	—	77	—
Barley	8	34	16	14	14	25
Oats	25	16	9	9	15	—
Rye	1	2	4	*	3	—
Corn	63	131	167	5	49	133
Tame hay	17	2	8	31	2	1
Feed crops	—	26	24	—	10	96
Other crops	5	1	2	[2] 49	31	6
Annual pasture	2	8	7	2	—	—
Fallow	—	89	36	1	105	4
Idle cropland	11	25	39	8	45	49
Former cropland	—	—	10	7	17	7
Native hay	15	1	3	3	1	—
Native pasture	74	94	126	120	505	310
Farmstead and waste	8	31	15	24	26	22

*Less than 0.5 acre.

[1] Total crop acreage exceeds cropland by 15 acres because of reseeded wheat.
[2] Includes 34 acres of sugar beets and 9 acres of potatoes.

Table 38.—Average Acreage of Important Crops on Selected Farms [1] in Representative Counties in the Central Great Plains, 1930–1934

County and year	Number of farms reporting	Average number of acres per farm							
		Wheat	Barley	Oats	Corn	Potatoes	Alfalfa	Sugar beets	Cane
SHERMAN									
1930	10	11	1	17	59	[2]	11	[2]	[2]
1931	25	12	9	23	80	[2]	10	[2]	[2]
1932	49	13	9	21	78	[2]	14	[2]	[2]
1933	55	11	7	22	79	[2]	14	[2]	[2]
1934	57	12	8	25	63	[2]	15	[2]	[2]
PERKINS									
Loam section									
1930	24	350	33	28	93	[2]	3	[2]	[2]
1931	27	337	33	29	125	[2]	2	[2]	[2]
1932	31	246	45	34	201	[2]	2	[2]	[2]
1933	35	255	47	39	175	[2]	2	[2]	[2]
1934	36	254	34	16	131	[2]	2	[2]	[2]
Sandy loam section									
1930	26	190	17	10	144	[2]	6	[2]	[2]
1931	29	171	26	12	176	[2]	3	[2]	[2]
1932	32	145	14	12	231	[2]	3	[2]	[2]
1933	35	146	20	15	212	[2]	4	[2]	[2]
1934	37	153	16	9	167	[2]	3	[2]	[2]
GOSHEN									
Irrigated section									
1930	23	2	14	7	3	8	34	28	[2]
1931	24	4	12	8	7	8	33	31	[2]
1932	28	3	13	7	6	9	32	32	[2]
1933	29	1	15	7	7	8	32	36	[2]
1934	29	3	14	9	5	9	31	34	[2]
Nonirrigated section									
1930	30	115	18	13	44	9	4	[2]	[2]
1931	39	179	19	9	50	9	3	[2]	[2]
1932	42	160	33	8	70	8	3	[2]	[2]
1933	43	150	32	19	73	8	3	[2]	[2]
1934	43	151	14	15	49	8	2	[2]	[2]
CHEYENNE									
1930	39	4	38	—	118	[2]	[2]	[2]	9
1931	51	2	35	—	169	[2]	[2]	[2]	10
1932	54	4	34	—	155	[2]	[2]	[2]	10
1933	56	4	53	—	163	[2]	[2]	[2]	9
1934	56	13	25	—	133	[2]	[2]	[2]	21

[1] Reporting acreage.
[2] Not calculated.

Table 39.—Number of Livestock on Hand April 1, 1935, and Normal Number on Selected Farms in Representative Counties in the Central Great Plains, by Size of Farm

County and size of farm	Average number of livestock																			
	All cattle		Milk cows		Beef cows		Other cattle		All hogs		Brood sows		Other hogs		Sheep		Poultry		Work stock	
	April 1, 1935	Normal	April 1, 1935	Normal	April 1, 1935	Normal	April 1, 1935	Normal	April 1, 1935	Normal	April 1, 1935	Normal	April 1, 1935	Normal	April 1, 1935	Normal	April 1, 1935	Normal	April 1, 1935	Normal
SHERMAN																				
Total farms	15	22	7	10	—	1	8	11	7	37	4	7	3	30	—	—	89	146	5	6
Less than 200 acres	12	16	6	8	—	—	6	8	5	26	2	6	3	20	—	—	83	129	5	5
200–279 acres	13	23	8	12	—	1	5	10	7	23	5	6	2	17	—	—	74	133	6	6
280–359 acres	21	26	8	9	1	2	12	15	6	46	4	8	2	38	—	—	113	186	7	8
360 acres or more	26	37	11	16	3	3	12	18	8	113	6	14	2	99	—	—	111	201	6	7
PERKINS																				
Loam section																				
Total farms	20	21	6	6	2	2	12	13	10	29	3	9	7	20	5	5	102	148	3	5
Less than 281 acres	—	—	—	—	—	—	—	—	—	—	—	—	—	—	—	—	—	—	—	—
281–400 acres	16	14	6	7	1	—	9	7	3	11	2	5	1	6	—	—	127	224	3	6
401–880 acres	18	19	6	7	1	1	11	11	11	33	3	9	8	24	—	—	101	139	3	4
881 acres or more	31	32	7	7	7	7	17	18	14	31	5	15	9	16	20	16	88	109	4	7
Sandy loam section																				
Total farms	23	31	7	7	4	5	12	19	8	38	3	10	5	28	—	—	88	106	5	5
Less than 281 acres	9	12	5	6	—	—	4	6	1	14	1	5	—	9	—	—	63	131	5	5
281–400 acres	12	14	6	6	—	—	6	8	4	18	3	7	1	11	—	—	51	67	3	3
401–880 acres	18	20	5	6	3	2	10	12	6	28	2	10	4	18	1	1	71	93	4	4
881 acres or more	46	72	9	10	12	16	25	46	18	91	5	18	13	73	1	—	165	149	10	01

Table 39.—Number of Livestock on Hand April 1, 1935, and Normal Number on Selected Farms in Representative Counties in the Central Great Plains, by Size of Farm—Continued

County and size of farm	Average number of livestock																			
	All cattle		Milk cows		Beef cows		Other cattle		All hogs		Brood sows		Other hogs		Sheep		Poultry		Work stock	
	April 1, 1935	Normal	April 1, 1935	Normal	April 1, 1935	Normal	April 1, 1935	Normal	April 1, 1935	Normal	April 1, 1935	Normal	April 1, 1935	Normal	April 1, 1935	Normal	April 1, 1935	Normal	April 1, 1935	Normal
GOSHEN																				
Irrigated section																				
Total farms	20	20	8	8	1	4	11	8	5	7	1	3	4	4	16	11	77	96	5	5
Less than 101 acres	5	6	3	4	—	—	2	2	—	4	—	2	—	2	—	—	74	130	4	4
101–280 acres	12	14	6	6	—	4	6	4	5	6	2	3	3	3	—	—	80	91	4	5
281–460 acres	31	29	11	12	2	6	21	11	1	1	—	1	1	—	55	40	80	82	7	7
461–640 acres	65	65	29	29	—	—	36	36	29	29	6	6	23	23	—	—	40	100	11	12
641 acres or more	—	—	—	—	—	—	—	—	—	—	—	—	—	—	—	—	—	—	—	—
Nonirrigated section																				
Total farms	19	22	5	7	5	7	9	8	3	12	1	5	2	7	—	—	70	116	4	5
Less than 101 acres	—	—	—	—	—	—	—	—	—	—	—	—	—	—	—	—	—	—	—	—
101–280 acres	10	6	4	4	—	—	6	2	1	2	1	2	—	—	—	—	48	75	3	5
281–460 acres	8	16	5	8	—	1	3	7	1	18	1	6	—	12	—	—	42	107	3	5
461–640 acres	8	21	3	11	—	—	5	13	—	12	—	2	—	10	—	—	78	203	5	5
641–960 acres	14	17	4	6	2	3	8	8	2	7	1	5	1	2	—	—	53	72	5	5
961 acres or more	40	36	6	6	15	20	19	10	7	14	1	6	6	8	—	—	111	145	5	6
CHEYENNE																				
Total farms	42	48	7	8	11	15	24	25	3	13	1	3	2	10	13	—	81	120	7	9
Less than 400 acres	29	34	5	7	6	9	18	18	2	9	1	2	1	7	—	—	64	99	6	7
400–559 acres	36	41	5	7	9	10	22	24	3	5	1	2	2	3	—	—	82	120	5	6
560–719 acres	50	66	5	8	18	26	27	32	1	24	—	5	1	19	53	1	71	111	11	13
720 acres or more	47	50	10	11	10	15	27	24	4	13	1	3	3	10	—	—	101	141	8	9

Table 40.—Number of Selected Farms With Livestock in Representative Counties in the Central Great Plains, April 1, 1935

Number of livestock	Number of farms reporting				
			Goshen		
	Sherman (57 farms)	Perkins (73 farms)	Irrigated section (29 farms)	Nonirrigated section (43 farms)	Cheyenne (56 farms)
MILK COWS					
None	2	4	2	8	13
1–5	19	30	13	16	16
6 or more	36	39	14	19	27
BEEF COWS					
None	55	58	20	31	28
1–5	—	5	3	4	3
6–15	1	5	3	2	9
16 or more	1	5	3	6	16
OTHER CATTLE					
None	—	1	—	3	1
1–10	22	29	11	15	6
11–25	25	23	7	15	21
26–50	10	13	7	6	12
51 or more	—	7	4	4	16
BROOD SOWS					
None	12	29	19	26	37
1–3	18	26	7	13	16
4 or more	27	18	3	4	3
OTHER HOGS					
None	22	36	13	27	41
1–5	26	13	10	12	9
6 or more	9	24	6	4	6
SHEEP					
None	57	69	28	41	55
1–10	—	2	—	2	—
11–50	—	1	—	—	—
51 or more	—	1	1	—	1
CHICKENS					
None	3	1	1	2	—
1–50	14	21	13	18	22
51–100	24	32	9	15	21
101 or more	16	19	6	8	13
WORK STOCK					
None	1	6	—	7	4
1–6	39	54	21	27	31
7 or more	17	13	8	9	21

Table 41.—Utilization of Labor on Selected Farms in Representative Counties in the Central Great Plains, by Size of Farm, 1934

County and size of farm	Number of farms reporting	Labor employed regularly (months)				Extra hired labor (days)
		Total	Operator	Family	Hired	
SHERMAN						
Total farms	57	17.0	11.8	4.7	0.5	6
Less than 200 acres	31	14.6	12.0	2.6	—	3
200–279 acres	11	15.0	12.0	2.7	0.3	9
280–359 acres	9	18.3	12.0	6.3	—	9
360 acres or more	6	30.2	10.0	16.2	4.0	16
PERKINS						
Loam section						
Total farms	36	21.6	10.9	8.4	2.3	33
Less than 281 acres	—	—	—	—	—	—
281–400 acres	7	13.1	11.0	2.1	—	23
401–880 acres	20	20.5	10.9	9.2	0.4	29
881 acres or more	9	30.3	10.9	11.3	8.1	51
Sandy loam section						
Total farms	37	16.4	10.8	4.1	1.5	38
Less than 281 acres	6	10.7	10.7	—	—	18
281–400 acres	10	15.1	10.5	4.6	—	18
401–880 acres	12	14.7	10.8	2.6	1.3	21
881 acres or more	9	23.7	11.1	8.1	4.5	95
GOSHEN						
Irrigated section						
Total farms	29	23.3	11.3	4.1	7.9	100
Less than 101 acres	6	19.5	12.0	3.0	4.5	19
101–280 acres	14	23.1	10.9	3.6	8.6	144
281–460 acres	6	27.3	11.5	8.3	7.5	77
461–640 acres	2	18.0	12.0	—	6.0	110
641 acres or more	1	36.0	12.0	—	24.0	80
Nonirrigated section						
Total farms	43	15.2	10.7	4.1	0.4	25
Less than 101 acres	—	—	—	—	—	—
101–280 acres	2	12.0	12.0	—	—	—
281–460 acres	11	12.6	9.6	3.0	—	5
461–640 acres	7	14.4	11.1	2.0	1.3	24
641–960 acres	9	16.7	10.2	6.5	—	4
961 acres or more	14	17.2	11.6	5.0	0.6	60
CHEYENNE						
Total farms	56	19.4	11.7	6.7	1.0	16
Less than 400 acres	13	16.0	11.1	4.9	—	9
400–559 acres	11	15.9	11.5	2.2	2.2	17
560–719 acres	14	22.0	10.9	9.6	1.5	5
720 acres or more	18	23.2	[1] 12.6	10.0	0.6	29

[1] 1 farm operated by 2 brothers.

Table 42.—Average Value of Farm Buildings and Estimated Cost of Needed Repairs per Farm on Selected Farms in Representative Counties in the Central Great Plains, by Size of Farm, 1935

County and size of farm	Number of farms reporting		Value of buildings			Cost of needed repairs		
	Total	Owned	Total	Dwelling	Other	Total	Dwelling	Other
SHERMAN								
Total farms	57	12	$2, 592	$1, 314	$1, 278	$270	$117	$153
Less than 200 acres	31	5	2, 218	1, 140	1, 078	217	102	115
200–279 acres	11	1	2, 737	1, 523	1, 214	191	36	155
280–359 acres	9	3	2, 437	1, 056	1, 381	343	160	183
360 acres or more	6	3	4, 488	2, 217	2, 271	581	283	298
PERKINS								
Loam section								
Total farms	36	22	4, 142	1, 643	2, 499	89	36	53
Less than 281 acres	—	—	—	—	—	—	—	—
281–400 acres	7	3	3, 241	1, 239	2, 002	128	31	97
401–880 acres	20	12	3, 762	1, 536	2, 226	86	42	44
881 acres or more	9	7	5, 684	2, 193	3, 491	63	26	37
Sandy loam section								
Total farms	37	21	3, 070	1, 305	1, 765	172	102	70
Less than 281 acres	6	3	2, 004	892	1, 112	105	72	33
281–400 acres	10	5	1, 921	875	1, 046	124	78	46
401–880 acres	12	6	3, 140	1, 313	1, 827	241	163	78
881 acres or more	9	7	4, 962	2, 047	2, 915	176	66	110
GOSHEN								
Irrigated section								
Total farms	29	20	2, 583	1, 199	1, 384	51	37	14
Less than 101 acres	6	4	1, 380	625	755	63	50	13
101–280 acres	14	10	2, 710	1, 523	1, 187	54	31	23
281–460 acres	6	4	3, 072	1, 150	1, 922	38	38	—
461–640 acres	2	2	3, 642	800	2, 842	13	13	—
641 acres or more	1	—	2, 975	1, 200	1, 775	100	100	—
Nonirrigated section								
Total farms	43	40	1, 604	655	949	141	96	45
Less than 101 acres	—	—	—	—	—	—	—	—
101–280 acres	2	2	1, 520	1, 100	420	106	70	36
281–460 acres	11	10	996	486	510	73	65	8
461–640 acres	7	6	1, 023	361	662	45	21	24
641–960 acres	9	8	1, 625	664	961	213	160	53
961 acres or more	14	14	2, 370	864	1, 506	200	120	80
CHEYENNE								
Total farms	56	36	2, 043	752	1, 291	104	52	52
Less than 400 acres	13	8	1, 638	588	1, 050	88	40	48
400–559 acres	11	8	2, 337	1, 005	1, 332	21	11	10
560–719 acres	14	9	2, 070	787	1, 283	104	61	43
720 acres or more	18	11	2, 131	690	1, 441	166	77	89

Table 46.—Percent of Farm Land Held by Resident and Nonresident Owners and Tenure of Operators in Representative Counties in the Central Great Plains, 1935

County and owner	Total	Tenure of operator	
		Owner	Tenant
SHERMAN			
Total	100	38	62
Resident	71	38	33
Nonresident	29	—	29
PERKINS			
Total	100	30	70
Resident	60	30	30
Nonresident	40	—	40
GOSHEN			
Irrigated section			
Total	100	54	46
Resident	42	31	11
Nonresident	58	23	35
Nonirrigated section			
Total	100	79	21
Resident	78	62	16
Nonresident	22	17	5
CHEYENNE			
Total	100	60	40
Resident	68	59	9
Nonresident	32	1	31

Source: Production control contracts of the Agricultural Adjustment Administration.

Table 47.—Average Value of Farm Assets, Amount of Liabilities, and Net Worth of Selected Farmers in Representative Counties in the Central Great Plains, by Tenure, 1935

Item	Owners							Tenants						
		Perkins		Goshen		Cheyenne			Perkins		Goshen		Cheyenne	
	Sherman (15 farms)	Loam section (23 farms)	Sandy loam section (20 farms)	Irrigated section (20 farms)	Nonirrigated section (40 farms)	Second-grade land (29 farms)	Third-grade land (7 farms)	Sherman (42 farms)	Loam section (13 farms)	Sandy loam section (17 farms)	Irrigated section (9 farms)	Nonirrigated section (3 farms)	Second-grade land (17 farms)	Third-grade land (3 farms)
Total assets	$12, 501	$21, 920	$18, 199	$11, 431	$7, 529	$7, 320	$6, 519	$1, 394	$2, 157	$1, 699	$3, 006	$762	$1, 301	$2, 059
Real estate	10, 394	17, 996	14, 187	8, 346	4, 776	4, 558	3, 593	—	—	—	—	—	—	—
Machinery	590	1, 815	1, 404	1, 070	965	641	578	336	1, 200	732	1, 593	249	306	724
Livestock	1, 052	1, 079	1, 294	1, 315	1, 276	1, 480	2, 097	978	697	810	1, 000	498	920	889
Farm products	92	180	173	95	240	180	135	22	96	46	105	15	59	104
Other	373	850	1, 141	605	272	461	116	58	164	111	308	—	16	342
Total liabilities	7, 213	7, 860	8, 302	4, 085	2, 540	2, 136	2, 172	1, 136	955	1, 117	882	776	819	395
Mortgages:														
Real estate	5, 891	6, 884	7, 352	3, 615	2, 000	1, 618	1, 735	—	—	—	—	—	—	—
Chattel	698	724	682	252	426	397	233	650	751	837	576	540	603	370
Delinquent taxes	48	68	9	133	58	43	35	16	29	18	36	95	7	—
Other debts	576	184	259	85	56	78	169	470	175	262	270	141	209	25
Net worth	5, 288	14, 060	9, 897	7, 346	4, 989	5, 184	4, 347	258	1, 202	582	2, 124	−14	482	1, 664

Table 48.—Normal Gross Cash Receipts, Source of Receipts, and Adequacy of Income on Selected Farms in Representative Counties in the Southern Great Plains, by Size of Farm

County and size of farm	Number of farms reporting	Normal gross cash receipts	Source of receipts (percent)			Average length of record (years)	Adequacy of income	
			Crops	Livestock and livestock products	Work off farm		Percent of years income was sufficient to meet expenses	Percent of years income was sufficient to increase capital
DALLAM								
Row-crop section								
Total farms	43	$2,895	66	33	1	11	68	56
Less than 281 acres	3	1,200	73	10	17	8	†	†
281–440 acres	9	1,106	69	31	—	8	69	55
441–880 acres	17	2,206	63	37	—	13	64	53
881–1,600 acres	9	2,772	66	34	—	11	74	54
1,601 acres or more	5	9,700	69	31	—	11	82	66
Grain section								
Total farms	[1] 35	3,800	84	16	—	13	52	38
Less than 281 acres	1	850	95	5	—	7	†	†
281–440 acres	13	1,996	86	14	—	11	45	31
441–880 acres	10	2,180	76	24	—	12	53	45
881–1,600 acres	5	4,880	94	6	—	20	58	47
1,601 acres or more	6	10,000	83	17	—	14	57	31
HALE								
Total farms	[2] 155	2,511	79	21	—	13	65	54
Less than 121 acres	12	1,096	74	25	1	16	62	52
121–200 acres	40	1,608	77	23	—	11	71	51
201–280 acres	8	1,669	81	19	—	9	58	55
281–400 acres	39	2,116	77	22	1	13	61	53
401–560 acres	17	2,789	82	18	—	15	73	60
561–720 acres	22	3,842	85	15	—	13	61	55
721 acres or more	17	4,935	79	21	—	17	66	59
CURRY								
Row-crop section								
Total farms	[3] 60	1,784	71	28	1	14	80	45
Less than 280 acres	9	847	63	37	—	14	89	36
280–379 acres	17	1,654	73	25	2	15	77	23
380–559 acres	13	1,966	74	25	1	13	74	54
560–719 acres	10	1,835	67	33	—	13	81	54
720–879 acres	6	2,250	78	20	2	16	79	44
880 acres or more	5	2,780	69	31	—	17	85	64
Grain section								
Total farms	[2] 46	2,299	77	22	1	18	82	56
Less than 280 acres	4	825	73	21	6	20	71	40
280–379 acres	9	1,589	89	11	—	18	75	33
380–559 acres	8	1,431	71	29	—	18	87	72
560–719 acres	8	2,375	71	29	—	20	85	60
720–879 acres	6	3,350	89	11	—	14	94	71
880 acres or more	11	3,418	68	29	3	19	80	42

† Percent not computed on a base of less than 50 years.

[1] Data not available for 2 farms.
[2] Data not available for 1 farm.
[3] Data not available for 3 farms.

Table 49.—Age of Farm Operators Receiving Relief [1] in Representative Counties in the Southern Great Plains and Number Unable to Work,[2] April–May 1935

Age	Dallam		Hale		Curry	
	Number of farm operators	Number unable to work	Number of farm operators [3]	Number unable to work	Number of farm operators	Number unable to work
Total	139	7	46	—	220	4
Under 21 years	—	—	—	—	3	—
21–25 years	10	—	6	—	26	—
26–30 years	24	—	5	—	31	1
31–35 years	27	—	6	—	29	—
36–40 years	18	1	10	—	32	1
41–45 years	11	1	2	—	21	2
46–50 years	21	2	7	—	16	—
51–55 years	11	—	3	—	28	—
56–60 years	6	—	2	—	13	—
61 years and over	11	3	1	—	18	—
Unknown	—	—	4	—	3	—

[1] For whom reports were available.
[2] Based on disabilities reported.
[3] Approved for rehabilitation.

Table 50.—Number of Children of Different Ages and Adult Members Other Than Parents in Farm Families Receiving Relief [1] in Representative Counties in the Southern Great Plains, April–May 1935

County and item	Total families	Number of families with specified number of persons											
		None	1	2	3	4	5	6	7	8	9	10	11
DALLAM													
Total children	139	36	21	31	23	6	6	9	4	—	2	1	—
Children under 16 years	139	44	25	31	23	2	6	5	2	1	—	—	—
Boys 16 years and over	139	106	18	13	2	—	—	—	—	—	—	—	—
Girls 16 years and over	139	123	12	4	—	—	—	—	—	—	—	—	—
Others	139	127	5	7	—	—	—	—	—	—	—	—	—
HALE													
Total children	[2] 46	4	13	6	7	5	1	3	3	2	2	—	—
Children under 12 years	46	10	16	6	5	4	4	1	—	—	—	—	—
Children 12 years and over	46	23	5	6	8	2	2	—	—	—	—	—	—
Others	46	34	2	2	5	—	2	—	1	—	—	—	—
CURRY													
Total children	220	56	34	46	25	19	14	13	4	6	1	1	1
Children under 16 years	220	86	32	41	22	11	16	8	1	2	1	—	—
Boys 16 years and over	220	159	37	16	6	2	—	—	—	—	—	—	—
Girls 16 years and over	220	186	23	5	5	1	—	—	—	—	—	—	—
Others	220	198	10	10	1	1	—	—	—	—	—	—	—

[1] For whom reports were available.
[2] Approved for rehabilitation.

Table 51.—Relative Importance of Different Causes of Crop Damage on Selected Farms in Representative Counties in the Southern Great Plains, by Degree of Loss

County and cause of damage	Total number of records	Length of record			Percent of years			
		Less than 10 years	10–19 years	20 years or more	Damage was reported	Degree of loss was		
						Total	Serious	Slight
DALLAM								
Row-crop section								
Drought					35	18	12	5
Hail					7	1	2	4
Soil blowing					12	1	2	9
Smut and rust	43	21	17	5	1	—	—	1
Insects					5	—	—	5
Frost					5	1	2	2
Excessive precipitation					2	—	—	2
Grain section								
Drought					22	14	5	3
Hail					9	2	2	5
Soil blowing					14	3	3	8
Smut and rust	37	22	7	8	4	1	—	3
Insects					4	—	1	3
Frost					1	—	—	1
Excessive precipitation					11	3	1	7
HALE								
Drought					49	11	21	17
Hail					33	8	9	16
Soil blowing					3	1	1	1
Smut and rust	[1] 154	77	67	10	1	—	—	1
Insects					4	—	1	3
Frost					4	1	1	2
Excessive precipitation					2	—	1	1
CURRY								
Row-crop section								
Drought					40	12	18	10
Hail					14	3	3	8
Soil blowing					7	2	1	4
Smut and rust	63	23	20	20	1	—	—	1
Insects					12	—	1	11
Frost					6	—	1	5
Excessive precipitation					4	2	1	1
Grain section								
Drought					44	11	17	16
Hail					17	3	3	11
Soil blowing					6	2	1	3
Smut and rust	47	9	16	22	2	—	—	2
Insects					1	—	—	1
Frost					1	—	—	1
Excessive precipitation					—	—	—	—

[1] Data not available for 2 farms.

Table 52.—Crop Yield per Harvested Acre in Selected Areas in the Southern Great Plains, 1905–1933

Area and crop	Period included	Total reports	Yield per harvested acre							
			Less than 2.5 bushels	2.5–7.4 bushels	7.5–12.4 bushels	12.5–17.4 bushels	17.5–22.4 bushels	22.5–27.4 bushels	27.5 bushels or more	Average yield (bushels)
SOUTHWESTERN KANSAS [1]										
Winter wheat	1911–1932	66	4	18	17	17	8	2	—	10.9
Corn	1905–1932	84	3	13	20	23	16	9	—	13.7
Barley	1905–1932	84	1	15	21	14	22	8	3	14.4
Kafir for grain	1915–1932	54	—	3	10	24	13	4	—	15.6
Milo for grain	1915–1932	54	—	1	7	19	27	—	—	16.8
Feterita for grain	1915–1932	53	—	4	12	22	13	2	—	14.7
SOUTHEASTERN COLORADO [2]										
Winter wheat	1923–1933	11	—	5	5	1	—	—	—	7.9
Spring wheat	1923–1933	11	1	9	1	—	—	—	—	5.5
Corn	1923–1933	11	—	4	4	2	1	—	—	10.1
Oats	1923–1933	11	—	3	4	4	—	—	—	10.4
Barley	1929–1933	5	—	2	3	—	—	—	—	8.2
Grain sorghums	1929–1933	5	—	2	2	1	—	—	—	9.6

[1] Southwestern Kansas Area includes Morton, Seward, and Stevens Counties.
[2] Southeastern Colorado Area includes Baca County, yields of irrigated crops being excluded.

Sources: *Biennial Reports*, Kansas State Board of Agriculture, Topeka, Kans., 1905–1906 to 1933–1934; and *Yearbooks of the State of Colorado*, State Board of Immigration, Denver, Colo., 1923–1933.

Table 53.—Average Yield per Seeded Acre of Important Crops on Selected Farms in Representative Counties in the Southern Great Plains, 1930–1934

County and crop	Average yield per seeded acre				
	1930	1931	1932	1933	1934
DALLAM					
Row-crop section					
Number of farms reporting	33	39	42	43	43
Wheat (bushels)	3	23	*	—	—
Corn (bushels)	23	20	8	2	—
Milo (bushels)	25	28	1	2	—
Hegari (tons)	0.9	1.5	0.9	0.5	0.2
Feed crops (tons)	0.7	0.7	0.4	0.4	—
Grain section					
Number of farms reporting	24	34	35	35	37
Wheat (bushels)	11	17	2	*	*
Corn (bushels)	17	18	6	1	—
Milo (bushels)	19	14	5	3	—
Hegari (tons)	0.4	0.5	0.2	0.2	—
Feed crops (tons)	1.1	0.7	0.2	0.2	—
HALE					
Number of farms reporting	82	121	144	153	156
Wheat (bushels)	8	13	6	6	13
Milo (bushels)	6	14	14	10	6
Grain sorghums (bushels)	10	17	14	21	1
Grain sorghums (tons)	0.8	0.9	0.8	0.9	0.2
Kafir (tons)	0.6	0.7	0.7	0.7	0.1
Cotton (pounds)	174	231	141	176	47
CURRY					
Row-crop section					
Number of farms reporting	33	53	59	60	63
Wheat (bushels)	6	18	5	4	3
Corn (bushels)	20	23	14	9	1
Milo, cane, and kafir (bushels)	16	22	14	7	—
Milo (tons)	—	1.0	0.5	0.3	0.1
Hegari (tons)	1.0	1.8	0.8	0.5	0.2
Cane and sorghums (tons)	0.7	1.0	0.5	0.3	0.2
Kafir (tons)	1.0	1.5	0.7	0.7	0.2
Grain section					
Number of farms reporting	25	45	45	46	47
Wheat (bushels)	4	24	2	3	1
Corn (bushels)	18	28	10	7	*
Milo, cane, and kafir (bushels)	10	22	6	9	—
Milo (tons)	0.4	1.8	0.4	0.2	—
Hegari (tons)	—	0.2	0.5	0.4	—
Cane and sorghums (tons)	0.1	1.0	0.2	0.3	0.1
Kafir (tons)	0.4	1.4	0.4	0.3	0.1

*Less than 0.5 bushel.

***Table 54.*—Average Yield per Seeded Acre of Important Crops on Selected Farms in Representative Counties in the Southern Great Plains and Frequency of Occurrence of Yields Which Were Good, Medium, Poor, or Failures**

Crop and county	Number of crops reported	Yield per seeded acre				Percent of years yield was obtained				Average yield per acre
		Good	Medium	Poor	Failure	Good	Medium	Poor	Failure	
WHEAT										
(bushels)										
Dallam:										
Row-crop section	48	22	14	7	2	11	8	4	77	5
Grain section	219	20	13	7	3	20	20	16	44	9
Hale	1,438	19	11	7	4	21	34	21	24	10
Curry:										
Row-crop section	217	21	13	5	2	15	19	29	37	8
Grain section	530	25	13	7	2	19	21	27	33	10
CORN										
(bushels)										
Dallam:										
Row-crop section	376	30	18	9	*	17	43	17	23	15
Grain section	228	26	18	8	5	20	42	14	24	15
Curry:										
Row-crop section	342	25	16	7	2	20	30	26	24	12
Grain section	357	31	17	7	*	18	31	35	16	13
GRAIN SORGHUMS										
(bushels)										
Dallam:										
Row-crop section	173	33	22	11	8	26	43	13	18	21
Grain section	174	33	22	13	9	25	33	20	22	20
Hale	136	26	16	9	7	14	42	23	21	14
Curry:										
Row-crop section	105	28	18	11	5	28	20	29	23	16
Grain section	244	32	19	9	6	30	30	23	17	18
FEED SORGHUMS										
(tons)										
Dallam:										
Row-crop section	60	1.5	1.0	0.5	0.2	15	35	17	33	0.7
Grain section	153	1.8	1.4	0.8	0.3	19	33	20	28	1.1
Hale	584	1.7	1.1	0.7	0.4	25	32	24	19	1.0
Curry:										
Row-crop section	183	2.0	1.5	0.8	0.4	29	34	16	21	1.3
Grain section	197	1.9	1.4	0.9	0.3	23	36	23	18	1.2
COTTON										
(pounds)										
Hale	182	293	191	123	88	25	34	23	18	182

*Less than 0.5 bushel.

Table 55.—Financial Progress of Selected Farmers in Representative Counties in the Southern Great Plains Since Beginning Farming in the Area, by Size of Farm, 1935

County and size of farm	Number of farms reporting	Financial status at beginning			Capital additions to business			Net put into business	Financial status in 1935			Average increase per farm	
		Assets	Liabilities	Net worth	Additions	Deductions	Net additions		Assets	Liabilities	Net worth	Total	Per year
DALLAM													
Row-crop section													
Total farms	43	$5,391	$610	$4,781	$294	$1,070	−$776	$4,005	$10,407	$6,016	$4,391	$386	$33
Less than 281 acres	3	1,083	83	1,000	433	91	342	1,342	2,986	3,511	−525	−1,867	−233
281–440 acres	9	3,869	667	3,202	—	1,036	−1,036	2,166	3,735	2,243	1,492	−674	−57
441–880 acres	17	4,299	753	3,546	209	1,113	−904	2,642	8,921	5,533	3,388	746	58
881–1,600 acres	9	1,572	22	1,550	533	678	−145	1,405	7,834	5,856	1,978	573	53
1,601 acres or more	5	21,300	1,400	19,900	600	2,277	−1,677	18,223	36,555	16,236	20,319	2,096	187
Grain section													
Total farms	37	5,297	603	4,694	512	1,407	−895	3,799	12,649	9,143	3,506	−293	−23
Less than 281 acres	1	1,500	—	1,500	1,200	300	900	2,400	2,800	4,246	−1,446	−3,846	−549
281–440 acres	13	5,352	108	5,244	218	639	−421	4,823	3,987	3,279	708	−4,115	−371
441–880 acres	11	3,910	464	3,446	255	625	−370	3,076	6,688	6,228	460	−2,616	−223
881–1,600 acres	5	4,844	—	4,844	620	6,226	−5,606	−762	12,186	8,991	3,195	3,957	195
1,601 acres or more	7	8,243	2,257	5,986	1,286	779	507	6,493	39,837	25,421	14,416	7,923	584
HALE													
Total farms	156	5,075	703	4,372	665	1,681	−1,016	3,356	9,022	2,688	6,334	2,978	199
Less than 121 acres	12	3,296	18	3,278	145	380	−235	3,043	4,332	821	3,511	468	27
121–200 acres	40	4,764	483	4,281	400	882	−482	3,799	5,708	1,371	4,337	538	46
201–280 acres	8	1,779	50	1,729	1,429	684	745	2,474	3,593	1,183	2,410	−64	−5
281–400 acres	40	5,369	285	5,084	681	1,815	−1,134	3,950	8,037	2,170	5,867	1,917	130
401–560 acres	17	3,059	172	2,887	476	1,955	−1,479	1,408	9,996	2,688	7,308	5,900	363
561–720 acres	22	3,682	1,205	2,477	944	1,747	−803	1,674	11,361	3,595	7,766	6,092	363
721 acres or more	17	11,444	2,797	8,647	1,106	4,145	−3,039	5,608	20,406	7,661	12,745	7,137	385

CURRY													
Row-crop section													
Total farms	63	3, 156	193	2, 963	335	1, 190	−855	2, 108	7, 331	2, 233	5, 098	2, 990	199
Less than 280 acres	9	588	67	521	1, 300	1, 092	208	729	2, 946	672	2, 274	1, 545	103
280–379 acres	17	2, 306	—	2, 306	38	1, 241	−1, 203	1, 103	5, 061	1, 056	4, 005	2, 902	165
380–559 acres	15	4, 973	—	4, 973	181	755	−574	4, 399	9, 091	2, 504	6, 587	2, 188	168
560–719 acres	10	4, 720	710	4, 010	305	1, 668	−1, 363	2, 647	6, 472	1, 338	5, 134	2, 487	199
720–879 acres	6	980	450	530	300	1, 248	−948	−418	9, 639	4, 267	5, 372	5, 790	344
880 acres or more	6	4, 908	200	4, 708	100	1, 286	−1, 186	3, 522	15, 276	6, 585	8, 691	5, 169	348
Grain section													
Total farms	47	1, 866	359	1, 507	389	1, 218	−829	678	8, 561	2, 796	5, 765	5, 087	263
Less than 280 acres	4	600	250	350	525	69	456	806	3, 844	1, 328	2, 516	1, 710	87
280–379 acres	9	1, 744	211	1, 533	22	1, 351	−1, 329	204	4, 898	1, 502	3, 396	3, 192	145
380–559 acres	9	1, 150	33	1, 117	111	1, 864	−1, 753	−636	5, 926	2, 330	3, 596	4, 232	228
560–719 acres	8	1, 025	—	1, 025	474	1, 325	−851	174	9, 734	2, 786	6, 948	6, 774	328
720–879 acres	6	2, 713	1, 917	796	—	957	−957	−161	10, 122	2, 264	7, 858	8, 019	523
880 acres or more	11	3, 159	198	2, 961	1, 018	1, 060	−42	2, 919	13, 725	5, 066	8, 659	5, 740	305

Table 56.—Cropland on Farms Having Corn-Hog Contracts in Representative Counties in the Southern Great Plains, by Size of Form, 1934

County and size of farm	Number of farms	Average number of acres per farm	
		Total	Cropland
DALLAM			
Total farms	502	588	404
Less than 281 acres	119	165	138
281–440 acres	153	329	254
441–880 acres	158	633	449
881–1,600 acres	51	1, 178	773
1,601 acres or more	21	3, 094	1, 767
HALE			
Total farms	481	325	255
Less than 121 acres	49	56	45
121–200 acres	131	166	133
201–280 acres	31	243	197
281–400 acres	151	325	261
401–560 acres	37	477	361
561–720 acres	67	637	488
721 acres or more	15	997	776
CURRY			
Total farms	491	557	340
Less than 280 acres	131	163	127
280–379 acres	121	319	237
380–559 acres	91	465	320
560–719 acres	65	629	422
720–879 acres	33	804	563
880 acres or more	50	2, 070	929

Source: Corn-hog production control contracts of the Agricultural Adjustment Administration.

Table 57.—Utilization of Land on Selected Farms in Representative Counties in the Southern Great Plains, by Size of Farm, 1934

County and size of farm	Number of farms reporting	Average number of acres per farm				
		Total	Cropland	Pasture	Former cropland	Farmstead and waste
DALLAM						
Row-crop section						
Total farms	43	904	534	352	5	13
Less than 281 acres	3	189	158	26	—	5
281–440 acres	9	329	211	101	6	11
441–880 acres	17	677	383	279	5	10
881–1,600 acres	9	1, 166	620	523	8	15
1,601 acres or more	5	2, 669	1, 696	943	—	30
Grain section						
Total farms	37	1, 056	768	267	4	17
Less than 281 acres	1	160	125	30	—	5
281–440 acres	13	352	252	89	—	11
441–880 acres	11	718	515	188	—	15
881–1,600 acres	5	1, 193	1, 035	128	7	23
1,601 acres or more	7	2, 917	2, 023	853	14	27
HALE						
Total farms	156	387	318	56	—	13
Less than 121 acres	12	77	66	6	—	5
121–200 acres	40	162	140	14	—	8
201–280 acres	8	238	189	38	—	11
281–400 acres	40	325	269	43	—	13
401–560 acres	17	479	378	86	—	15
561–720 acres	22	636	521	99	—	16
721 acres or more	17	932	763	141	—	28
CURRY						
Row-crop section						
Total farms	63	511	353	135	8	15
Less than 280 acres	9	175	123	45	—	7
280–379 acres	17	318	243	61	—	14
380–559 acres	15	479	355	103	—	21
560–719 acres	10	634	438	171	8	17
720–879 acres	6	779	611	154	—	14
880 acres or more	6	1, 172	612	470	73	17
Grain section						
Total farms	47	699	482	201	3	13
Less than 280 acres	4	225	153	65	—	7
280–379 acres	9	320	226	84	—	10
380–559 acres	9	485	342	129	3	11
560–719 acres	8	630	437	183	—	10
720–879 acres	6	806	671	109	7	19
880 acres or more	11	1, 350	858	470	5	17

86869°—38——14

Table 58.—Utilization of Land on 1,496 Farms Having Cotton Contracts in Hale County, Tex., by Size of Farm, 1934

Size of farm	Number of farms	Average number of acres per farm		
		Total	Cropland	Pasture and farmstead
Total farms	1,496	282	233	49
Less than 121 acres	229	70	64	6
121–200 acres	523	163	140	23
201–280 acres	108	238	194	44
281–400 acres	374	324	270	54
401–560 acres	75	477	381	96
561–720 acres	142	635	503	132
721 acres or more	45	1,085	868	217

Source: Cotton production control contracts of the Agricultural Adjustment Administration.

Table 59.—Size of Farm, Number of Livestock per Farm, and Tenure of Farm Operators Receiving Relief in Representative Counties in the Southern Great Plains, April–May 1935

County and size of farm	Number of farms reporting	Average size of farm (acres)		Average number of livestock				Tenure of operator	
		Total	Crop-land	Cattle	Hogs	Chick-ens	Horses	Owner	Tenant
DALLAM									
Total farms	[1] 81	([2])	([2])	5	1	34	2	22	59
HALE									
Total farms	[3] 46	71	69	5	1	21	2	1	45
Less than 61 acres	30	37	36	5	1	22	2	1	29
61–160 acres	13	112	108	6	2	21	2	—	13
161–300 acres	3	234	234	7	—	18	5	—	3
CURRY									
Total farms	[4] 198	284	207	5	1	40	3	44	154
Less than 280 acres	87	154	132	4	1	38	3	19	68
280–379 acres	60	312	218	5	1	46	3	18	42
380–559 acres	30	458	320	6	1	47	2	6	24
560–719 acres	7	631	381	7	1	46	5	—	7
720–879 acres	3	800	540	23	—	46	1	—	3
Unknown	11	—	—	2	1	14	1	1	10

[1] Reports available for only 81 of the 199 farmers receiving relief in May 1935.
[2] Size not given.
[3] Reports available only for farmers approved for rehabilitation loans. In April 1935, 219 farmers in the county were receiving relief.
[4] Reports available for only 198 of the 220 farmers receiving relief in May 1935.

Table 60.—Percent of Owned and Rented Land in Crops and Grass on Selected Farms in Representative Counties in the Southern Great Plains, 1934

Item	Dallam		Hale (156 farms)	Curry	
	Row-crop section (43 farms)	Grain section (37 farms)		Row-crop section (63 farms)	Grain section (47 farms)
Total operated land [1]	100.0	100.0	100.0	100.0	100.0
Cropland	59.0	72.8	82.1	69.3	69.0
Hay and pasture	39.0	25.3	14.4	26.1	28.8
Former cropland	0.5	0.3	0.1	1.6	0.4
Other	1.5	1.6	3.4	3.0	1.8
Total owned land	55.3	58.1	51.3	64.5	67.7
Cropland	32.9	42.3	42.2	44.1	46.6
Hay and pasture	21.5	14.7	7.2	16.6	19.5
Former cropland	—	0.2	0.1	1.6	0.3
Other	0.9	0.9	1.8	2.2	1.3
Total share-rented land	40.8	39.8	50.7	29.1	28.6
Cropland	26.1	30.6	42.3	24.4	22.9
Hay and pasture	13.6	8.4	6.7	3.9	5.1
Former cropland	0.5	0.1	—	—	0.1
Other	0.6	0.7	1.7	0.8	0.5
Total cash-rented land	3.9	3.7	1.7	7.6	5.8
Cropland	—	1.5	0.7	2.0	1.3
Hay and pasture	3.9	2.2	1.0	5.6	4.5
Former cropland	—	—	—	—	—
Other	—	—	*	—	—
Land rented out	—	1.6	3.7	1.2	2.1
Cropland	—	1.6	3.1	1.2	1.8
Hay and pasture	—	—	0.5	—	0.3
Former cropland	—	—	—	—	—
Other	—	—	0.1	—	—

* Less than 0.05 percent.

[1] Total operated land is the sum of owned and rented land less land rented out.

Table 61.—Use of Farm Land on Selected Farms in Representative Counties in the Southern Great Plains, 1934

Use of farm land	Average number of acres per farm				
	Dallam		Hale (156 farms)	Curry	
	Row-crop section (43 farms)	Grain section (37 farms)		Row-crop section (63 farms)	Grain section (47 farms)
Total land operated	904	1,056	387	511	699
Total cropland [1]	534	768	318	353	482
Reseeded acres	*16*	*10*	—	*9*	*7*
Wheat	97	254	112	105	213
Wheat on fallow	—	128	8	10	53
Forage sorghums	74	34	46	45	59
Milo and kafir	46	83	21	53	21
Hegari	16	9	19	64	36
Corn	32	23	1	22	9
Broom corn	10	6	—	8	19
Other crops	20	12	[2] 67	30	10
Fallow	48	49	30	13	38
Idle cropland	207	180	14	12	31
Former cropland	5	4	—	8	3
Native pasture	352	267	56	135	201
Farmstead and waste	13	17	13	15	13

[1] The reseeded acres are not included in the total cropland item.
[2] Includes 46 acres of cotton.

Table 62.—Average Acreage of Important Crops on Selected Farms [1] in Representative Counties in the Southern Great Plains, 1930–1934

County and year	Number of farms reporting	Average number of acres per farm			
		Wheat	Corn	Sorghums	Cotton
DALLAM					
Row-crop section					
1930	33	159	195	180	—
1931	39	112	221	225	—
1932	42	99	161	235	—
1933	43	92	69	138	—
1934	43	97	32	140	—
Grain section					
1930	24	439	51	162	—
1931	34	496	65	182	—
1932	35	524	74	220	—
1933	35	405	45	191	—
1934	37	382	23	134	—
HALE					
1930	82	196	(2)	82	43
1931	121	163	(2)	70	53
1932	144	152	(2)	77	59
1933	153	138	(2)	71	44
1934	156	120	1	86	46
CURRY					
Row-crop section					
1930	33	85	44	162	—
1931	53	128	42	149	—
1932	59	123	41	157	—
1933	60	117	33	146	—
1934	63	115	22	163	—
Grain section					
1930	25	202	17	99	—
1931	45	330	23	106	—
1932	45	296	18	114	—
1933	46	282	10	96	—
1934	47	266	9	115	—

[1] Reporting acreage.
[2] Not calculated.

Table 63.—Number of Livestock on Hand April 1, 1935, and Normal Number on Selected Farms in Representative Counties in the Southern Great Plains, by Size of Farm

County and size of farm	Average number of livestock																			
	All cattle		Milk cows		Beef cows		Other cattle		All hogs		Brood sows		Other hogs		Sheep		Poultry		Work stock	
	April 1, 1935	Normal	April 1, 1935	Normal	April 1, 1935	Normal	April 1, 1935	Normal	April 1, 1935	Normal	April 1, 1935	Normal	April 1, 1935	Normal	April 1, 1935	Normal	April 1, 1935	Normal	April 1, 1935	Normal
DALLAM																				
Row-crop section																				
Total farms	17	30	5	9	6	16	6	5	2	9	1	3	1	6	—	—	69	122	4	6
Less than 281 acres	4	7	3	5	—	—	1	2	2	3	1	1	1	2	—	—	41	78	3	5
281–440 acres	3	17	2	6	—	11	1	—	—	2	—	2	—	—	—	—	52	107	3	5
441–880 acres	12	26	6	9	2	12	4	5	3	4	1	3	2	1	—	—	61	126	4	5
881–1,600 acres	25	42	8	13	8	19	9	10	4	23	1	4	3	19	—	—	70	121	5	9
1,601 acres or more	63	64	6	11	32	45	25	8	1	16	—	4	1	12	—	—	139	163	3	6
Grain section																				
Total farms	13	21	4	8	4	5	5	8	3	9	1	2	2	7	—	—	46	95	2	3
Less than 281 acres	1	14	1	6	—	—	—	8	—	7	—	1	—	6	—	—	50	125	—	—
281–440 acres	4	14	2	7	—	—	2	7	1	7	—	1	1	6	—	—	35	90	1	4
441–880 acres	8	15	5	7	—	5	3	3	2	3	1	2	1	1	—	—	40	88	2	3
881–1,600 acres	18	31	8	13	2	4	8	14	2	10	1	1	1	9	—	—	70	117	2	4
1,601 acres or more	40	43	5	10	21	17	14	16	4	18	1	4	3	14	—	—	58	99	3	5
HALE																				
Total farms	11	16	6	9	*	*	5	7	4	8	1	2	3	6	11	14	61	96	4	4
Less than 121 acres	8	9	3	4	—	—	5	5	2	2	—	1	2	1	—	—	61	88	3	2
121–200 acres	8	9	5	7	—	—	3	2	3	4	1	1	2	3	—	—	44	75	2	3
201–280 acres	8	14	4	5	—	—	4	9	2	7	—	1	2	6	—	—	71	102	4	5
281–400 acres	10	15	6	8	—	—	4	7	4	8	1	2	3	6	—	—	58	94	4	4
401–560 acres	10	16	5	9	—	—	5	7	3	4	1	2	2	2	28	38	74	109	5	6
561–720 acres	18	26	9	12	1	2	8	12	8	10	2	3	6	7	29	31	66	109	4	4
721 acres or more	21	30	10	17	—	1	11	12	11	25	3	4	8	21	36	44	79	125	4	4

CURRY																				
Row-crop section																				
Total farms	17	17	8	9	1	2	8	6	4	7	1	2	3	5	—	—	81	125	3	4
Less than 280 acres	8	9	5	6	—	—	3	3	2	6	1	1	1	5	—	—	61	82	4	5
280–379 acres	9	12	5	8	—	—	4	4	3	4	1	1	2	3	—	—	69	89	3	4
380–559 acres	17	14	7	7	1	2	9	5	4	7	1	2	3	5	—	—	107	141	4	4
560–719 acres	19	18	9	11	1	2	9	5	3	5	1	2	2	3	—	—	84	129	3	4
720–879 acres	19	30	9	14	—	—	10	16	6	21	1	2	5	19	—	—	94	215	2	5
880 acres or more	44	35	18	15	9	14	17	6	6	3	1	3	5	—	—	—	62	155	2	2
Grain section																				
Total farms	19	25	7	10	4	5	8	10	3	4	*	1	3	3	—	—	97	141	3	4
Less than 280 acres	4	9	3	4	—	—	1	5	3	6	—	1	3	5	—	—	76	119	5	5
280–379 acres	6	11	4	6	—	—	2	5	—	1	—	—	—	1	—	—	72	122	3	3
380–559 acres	10	18	6	8	—	4	4	6	2	5	1	3	1	2	—	—	96	157	4	3
560–719 acres	18	23	7	11	3	4	8	8	4	5	—	2	4	3	—	—	102	140	2	3
720–879 acres	14	29	5	6	—	7	9	16	1	2	—	—	1	2	—	—	136	186	1	3
880 acres or more	46	46	12	18	15	12	19	16	5	7	1	1	4	6	—	—	101	140	4	5

*Less than 0.5.

Table 64.—Number of Selected Farms With Livestock in Representative Counties in the Southern Great Plains, April 1, 1935

Number of livestock	Number of farms reporting				
	Dallam		Hale (156 farms)	Curry	
	Row-crop section (43 farms)	Grain section (37 farms)		Row-crop section (63 farms)	Grain section (47 farms)
MILK COWS					
None	1	6	4	3	3
1–5	29	20	81	24	25
6 or more	13	11	71	36	19
BEEF COWS					
None	33	33	155	56	40
1–5	4	1	—	4	1
6–15	1	1	1	1	2
16 or more	5	2	—	2	4
OTHER CATTLE					
None	—	5	2	1	3
1–10	27	22	88	25	23
11–25	9	5	56	27	10
26–50	4	1	8	8	6
51 or more	3	4	2	2	5
BROOD SOWS					
None	25	28	94	36	34
1–3	17	8	56	25	12
4 or more	1	1	6	2	1
OTHER HOGS					
None	26	26	85	29	25
1–5	13	8	47	26	16
6 or more	4	3	24	8	6
SHEEP					
None	43	37	141	60	47
1–10	—	—	8	3	—
11–50	—	—	—	—	—
51 or more	—	—	7	—	—
CHICKENS					
None	—	5	5	—	1
1–50	22	20	83	27	16
51–100	13	8	50	23	17
101 or more	8	4	18	13	13
WORK STOCK					
None	13	20	24	13	13
1–6	22	13	109	44	30
7 or more	8	4	23	6	4

Table 65.—Acreage Operated by Specified Number of Men, With or Without Tractors, on Selected Farms in Representative Counties in the Southern Great Plains, 1934

County and item	Number of farms reporting			Average acreage in farms operated by specified number of men											
				1			2			3			4		
	Total	With tractor	Without tractor	Total	With tractor	Without tractor	Total	With tractor	Without tractor	Total	With tractor	Without tractor	Total	With tractor	Without tractor
DALLAM															
Row-crop section															
Total farms	43	26	17	31	17	14	9	6	3	2	2	—	1	1	—
Total acres operated	903	1,037	700	698	772	609	1,509	1,700	1,127	1,276	1,276	—	1,093	1,093	—
Crop acres operated	533	738	221	405	559	218	925	1,269	237	585	585	—	896	896	—
Grain section															
Total farms	37	33	4	27	23	4	7	7	—	2	2	—	1	1	—
Total acres operated	1,055	1,127	457	827	891	457	1,241	1,241	—	1,746	1,746	—	4,515	4,515	—
Crop acres operated	768	829	261	596	654	261	1,092	1,092	—	1,486	1,486	—	1,702	1,702	—
HALE															
Total farms	156	97	59	88	55	33	40	21	19	22	16	6	6	5	1
Total acres operated	387	494	210	348	459	162	385	511	246	505	555	371	534	609	160
Crop acres operated	318	407	171	284	376	131	322	429	203	403	445	291	467	533	140
CURRY															
Row-crop section															
Total farms	63	41	22	39	19	20	22	20	2	2	2	—	—	—	—
Total acres operated	511	612	324	477	649	312	558	569	443	678	678	—	—	—	—
Crop acres operated	355	431	211	319	445	199	393	400	333	623	623	—	—	—	—
Grain section															
Total farms	[1] 46	33	13	29	19	10	15	12	3	1	1	—	1	1	—
Total acres operated	703	832	376	668	818	385	735	832	347	980	980	—	960	960	—
Crop acres operated	483	577	242	486	611	249	468	530	220	700	700	—	390	390	—

[1] Data not available for 1 farm.

***Table 66.*—Average Value of Farm Buildings and Estimated Cost of Needed Repairs per Farm on Selected Farms in Representative Counties in the Southern Great Plains, by Size of Farm, 1935**

County and size of farm	Number of farms reporting		Value of buildings			Cost of needed repairs		
	Total	Owned	Total	Dwelling	Other	Total	Dwelling	Other
DALLAM								
Row-crop section								
Total farms	43	30	$2, 331	$909	$1, 422	$105	$63	$42
Less than 281 acres	3	3	879	342	537	102	50	52
281–440 acres	9	4	1, 506	606	900	57	41	16
441–880 acres	17	13	2, 137	857	1, 280	69	47	22
881–1,600 acres	9	5	2, 412	825	1, 587	207	129	78
1,601 acres or more	5	5	5, 202	2, 120	3, 082	131	43	88
Grain section								
Total farms	37	28	1, 956	776	1, 180	143	76	67
Less than 281 acres	1	1	735	350	385	115	15	100
281–440 acres	13	10	1, 395	560	835	107	70	37
441–880 acres	11	7	2, 087	893	1, 194	174	97	77
881–1,600 acres	5	3	2, 739	1, 000	1, 739	157	70	87
1,601 acres or more	7	7	2, 408	894	1, 514	158	68	90
HALE								
Total farms	156	95	1, 953	838	1, 115	78	47	31
Less than 121 acres	12	8	1, 142	514	628	54	40	14
121–200 acres	40	23	1, 702	693	1, 009	29	18	11
201–280 acres	8	4	1, 363	587	776	107	78	29
281–400 acres	40	23	1, 745	876	869	80	50	30
401–560 acres	17	11	1, 796	829	967	92	53	39
561–720 acres	22	11	2, 396	959	1, 437	94	61	33
721 acres or more	17	15	3, 467	1, 290	2, 177	159	78	81
CURRY								
Row-crop section								
Total farms	63	47	1, 615	660	955	93	53	40
Less than 280 acres	9	6	843	358	485	90	71	19
280–379 acres	17	11	1, 436	565	871	84	51	33
380–559 acres	15	13	2, 077	862	1, 215	80	33	47
560–719 acres	10	7	1, 828	770	1, 058	45	25	20
720–879 acres	6	5	1, 572	854	718	183	62	121
880 acres or more	6	5	1, 816	500	1, 316	148	118	30
Grain section								
Total farms	[1] 46	39	1, 334	557	777	159	93	66
Less than 280 acres	4	4	1, 071	625	446	40	14	26
280–379 acres	9	8	792	389	403	98	59	39
380–559 acres	9	5	1, 469	494	975	116	54	62
560–719 acres	8	7	1, 564	556	1, 008	157	111	46
720–879 acres	6	4	1, 370	558	812	302	93	209
880 acres or more	10	11	1, 599	735	864	215	174	41

[1] Data not available for 1 farm.

Table 67.—Percent of Acreage With Mortgages of Record Held by Different Types of Lending Agencies in Representative Counties in the Southern Great Plains, 1935

Type of lending agency	Percent of mortgaged acres		
	Dallam	Hale	Curry
ALL MORTGAGES			
Total	100.0	100.0	100.0
Private	23.0	2.8	18.9
Corporate	13.6	12.9	5.4
Commercial banks	1.7	0.4	0.7
Federal Land Bank	38.4	52.5	43.6
Federal Land Bank Commissioner	23.3	31.4	31.1
State lending agencies	—	—	0.3
Other	—	—	—
FIRST MORTGAGES			
Total	100.0	100.0	100.0
Private	27.3	2.7	18.3
Corporate	17.4	17.1	5.1
Commercial banks	—	0.5	0.5
Federal Land Bank	51.4	70.8	55.4
Federal Land Bank Commissioner	3.9	8.9	20.5
State lending agencies	—	—	0.2
Other	—	—	—

Source: County records.

Table 68.—Federal Emergency Loans to Farmers in Representative Counties in the Southern Great Plains, 1934–1935

County	All Federal emergency loans		1934 crop and feed loans[1]		1934–1935 feed loans[2]	
	Total	Average per farm	Total	Average per farm	Total	Average per farm
Dallam	$284,405	$401	$253,571	$358	$30,834	$43
Hale	105,466	57	61,125	33	44,341	24
Curry	217,217	151	172,589	120	44,628	31

[1] Outstanding December 31, 1934.
[2] Outstanding February 28, 1935.

Source: Compiled from data supplied by the Farm Credit Administration.

Table 69.—Acreage and Percent of Total Land Area Tax-Delinquent in Representative Counties in the Southern Great Plains, 1935

County	Total acreage tax-delinquent, 1935		Acreage tax-delinquent			
	Number of acres	Percent of total land area	1934	1933	1932	1931
Dallam	252,011	26	—	203,847	4,485	43,679
Hale	262,239	40	98,283	74,724	58,134	31,098
Curry	105,639	12	—	38,411	13,766	53,462

Source: Records in offices of county tax assessors.

Table 70.—Average Indebtedness of Farm Operators Receiving Relief [1] in Representative Counties in the Southern Great Plains, by Tenure, April–May 1935

County and size of farm	Owners					Tenants			
	Number of farms reporting	Average indebtedness	Kind of indebtedness (percent)			Number of farms reporting	Average indebtedness	Kind of indebtedness (percent)	
			Real-estate mortgages	Chattel mortgages	Other debts			Chattel mortgages	Other debts
DALLAM									
Total farms [2]	24	$4,569	84	16	—	44	$698	100	—
HALE									
Total farms	1	1,000	100	—	—	45	67	69	31
Less than 61 acres	1	1,000	100	—	—	29	22	55	45
61–160 acres	—	—	—	—	—	13	96	66	34
161–300 acres	—	—	—	—	—	3	370	81	19
CURRY									
Total farms	44	1,988	80	12	8	154	352	68	32
Less than 280 acres	19	1,138	78	12	10	68	257	58	42
280–379 acres	18	2,222	80	13	7	42	374	68	32
380–559 acres	6	4,284	84	10	6	24	562	81	19
560–719 acres	—	—	—	—	—	7	506	76	24
720–879 acres	—	—	—	—	—	3	881	91	9
Unknown	1	119	—	65	35	10	136	22	78

[1] For whom reports were available.
[2] Size not available.

Table 71.—Indebtedness of Selected Farmers and of Relief Clients [1] in Curry County, N. Mex., by Tenure and Size of Farm, May 1935

Size of farm	Selected farmers [2]				Relief clients			
	Owners		Tenants		Owners		Tenants	
	Number of farms	Average indebtedness	Number of farms	Average indebtedness	Number of farms	Average indebtedness	Number of farms	Average indebtedness
Total farms	85	$2,944	22	$692	44	$1,988	154	$352
Less than 280 acres	10	1,081	3	186	19	1,138	68	257
280–379 acres	20	1,396	5	502	18	2,222	42	374
380–559 acres	17	2,968	5	613	6	4,284	24	562
560–719 acres	13	2,427	5	826	—	—	7	506
720–879 acres	9	3,905	3	1,346	—	—	3	881
880 acres or more	16	5,895	1	917	—	—	—	—
Unknown	—	—	—	—	1	119	10	136

[1] For whom reports were available.
[2] Data not available for 3 farmers.

Table 72.—**Average Value of Farm Assets, Amount of Liabilities, and Net Worth of Selected Farmers in Representative Counties in the Southern Great Plains, by Tenure, 1935**

Item	Owners					Tenants				
	Dallam		Hale [1] (94 farms)	Curry		Dallam		Hale [1] (60 farms)	Curry	
	Row-crop section (30 farms)	Grain section (28 farms)		Row-crop section [2] (46 farms)	Grain section (39 farms)	Row-crop section (13 farms)	Grain section (9 farms)		Row-crop section [2] (14 farms)	Grain section (8 farms)
Total assets	$14,086	$16,265	$13,522	$9,089	$10,104	$1,917	$1,397	$1,971	$1,557	$1,038
Real estate	10,704	12,378	9,289	6,706	7,235	—	—	—	—	—
Machinery	1,191	2,021	1,298	927	1,195	779	904	1,002	781	646
Livestock	982	578	787	744	1,015	591	279	578	488	265
Farm products	36	80	152	141	108	13	24	68	68	12
Other	1,173	1,208	1,996	571	551	534	190	323	220	115
Total liabilities	8,225	11,490	4,090	2,723	3,204	917	1,839	491	627	806
Mortgages:										
Real estate	6,828	8,201	3,615	2,345	2,371	—	—	—	—	—
Chattel	1,136	2,430	275	286	711	863	1,687	354	477	654
Delinquent taxes	160	160	37	28	14	11	14	1	—	1
Other debts	101	699	163	64	108	43	138	136	150	151
Net worth	5,861	4,775	9,432	6,366	6,900	1,000	−442	1,480	930	232

[1] Data not available for 2 farms.
[2] Data not available for 3 farms.

Appendix B

METHOD AND SCOPE OF THE STUDY

AN ACUTE need for reliable data to be used in formulating feasible rehabilitation policies in the drought area of the Great Plains was first manifested in 1934 and the early part of 1935 when, as a result of a succession of exceedingly unfavorable crop seasons, large numbers of farmers in the Great Plains turned to relief organizations to obtain food for their families and their livestock. Accordingly, in February 1935 a project was outlined by a research committee set up by a conference of State and regional rehabilitation directors and agricultural economists from State colleges to obtain data which would show:

(1) In which sections of the area a rural rehabilitation program is needed;
(2) What is needed to rehabilitate farmers;
(3) What use can best be made of the natural resources in the area;
(4) What the burden of fixed costs to be met is and whether or not the normal farm income is sufficient to meet them;
(5) Whether or not permanent rehabilitation will involve an increase in the size of farms;
(6) What percent of the farmers have a chance to be rehabilitated in their present location;
(7) What disposition can be made of farmers who do not remain in the area.

Available information pertaining to the drought area was assembled from weather reports, soil surveys, reports of the United States Census, and farm practice studies previously made. The State colleges, State Agricultural Experiment Stations, State Planning Boards, State relief and rehabilitation organizations, and other agencies in the drought area were visited and data collected from them that were applicable to the study were assembled. To provide a more complete picture of the situation in the different sections of the Great Plains,

13 counties (table A) distributed throughout the drought area[1] were selected from which more detailed information was obtained. The counties studied were selected to represent different conditions in the Great Plains, and an attempt was made to select counties which would be representative of the larger surrounding areas. Two counties located in reasonably good farming areas, Traill County, N. Dak., and Moody County, S. Dak., and one county embracing a portion of an irrigated area, Goshen County, Wyo., were included in the selected counties to determine if possible areas wherein farmers from the stricken areas might relocate.

Factors considered in selecting counties for special study were:

(1) Climatic conditions;
(2) Soil type;
(3) Systems of farming;
(4) Proportion of farmers on relief;
(5) Available data for the area.

Data assembled in each of the selected counties were:

A. From county records:

(1) Tax delinquency in 1934, and previous years' delinquency where available;
(2) Farm mortgages of record;
(3) A map showing the location of taxing units and a record of tax rates for recent years.

B. From Agricultural Adjustment Administration contracts:

(1) Land-use map showing cropland and grass land;
(2) Size of units operated in the county and acres of crop and grass land in each unit;
(3) Land owner and address;
(4) Land operator and address.

C. From records of county director of the Emergency Relief Administration or the poor commissioner:

(1) Number and location of farmers on relief;
(2) Size of farm operated by client;
(3) Tenure;
(4) Number of livestock;
(5) Number of dependents;
(6) Financial status;
(7) Relief history.

[1] No county was selected in Montana because basic information had already been assembled by the State Agricultural Experiment Station. No county from the wheat areas in Kansas was studied because conditions in the distressed areas were fairly well represented by counties in adjoining States.

D. From records of the State or local rehabilitation office:

(1) Number and location of applicants for rehabilitation;
(2) Data similar to those obtained for relief clients.

E. From records of the county agricultural agent:

(1) Number of livestock purchased by the Government during the Emergency Livestock Purchase Program;
(2) Payments made to the farmers and to those holding liens and mortgages on livestock sold.

F. From farm survey records (see schedule):

(1) Data on the organization of farms;
(2) History of crop production;
(3) Adequacy and condition of buildings, machinery, and equipment;
(4) Production of livestock,
(5) Income for the year 1934 and for normal years;
(6) Financial condition of the farm operators;
(7) Financial progress made by farmers in the area.

The farms surveyed in each county were selected at random within the crop-producing areas. Sufficient farms were surveyed in each area to give a reliable sample. In those counties where different type-of-farming areas prevailed as a result of a marked difference in soil or topographic features, each farming area was sampled and tabulated separately. The counties surveyed, the number of farms reported in the selected counties by the United States Census of Agriculture in 1935, the number of sample farms surveyed, and the percentage of all farms surveyed are shown in table A.

Table A.—Total Farms in Representative Counties in 1935 and Number of Farms Surveyed

Representative counties	Total farms, 1935	Sample farms	
		Number	Percent of total
Divide County, N. Dak.	1,576	66	4.2
Hettinger County, N. Dak.	1,235	63	5.1
Sheridan County, N. Dak.	1,147	57	5.0
Hyde County, S. Dak.	581	48	8.3
Traill County, N. Dak.	1,557	52	3.3
Moody County, S. Dak.	1,358	87	6.4
Sherman County, Nebr.	1,444	57	3.9
Perkins County, Nebr.	958	73	7.6
Goshen County, Wyo.	1,538	75	4.9
Cheyenne County, Colo.	671	56	8.3
Dallam County, Tex.	709	80	11.3
Hale County, Tex.	1,859	156	8.4
Curry County, N. Mex.	1,436	110	7.7

86869°—38——15

The averages for size of farm, acres of crops, and number of livestock per farm obtained from the sample conform closely to data reported by the census except in those counties having extreme differences in types of farming. As the sample obtained in this study was one primarily of family-sized crop-producing farms, some variation from the county average is to be expected in areas containing large tracts of ranch land.

Because of differences in climate, soils, and types of farming practiced, the Great Plains region was divided into three areas for the analysis of the data and the preparation of reports. Divide, Hettinger, Sheridan, and Traill Counties, N. Dak., and Hyde and Moody Counties, S. Dak., were considered representative of the Northern Great Plains; Sherman and Perkins Counties, Nebr., Goshen County, Wyo., and Cheyenne County, Colo., were considered representative of the Central Great Plains; and Dallam and Hale Counties, Tex., and Curry County, N. Mex., were considered representative of the Southern Great Plains.

FARM REHABILITATION SURVEY

[DROUGHT AREAS]

State..........
County..........
M. C. D..........
Record..........

Operator.......... Landlord..........
Address.......... Address..........

USE OF LAND

	Rental	Crop-land	Native grass		Former crop-land	Waste	Farm-stead	Total
			Hay	Pasture				
	Acres	*Acres*	*Acres*	*Acres*	*Acres*	*Acres*	*Acres*	*Acres*
Owned								
Share rent								
Cash rent								
Free land								
Total								
Rented out								
Total operated								
Irrigated:								
Owned								
Rented								

Legal description: S.......... T.......... R..........
Type of soil: S. acres.......... Sl. acres.......... L. acres.......... C. acres..........
Type of subsoil..........
Topography: Level acres.......... Rolling acres.......... Rough acres..........
Water erosion:
Gullied acres.......... Top.......... Soil type..........
Washed acres.......... Top.......... Soil type..........
Sheet acres.......... Top.......... Soil type..........
Wind erosion:
Severely damaged acres.......... Soil type..........
Slightly damaged acres.......... Soil type..........
Weed problem:
Kind.......... Notes.......... Acres..........
Kind.......... Notes.......... Acres..........
Alkali land: Acres.......... Soil type.......... Use..........
Former cropland: Last cultivated.......... Why abandoned..........
Present vegetation.......... Physical condition..........
Condition of pastures.......... Percent of normal..........
Kinds of grass..........
Carrying capacity: Acres per head mature cattle, 1935.......... Normal..........

State
County
Record

BUILDINGS

Kind	Number	Size	Material	Future life	Advised repairs	Value of building (1935)
				Years	*Dollars*	
Dwelling						
Barn						
Dairy building						
Poultry house						
Hog house						
Machine shed						
Granary						
Corn crib						
Garage						
Silo						
Fences						
Water system						

FREQUENCY OF CROP DAMAGE

Kind	Crop	Damage			Occurrence	Total
		Total	Half or more	Less than half		
		Years	*Years*	*Years*	*Years*	*Years*
Hail						
Rust						
Flood						
Drought						
Soil blowing						
Frost						
Hoppers						
Other insects						

FREQUENCY OF YIELDS (PER SEEDED ACREAGE)

Crop	Failure	Low	Average	Good	Total
Wheat:					
Bushels					
Years					
Barley:					
Bushels					
Years					
Oats:					
Bushels					
Years					
Corn:					
Bushels					
Years					

State..............................
County...........................
Record...........................

GROSS INCOME, 1934

Source	*Dollars*
Crop sales..............................	....
Livestock sales..............................	....
Livestock products..............................	....
AAA wheat contract..............................	....
AAA hog contract..............................	....
ERA..............................	....
Other..............................	....
Total..............................	....

VALUE OF PRODUCTS USED IN HOME

Kind	*Dollars*
Dairy products..............................	....
Poultry products..............................	....
Meat..............................	....
Crop and garden..............................	....

Was this income sufficient to pay living expenses...
....

Was it sufficient to accumulate capital or reduce debts..

[1] Question on original schedule.

USUAL GROSS INCOME

What was usual gross cash income $..................
Sources of income:
Crops %.................. Livestock %..........
Nonfarm %..............................
Was income sufficient to pay expenses[1]..........
Accumulate capital..............................
Reduce debts..............................
In how many years was farm income sufficient to:[2]
Pay farm and living expenses..................
Accumulate capital or reduce debts..............
Total years reported..............................
What size of farm should one man operate to provide adequate family income..............................
....
....
....
....
What type of farm..............................
....
....
....

[2] Question on revised schedule.

COMMUNITY INSTITUTIONS, 1934[1]

Institution	Contributions			Membership		Regular attendance[2]	
	Money	Goods	Time				
		Dollars	*Hours*	*Yes*	*No*	*Yes*	*No*
Church..............................	....	....	....	....	....	....	....
School..............................	....	....	....	....	....	....	....
Clubs..............................	....	....	....	....	....	....	....
Others..............................	....	....	....	....	....	....	....

[1] Any member or members of household. [2] Half or more of meetings.

FAMILY COMPOSITION[1]

Relationship to head	Age	Sex	Working on this farm	Working elsewhere	Seeking work
1. Head..............................	....	....	....	....	....
2.	....	....	....	....	....
3.	....	....	....	....	....
4.	....	....	....	....	....
5.	....	....	....	....	....
6.	....	....	....	....	....
7.	....	....	....	....	....
8.	....	....	....	....	....
9.	....	....	....	....	....
10.	....	....	....	....	....
11.	....	....	....	....	....
12.	....	....	....	....	....

[1] Include all members of household as of April 1, 1935.

State
County
Record

CROP ACRES AND PRODUCTION, 1930–1935

Crop	1935	1934		1933		1932		1931		1930	
	Acres seeded	Acres seeded	Production [1]	Acres seeded	Production [1]	Acres seeded	Production [1]	Acres seeded	Production [1]	Acres seeded	Production [1]
Wheat on fallow:											
Spring											
Durum											
Winter											
Other wheat:											
Spring											
Durum											
Winter											
Flax											
Barley											
Oats											
Rye											
Corn:											
Grain											
Fodder											
Silage											
Grain sorghum											
Sorgo											
Hay:											
Small grain											
Sweet clover											
Alfalfa											
Alfalfa seed											
Sweet clover seed											
Potatoes											
Fallow											
Idle cropland											
Annual pasture											
Total cropland											
Native hay											
Native pasture											

[1] Report total bushels, tons, or pounds produced.

NOTE.—Write in crops not specified but grown on farm.

State______________________
County_____________________
Record_____________________

LIVESTOCK RECORD FOR 1934–35

Kind	April 1, 1934	Died	Sold		Killed for use	Bought	Born	April 1, 1935	Value	Normal number April 1
			To Government	Other						
	Number	*Number*	*Number*	*Number*	*Number*	*Number*	*Number*	*Number*		
Milk cows______	______	______	______	______	______	______	______	______	______	______
Beef cows______	______	______	______	______	______	______	______	______	______	______
Steers:										
2 years or older_	______	______	______	______	______	______	______	______	______	______
1 year______	______	______	______	______	______	______	______	______	______	______
Heifers______	______	______	______	______	______	______	______	______	______	______
Calves______	______	______	______	______	______	______	______	______	______	______
Bulls______	______	______	______	______	______	______	______	______	______	______
Brood sows______	______	______	______	______	______	______	______	______	______	______
Shoats______	______	______	______	______	______	______	______	______	______	______
Pigs______	______	______	______	______	______	______	______	______	______	______
Boar______	______	______	______	______	______	______	______	______	______	______
Breeding ewes______	______	______	______	______	______	______	______	______	______	______
Lambs______	______	______	______	______	______	______	______	______	______	______
Rams______	______	______	______	______	______	______	______	______	______	______
Chickens______	______	______	______	______	______	______	______	______	______	______
Turkeys______	______	______	______	______	______	______	______	______	______	______
Ducks______	______	______	______	______	______	______	______	______	______	______
Work stock______	______	______	______	______	______	______	______	______	______	______
Colts______	______	______	______	______	______	______	______	______	______	______
Other horses______	______	______	______	______	______	______	______	______	______	______

Notes on livestock	Cattle	Sheep	Hogs	Poultry	Horses
Breeds______	______	______	______	______	______
Age marketed______	______	______	______	______	______
Feeding practice______	______	______	______	______	______

Are cattle confined to pasture recorded on p. 1______________________________
If not, what acreage is used______________________________
____

Age of work stock on hand April 1, 1935:

Less than 7 years No. ______________
8 to 12 years No. ______________
13 years and older No. ______________

State
County
Record

MACHINERY AND EQUIPMENT

Kind	Make	Size	Age	Necessary repairs	Present value
				Dollars	*Dollars*
Tractor					
Stationary engine					
Combine					
Binder					
Header					
Thresher					
Windrower					
Moldboard plow					
Lister					
1-way disk					
Tandem disk					
Single disk					
Field cultivator					
Duck foot					
Spring tooth					
Rod weeder					
Disk drill					
Press drill					
Deep-furrow drill					
Row planter					
Row binder					
Corn picker					
Corn sheller					
Ensilage cutter					
Row cultivator					
Lister cultivator					
Stalk cutter					
Packer					
Spike-tooth harrow					
Mower					
Dump rake					
Side rake					
Sweep rake					
Hay stacker					
Truck					
Auto					
Wagon					
Pack wagon					
Manure spreader					
Cream separator					

State
County
Record

FINANCIAL CONDITION

Indebtedness		Interest rate	Due date	Unpaid		Total due	Creditor	Debt adjustment
Kind	Original amount			Interest	Principal			
Real estate:	*Dollars*	*Percent*		*Dollars*	*Dollars*	*Dollars*		
First mortgage								
Second mortgage								
Land purchase contract								
Chattel mortgages:								
Livestock								
Machinery								
Crops								
Crop loans								
Judgment								
Unsecured notes								
Open accounts								
Taxes delinquent								
Water assessment								
Other								
Total								

ASSETS

Kind	Value	Equity	Notes
Real estate (this farm)			Acres.
Machinery			
Livestock			
Farm products			
Cash on hand			
Notes receivable			
Accounts receivable			
Insurance (cash value)			
Other real estate			
Personal property			
Other assets			
Total			

When did you begin farming in area Year
Tenant Owner
Approximate resources Approximate debt
How much additional capital went into farm
Source of these funds
How much above living expenses was taken out
Education Investments Bank failure
Other

Appendix C

LIST OF TABLES

TEXT TABLES

Table *Page*

1. Average gross receipts per farm on selected farms in representative counties in the Northern Great Plains, by source of receipts, 1934 — 3
2. Date of first relief to farm operators on relief in April–May 1935 in representative counties in the Northern Great Plains — 5
3. Percent of years different causes of crop damage were reported on selected farms in representative counties in the Northern Great Plains — 16
4. Average yield per harvested acre of important crops in representative counties in the Northern Great Plains, 1911–1931 — 18
5. Utilization of land on selected farms in representative counties in the Northern Great Plains, 1934 — 23
6. Average value of farm buildings and estimated cost of needed repairs per farm on selected farms in representative counties in the Northern Great Plains, 1935 — 32
7. Acreage mortgaged and average indebtedness per acre, mortgages of record in representative counties in the Northern Great Plains, 1935 — 33
8. Farm tenancy in representative counties in the Northern Great Plains, 1920, 1930, and 1935 — 37
9. Percent of land owned by different types of owners in representative counties in the Northern Great Plains, 1935 — 39
10. Average gross receipts per farm on selected farms in representative counties in the Central Great Plains, by source of receipts, 1934 — 43
11. Date of first relief to farm operators on relief in April–May 1935 in representative counties in the Central Great Plains — 46
12. Percent of years different causes of crop damage were reported on selected farms in representative counties in the Central Great Plains — 55
13. Average yield per harvested acre of important crops in representative counties in the Central Great Plains, 1910–1932 — 57
14. Utilization of land on selected farms in representative counties in the Central Great Plains, 1934 — 62
15. Average value of farm buildings and estimated cost of needed repairs per farm on selected farms in representative counties in the Central Great Plains, 1935 — 66
16. Acreage mortgaged and average indebtedness per acre, mortgages of record in representative counties in the Central Great Plains, 1935 — 68
17. Percent of land owned by different types of owners in representative counties in the Central Great Plains, 1935 — 70

Table *Page*

18. Farm tenancy in representative counties in the Central Great Plains, 1920, 1930, and 1935 ... 71
19. Average gross receipts per farm on selected farms in representative counties in the Southern Great Plains, by source of receipts, 1934 ... 74
20. Percent of years different causes of crop damage were reported on selected farms in representative counties in the Southern Great Plains ... 83
21. Percent of years poor yields or failures of important crops were reported by selected farmers in representative counties in the Southern Great Plains ... 86
22. Utilization of land on selected farms in representative counties in the Southern Great Plains, 1934 ... 89
23. Average value of farm buildings and estimated cost of needed repairs per farm on selected farms in representative counties in the Southern Great Plains, 1935 ... 95
24. Acreage mortgaged and average indebtedness per acre, mortgages of record in representative counties in the Southern Great Plains, 1935 ... 97
25. Type and residence of owners of land in representative counties in the Southern Great Plains, 1935 ... 100
26. Tenure of operators of farm land in representative counties in the Southern Great Plains, 1934 ... 101
27. Farm tenancy in representative counties in the Southern Great Plains, 1920, 1930, and 1935 ... 101

SUPPLEMENTARY TABLES

1. Normal gross cash receipts, source of receipts, and adequacy of income on selected farms is representative counties in the Northern Great Plains, by size of farm ... 123
2. Age of farm operators receiving relief in representative counties in the Northern Great Plains and number unable to work, April–May 1935 ... 124
3. Number of children of different ages and adult members other than parents in farm families receiving relief in representative counties in the Northern Great Plains, April–May 1935 ... 125
4. Relative importance of different causes of crop damage on selected farms in representative counties in the Northern Great Plains, by degree of loss ... 126
5. Average annual yield per harvested acre of important crops in representative counties in the Northern Great Plains, 1911–1931 ... 127
6. Percent of years specified crop yield per harvested acre was obtained in selected areas in the Northern Great Plains, 1911–1931 ... 128
7. Average yield per seeded acre of important crops on selected farms in representative counties in the Northern Great Plains and frequency of occurrence of yields which were good, medium, poor, or failures ... 129
8. Average yield per seeded acre of important crops on selected farms in representative counties in the Northern Great Plains, 1930–1934 ... 130
9. Financial progress of selected farmers in representative counties in the Northern Great Plains since beginning farming in the area, by size of farm, 1935 ... 131
10. Size of farm, number of livestock per farm, and tenure of farm operators receiving relief in representative counties in the Northern Great Plains, April–May 1935 ... 133

Table | Page

11. Utilization of land on selected farms in representative counties in the Northern Great Plains, by size of farm, 1934 ... 134
12. Use of farm land on selected farms in representative counties in the Northern Great Plains, 1934 ... 135
13. Average acreage of important crops on selected farms in representative counties in the Northern Great Plains, 1930–1934 ... 136
14. Percent of owned and rented land in crops and grass on selected farms in representative counties in the Northern Great Plains, 1934 ... 137
15. Number of livestock on hand April 1, 1935, and normal number on selected farms in representative counties in the Northern Great Plains, by size of farm ... 138
16. Number of selected farms with livestock in representative counties in the Northern Great Plains, April 1, 1935 ... 140
17. Utilization of labor and tractors on selected farms in representative counties in the Northern Great Plains, by size of farm, 1935 ... 141
18. Acreage operated by specified number of men, with or without tractors, on selected farms in Sheridan and Traill Counties, N. Dak., by size of farm, 1935 ... 142
19. Average value of farm buildings and estimated cost of needed repairs per farm on selected farms in representative counties in the Northern Great Plains, by size of farm, 1935 ... 143
20. Percent of acreage with mortgages of record held by different types of lending agencies in representative counties in the Northern Great Plains, 1935 ... 144
21. Federal emergncy loans to farmers in representative counties in the Northern Great Plains and loans outstanding, December 31, 1934 ... 144
22. Average indebtedness of farm operators receiving relief in representative counties in the Northern Great Plains, by tenure, April–May 1935 ... 145
23. Average value of farm assets, amount of liabilities, and net worth of selected farmers in representative counties in the Northern Great Plains, by tenure, 1935 ... 147
24. Normal gross cash receipts, source of receipts, and adequacy of income on selected farms in representative counties in the Central Great Plains, by size of farm ... 148
25. Age of farm operators receiving relief in representative counties in the Central Great Plains and number unable to work, April–May 1935 ... 149
26. Number of children of different ages and adult members other than parents in farm families receiving relief in representative counties in the Central Great Plains, April–May 1935 ... 149
27. Relative importance of different causes of crop damage on selected farms in representative counties in the Central Great Plains, by degree of loss ... 150
28. Average annual yield per harvested acre of important crops in representative counties in the Central Great Plains, 1910–1932 ... 151
29. Percent of years specified crop yield per harvested acre was obtained in selected areas in the Central Great Plains, 1905–1934 ... 152
30. Average yield per seeded acre of important crops on selected farms in representative counties in the Central Great Plains and frequency of occurrence of yields which were good, medium, poor, or failures ... 153
31. Average yield per seeded acre of important crops on selected farms in representative counties in the Central Great Plains, 1930–1934 ... 154

Table *Page*

32. Financial progress of selected farmers in representative counties in the Central Great Plains since beginning farming in the area, by size of farm, 1935 155
33. Size of farm, number of livestock per farm, and tenure of farm operators receiving relief in representative counties in the Central Great Plains, April–May 1935 157
34. Utilization of land on farms having corn-hog contracts in representative counties in the Central Great Plains, by size of farm, 1934 158
35. Utilization of land on selected farms in representative counties in the Central Great Plains, by size of farm, 1934 159
36. Percent of owned and rented land in crops and grass on selected farms in representative counties in the Central Great Plains, 1934 160
37. Use of farm land on selected farms in representative counties in the Central Great Plains, 1934 161
38. Average acreage of important crops on selected farms in representative counties in the Central Great Plains, 1930–1934 162
39. Number of livestock on hand April 1, 1935, and normal number on selected farms in representative counties in the Central Great Plains, by size of farm 163
40. Number of selected farms with livestock in representative counties in the Central Great Plains, April 1, 1935 165
41. Utilization of labor on selected farms in representative counties in the Central Great Plains, by size of farm, 1934 166
42. Average value of farm buildings and estimated cost of needed repairs per farm on selected farms in representative counties in the Central Great Plains, by size of farm, 1935 167
43. Percent of acreage with mortgages of record held by different types of lending agencies in representative counties in the Central Great Plains, 1935 168
44. Federal emergency loans to farmers in representative counties in the Central Great Plains, 1934–1935 168
45. Average indebtedness of farm operators receiving relief in representative counties in the Central Great Plains, by tenure, April–May 1935 169
46. Percent of farm land held by resident and nonresident owners and tenure of operators in representative counties in the Central Great Plains, 1935 170
47. Average value of farm assets, amount of liabilities, and net worth of selected farmers in representative counties in the Central Great Plains, by tenure, 1935 171
48. Normal gross cash receipts, source of receipts, and adequacy of income on selected farms in representative counties in the Southern Great Plains, by size of farm 172
49. Age of farm operators receiving relief in representative counties in the Southern Great Plains and number unable to work, April–May 1935 173
50. Number of children of different ages and adult members other than parents in farm families receiving relief in representative counties in the Southern Great Plains, April–May 1935 173
51. Relative importance of different causes of crop damage on selected farms in representative counties in the Southern Great Plains, by degree of loss 174
52. Crop yield per harvested acre in selected areas in the Southern Great Plains, 1905–1933 175

Table *Page*

53. Average yield per seeded acre of important crops on selected farms in representative counties in the Southern Great Plains, 1930–1934 ... 176
54. Average yield per seeded acre of important crops on selected farms in representative counties in the Southern Great Plains and frequency of occurrence of yields which were good, medium, poor, or failures ... 177
55. Financial progress of selected farmers in representative counties in the Southern Great Plains since beginning farming in the area, by size of farm, 1935 ... 178
56. Cropland on farms having corn-hog contracts in representative counties in the Southern Great Plains, by size of farm, 1934 ... 180
57. Utilization of land on selected farms in representative counties in the Southern Great Plains, by size of farm, 1934 ... 181
58. Utilization of land on 1,496 farms having cotton contracts in Hale County, Tex., by size of farm, 1934 ... 182
59. Size of farm, number of livestock per farm, and tenure of farm operators receiving relief in representative counties in the Southern Great Plains, April–May 1935 ... 182
60. Percent of owned and rented land in crops and grass on selected farms in representative counties in the Southern Great Plains, 1934 ... 183
61. Use of farm land on selected farms in representative counties in the Southern Great Plains, 1934 ... 184
62. Average acreage of important crops on selected farms in representative counties in the Southern Great Plains, 1930–1934 ... 185
63. Number of livestock on hand April 1, 1935, and normal number on selected farms in representative counties in the Southern Great Plains, by size of farm ... 186
64. Number of selected farms with livestock in representative counties in the Southern Great Plains, April 1, 1935 ... 188
65. Acreage operated by specified number of men, with or without tractors, on selected farms in representative counties in the Southern Great Plains, 1934 ... 189
66. Average value of farm buildings and estimated cost of needed repairs per farm on selected farms in representative counties in the Southern Great Plains, by size of farm, 1935 ... 190
67. Percent of acreage with mortgages of record held by different types of lending agencies in representative counties in the Southern Great Plains, 1935 ... 191
68. Federal emergency loans to farmers in representative counties in the Southern Great Plains, 1934–1935 ... 191
69. Acreage and percent of total land area tax-delinquent in representative counties in the Southern Great Plains, 1935 ... 191
70. Average indebtedness of farm operators receiving relief in representative counties in the Southern Great Plains, by tenure, April–May 1935 ... 192
71. Indebtedness of selected farmers and of relief clients in Curry County, N. Mex., by tenure and size of farm, May 1935 ... 192
72. Average value of farm assets, amount of liabilities, and net worth of selected farmers in representative counties in the Southern Great Plains, by tenure, 1935 ... 193

Index

INDEX

Page

Agricultural Adjustment Administration (*see also* Livestock Purchase Program, Emergency):
- Livestock purchased by 26, 27, 92, 93
- Payments 2, 3, 4, 42–44, 74–75

Agriculture, development of, in Great Plains .... XIII–XIV
Assets, farm, by tenure 37–39, 71, 72, 101–102, 147, 171, 193
Automobiles, farmers' ownership of 29

Brown, L. A., Gemmell, R. L., and Hayes, F. A.: *Soil Survey of Sherman County, Nebraska* 49n
Brown, L. A. *See* Mathews, O. R.
Buildings, farm:
- Repairs needed, average cost of 31–32, 66–67, 95–96, 143, 167, 190
- Value, average estimated 31–32, 66–67, 95, 143, 167, 190

Carter, William T., Jr.: *The Soils of Texas* 77n
——— and Others: *Reconnaissance Soil Survey of Northwest Texas* 79n
Census, Bureau of the:
- *Fifteenth Census of the United States: 1930* 68n, 100n
- *Fourteenth Census of the United States: 1920* 37n, 71n, 101n
- *United States Census of Agriculture: 1935* 20n, 22n, 27n, 33n, 37n, 58n, 59n, 60n, 61n, 71n, 88n, 89n, 97n, 100n, 101n

Chemistry and Soils, Bureau of: *Atlas of American Agriculture* 7n, 8n, 10n, 48n, 79n, 80n
Climate:
- Crop production related to. *See* Crop, yield.
- Drought. *See* Drought.
- Growing season, length of 7, 10, 11, 12, 50, 52, 80
- Rainfall (*see also* Population movements) 7, 10, 12–16, 50–53, 80–83
- Temperature 10, 50, 52, 79–80

Colorado, Yearbooks of the State of 57n, 151n, 175n
Crop:
- Damage, causes of, degree of loss, and frequency of 16–17, 55–56, 83–84, 126, 150, 174
- Failure, by type 85–86, 177
- Loans. *See* Loans, Federal emergency.
- Sales, as source of income 3–4, 43–44, 74, 75, 123–124, 148, 172
- Types of (*see also* Land use) .... XIII, XIV, XVI, 6–7, 23, 24–25, 41, 46–47, 63–64, 77–78, 90–92, 135, 136, 161, 162, 184, 185.
- Yield:
  - Average per harvested acre 17–18, 56–57, 85, 127, 151, 175
  - Average per seeded acre 17, 18, 57, 85–86, 129, 130, 153, 154, 176, 177
  - Reporting, method of 17n, 57n
  - Variation, by year 17, 18, 19, 56, 57, 84–86, 128, 152, 177

Drought: Page
Crop damage caused by 16, 55, 83, 84, 126, 150, 174
Effects of 5, 42, 53–54
Occurrence 12, 13, 14, 15, 16, 51, 52–53, 80–83

Elliott, F. F.: *Types of Farming in the United States* 6n, 46n, 47n, 78n
Employment, off-the-farm. *See* Income.
Erosion. *See* Soils.

Farm products, home use 3, 43, 44, 74, 75
Farms (*see also* Irrigated areas; Land use; Tractor-operated farms):
Size of 20–23, 58–60, 87–89, 123–124, 133, 148, 157, 182
Type of xiv, xvi, 6–7, 46–47, 77–78
Federal emergency loans. *See* Indebtedness.
Federal Emergency Relief Administration. *See* Relief.
Federal Land Bank, mortgages held by 34, 68, 97–98, 144, 168, 191
Federal Land Bank Commissioner, mortgages held by 34, 68, 97–98, 144, 168, 191
Feed and seed loans. *See* Loans, Federal emergency.
Financial progress, farm operators (*see also* Land use):
Insolvency 4, 37–38, 39, 72
Net worth, average, by tenure 38, 39, 45, 71, 72, 101–102, 147, 171, 193
Size of farm and 19–21, 58–60, 86–87 131–132, 155–156, 178–179
Frost. *See* Climate, growing season.
Fuller, O. M. *See* Willard, Rex E.

Gemmell, R. L. *See* Brown, L. A.

Hayes, F. A. *See* Brown, L. A.

Income:
By adequacy, size of farm, and source 2–4, 42–44, 74–76, 123–124, 148, 172
Employment, off-the-farm, as source of 123–124, 148, 172
Federal Government as source of 2–4, 42–44, 74, 75
Reduction in 2–4, 42–44, 74–76
Indebtedness (*see also* Tax delinquency; Tax rates):
Amount per farm, by tenure 32, 37, 38–39, 71, 101–102, 147, 171, 193
Loans, Federal emergency:
Average number and amount per farm:
Crop, feed, and seed 34–35, 68, 96, 98, 144, 168, 191
Mortgages (*see also* Federal Land Bank; Federal Land Bank Commissioner):
Chattel 32–33, 67, 75, 96, 147, 171, 193
Lending agencies and acreage mortgaged 34, 67–68, 97–98, 144, 168, 191
Real estate:
Acreage mortgaged and average amount per acre 32–33, 34, 67–68, 96, 97–98
Foreclosures, average number per year 33
Relief and nonrelief families compared, by size of farm and tenure 36, 69, 99, 145–146, 147, 169, 171, 192

Irrigated areas: *Page*
Crop:
Acreage 63, 64, 161, 162
Damage 55–56, 150
Yields 56–57, 153, 154
Farm:
Buildings 66, 167
Income 42–44, 148
Size:
Financial progress and 59, 155–156
Land utilization and 59, 61–62, 158, 159
Farming, types of, in 47
Financial condition, farm operators in 71–72, 171
Labor requirements and size of farm 66, 166
Land utilization and tenure 61–64, 160, 161
Livestock 64–65, 163–164, 165
Ownership, type of 69–70, 170
Water supply 55

Johnson, W. D.: *The High Plains and Its Utilization* 48n

Kansas State Board of Agriculture: *Biennial Reports* 54n, 152n, 175n
Kincaid Act 58

Labor requirements, farm (*see also* Irrigated areas):
Acreage operated and 30–31, 65–66, 94–95, 142, 166, 189
Machinery, ownership of, and. *See* Machinery.
Tractors, use of, and. *See* Tractor-operated farms.
Land owners, type of 39–40, 69–70, 99–100, 170
Land retirement areas 2, 41–42, 56
Land use:
Crops, percent in, by type 23–25, 60–64, 89–92, 135, 161, 184
Size of operating unit and:
Financial progress, relation to 20–21, 58–60, 87, 88, 131–132, 155–156, 178–179
Relief status, relation to 21–23, 60, 88–89, 133, 157, 182
Variation in xiii, xiv–xvi, 1, 2, 20, 22–24, 60–62, 87–92, 134, 158, 159, 180, 181, 182
Tenure and 25, 61, 62, 63, 90, 137, 160, 183
Larson, G. A. *See* Watkins, W. I.
Liabilities. *See* Indebtedness.
Livestock (*see also* Agricultural Adjustment Administration):
As source of income xiv, 3–4, 43–44, 74–75, 123–124, 148, 172
Number:
Farms reporting, by type 26–28, 64–65, 92–93, 140, 165, 188
Reduction in xiv, 26, 27, 42, 45, 58, 64–65, 75, 92–93, 138–139, 163–164, 186–187
Ownership and relief status (*see also* Relief families) 28, 65, 93, 133, 157, 182
Production, areas of xiii, xiv, xvi, 26, 64–65, 92
Livestock Purchase Program, Emergency 3–4, 42–44, 75, 92–93

McClure, R. W. *See* Veatch, J. O.

Machinery (*see also* Tractor-operated farms): Page
Repairs, needed, average cost of 29, 94
Type and extent of use 29, 94
Use, extent of, and labor requirements 29–31, 65–66, 94–95, 141, 142, 189
Value, average estimated, per farm 29–30, 66, 94, 147, 171, 193
Machlis, J. A. and Williams, B. H.: *Soil Survey of Hyde County, South Dakota* 10n
Maladjustments in Land Use in the United States 2n
Mathews, O. R. and Brown, L. A.: *Winter Wheat and Sorghum Production Under Limited Rainfall* 105n
Methodology:
Areas represented xv, 1–2, 41–42, 73–74, 198
Counties in area studied 1–2, 41–42, 73–74
Farms, sample, number in study xvi, 197
Method and scope of study xvi, 195–198
Sample counties in study xv, 1–2, 41–42, 73–74, 195–196, 197
Representativeness of xvi, 1–2, 41–42, 73–74, 196, 197–198
Sources of data 195–197
Mortgages. *See* Indebtedness.

National Resources Board 2n, 19n
Nebraska Agricultural Statistics 57n, 151n, 152n
Nebraska State Board of Agriculture: *Annual Reports* 57n, 151n, 152n

Owners, farm:
Farm assets, value of. *See* Assets, farm.
Indebtedness. *See* Indebtedness.
Net worth, average. *See* Financial progress.
Type of 39–40, 69–70, 99–100, 170

Population movements 53–54
Poulson, E. N. *See* Sweet, A. T.

Rainfall. *See* Climate.
Real estate, average estimated value per farm 32, 66–67, 96, 147, 171, 193
Rehabilitation families:
Age:
Children, number and 77, 173
Heads 173
Average loan budgeted 76n
Composition 77, 173
Disabilities of heads 77, 173
Livestock ownership 93, 182
Number of 44, 76
Size of farm 88–89, 182
Rehabilitation problems, by region 19, 58, 86–87, 103–106
Rehabilitation, suggestions for, in representative counties 106–119
Relief:
Accessions:
Date of first 5, 45, 46, 76–77
Reasons for 5–6, 45–46, 76–77
As source of income 2–3, 4, 42–44, 74–75
Grants, average monthly 76n
Intensity 1–2, 5, 41–42, 44, 76–77
Tenancy and need for 38–39, 77, 101, 145–146, 169, 182

Relief families (*see also* Indebtedness): *Page*
Age:
Children, number and 6, 46, 77, 125, 149, 173
Heads 5–6, 46, 77, 124, 149, 173
Disabilities of heads 5–6, 46, 77, 124, 149, 173
Farms, size of, compared to nonrelief farms 21–23, 60, 88–89
Livestock ownership 28, 65, 93, 133, 157, 182
Net worth 45
Russom, V. M. *See* Wolfganger, Louis A.

Sample counties in study. *See* Methodology.
Size of farms. *See* Land use.
Soils:
Crop production, related to 7, 10, 49–50, 79
Erosion, wind, extent of 7, 9, 16–17, 48, 56, 84
Types of 7, 8, 10, 48–50, 79
Steele, Harry A.: *Farm Mortgage Foreclosures in South Dakota, 1921–1932* 34n
Strieter, E. H. *See* Wolfganger, Louis A.
Sweet, A. T. and Poulson, E. N.: *Soil Survey of the Fort Sumner Area, New Mexico* 79n

Tables, list of text and supplementary 207–211
Taeuber, Conrad and Taylor, Carl C.: *The People of the Drought States* 54n
Tax delinquency 35–36, 68–69, 98–99, 191
Tax Delinquency of Rural Real Estate in 15 Oklahoma Counties, 1928–33 98n
Tax Delinquency of Rural Real Estate in 55 Texas Counties, 1928–33 98n
Tax Delinquency of Rural Real Estate in 10 New Mexico Counties, 1928–33 98n
Tax rates 69, 99
Taylor, Carl C. *See* Taeuber, Conrad.
Temperature. *See* Climate.
Tenancy, farm:
Farm assets, value of, and. *See* Assets, farm.
Problems related to 37–39, 69–70, 100
Ratio:
By region and year 37–38, 70–71, 100–101
Residence of owner and 99–100
Relief status and 38–39, 72, 76–77, 101, 145–146, 169, 182
Tenants, farm:
Farm land, percent operated by 25, 37, 38, 39, 61, 62, 63, 70, 90, 100–101, 137, 160, 183
Indebtedness. *See* Indebtedness.
Net worth, average. *See* Financial progress.
Topography 7, 47–48, 78–79
Tractor-operated farms 30–31, 94–95, 141, 142, 189

Veatch, J. O. and McClure, R. W.: *Soil Survey of the Fort Laramie Area, Wyoming-Nebraska* 49n, 50n

Watkins, W. I. and Larson, G. A.: *Soil Survey of Moody County, South Dakota* 7n
Willard, Rex E. and Fuller, O. M.: *Type-of-Farming Areas in North Dakota* 18n, 127n, 128n
Williams, B. H. *See* Machlis, J. A.
Wolfanger, Louis A., Russom, V. M., and Strieter, E. H.: *Soil Survey of Perkins County, Nebraska* 49n, 50n
Wyoming Agricultural Statistics 57n, 151n, 152n